DATE DUE

BRODART   Cat. No. 23-221

C. Wright Mills

A Native Radical and His
American Intellectual Roots

C. WRIGHT MILLS

A Native Radical and His American Intellectual Roots

Rick Tilman

THE PENNSYLVANIA STATE UNIVERSITY PRESS
UNIVERSITY PARK AND LONDON

Library of Congress Cataloging in Publication Data

Tilman, Rick.
C. Wright Mills : a native radical and
his American intellectual roots.

Includes bibliography and index.
1. Mills, C. Wright (Charles Wright), 1916–1962.
2. Sociology. I. Title.
HM22.U6M466 1984   301'.092'4   83-43034
ISBN 0-271-00360-X

Contents

Preface   vii

Acknowledgments   ix

Introduction: Our Foremost Dissenter   1

1   C. Wright Mills and His Critics   5

2   Mills' Eclectic Theory of Stratification and Power in America   14

3   Mills and European Social Thought: A Reappraisal   30

4   Thorstein Veblen and the Institutionalist Influence on Mills   61

5   Mills' Critique of Veblen and the Conservative Institutionalists   90

6   George H. Mead and Mills' Social Psychology   107

7   John Dewey and the Pragmatic Influence on Mills   121

8   Mills' Attack on Dewey and American Liberalism   143

9   Native Doctrine and Indigenous Insurgency in Mills, Veblen, Dewey and Mead   173

10   Protestantism, Pragmatism and the American Radical Intellectual Tradition   193

Citations 203
Bibliography 225
Index 241

Preface

C. Wright Mills is the most influential American radical social theorist since Thorstein Veblen. This alone should make his intellectual pedigree and ideological genesis significant. But this book erects no icons to Mills, who is its central figure, nor does it attempt to elevate him to sainthood. It has other objectives. The first is to show the inadequacy of monistic interpretations of his intellectual perspective, especially those that ignore the influence of American thinkers. His primary interpreters have exaggerated the influences of several European schools of social thought and their leading theoreticians: thus Mills is inaccurately labeled a "Marxist," a "Machiavellian," a "Weberian," and even a "Freudian." In the strict sense of the terms, none of these labels are adequate.

My second objective is to show the important influence on Mills of Veblen, Dewey and to a lesser extent George H. Mead, and thereby to illustrate his deep roots in the American past. Even though Mills was an important radical critic of all three men, his work cannot be understood without recognizing their great impact on him. While exaggerating certain tendencies in their thought, Mills was an original and penetrating user and critic of the ideas of Dewey, Veblen, and Mead. His use and abuse of their work, especially Dewey's later writings, is unique in contemporary intellectual history and social theory.

My third objective is to show how American radical intellectual traditions are incorporated into Mills' creative theorizing about American society. Few if any thinkers have had Mills' influence on the left's perception of power and stratification, and it is important to recognize why this is so. Mills' impact on American radicalism can only be understood if it is viewed as an outgrowth and an offshoot of our radical intellectual tradition itself.

Acknowledgments

I would like to acknowledge the aid of the following people for giving me insightful critiques when the manuscript was in draft form: Andy Fry, John Diggins, Richard Pells, Larry Spence, David Westby, Vernon Mattson, Frank Nutch, Bill Dugger and Gene Shoemaker. For providing me with useful information about the central figures in this book I thank David Miller, Herbert Blumer, William Leonard, Harold Orbach and H. H. Liebhafsky; their correspondence with me has been invaluable.

Mention must be made of the following undergraduate professors of mine at Oregon State University 1957–1961 for their contributions to my intellectual growth and development: Charles Green, Jack Putnam, Faith Norris, Sid White, Frank Shaw, Ken Patterson, Cyrus Mayshark, E. D. Smith, R. D. Brown, and Melvin Walker La Follette. I would also like to thank my fellow graduate students at the University of Arizona for many stimulating discussions on various facets of the American political system during the years 1961–1966. This includes Vince Peloso, Don Baldrige, Gus Seligman, C. K. McFarlane, Hal Rhodes, Paul Goldstene, Ted Putterman, Bill Elkins, Ed Baumgard, John Ingersoll, John Fonte, Ward Albro, Jerry Polinard, Bob Wrinkle, and Charles Cotrel. The graduate faculty at Arizona was more than helpful during my stay there, especially Herman E. Bateman who directed my doctoral dissertation, Don Lammers, James Donahoe, R. Jack Wilson and Neal Houghton.

Thanks are also due my colleagues at the University of Nevada, Las

Vegas for their aid and encouragement, including Maurice Finnochiaro, Craig Walton, Jim Frey, Marilyn Lester, Lynn Osborne, Andy Fontana, Loren Reichert, and Gary Jones. I have drawn moral support and a modest amount of cultural stimulation from Chuck Rasmussen, Lorne Seidman, Dick Peet, Mike Sheehan, and Michael Clarke.

Special thanks are due John Pickering, editorial director of the Penn State Press, for his patience and his special interest in my project, and to W. L. Parker, the copy editor. I am grateful to Pat Hudson, Gay Gubler, and Lynne T. Jackson for typing drafts of the manuscript. I am also in the debt of Yaroslava Mills, wife of the late C. Wright Mills, for giving me access to his papers and permission to quote from them. Finally, I would like to dedicate this book to my long-suffering parents Lee R. and Noma J. Tilman of Boulder City, Nevada, who have learned more about Mills, Veblen, and Dewey than they ever wanted to know.

I would like to thank the following for permission to reprint articles originally published elsewhere: Dean Mann, editor of the *Western Political Quarterly*, for permission to reprint "The Intellectual Pedigree of C. Wright Mills: A Reappraisal," 32 (December 1979); and Will Lissner, editor of the *American Journal of Economics and Sociology*, for permission to reprint "Radicalism Versus Liberalism: C. Wright Mills' Critique of John Dewey's Ideas," 37 (Fall 1978), and "On the Use and Abuse of Thorstein Veblen in Contemporary American Sociology," 11, 42 (Fall 1983).

Introduction:
Our Foremost Dissenter

The term "radical" is used here in its literal sense to mean those who would change society at its roots rather than gradually reform it. Radicalism aims at transforming the political and economic structure of the society through changing the relations of property ownership and political power. "Radical" is applied to those who want a basic change in the social order—even if their efforts have no effect, and regardless of whether their tactics are violent or peaceful. Radicalism is a term that is subject to abuse on several counts, not least of which is the inability of many critics to distinguish it from liberalism. That durable and tenacious American radical historian William Appleman Williams has argued that radicals, if worth their salt, must do four things.[1] First, they must get to the root of things by finding the actual rather than the apparent nature of the political economy and social structure. Second, they must offer an explanation of the constantly changing relationships among basic social institutions. Third, they must provide an alternative hierarchy to the socially dominant values. Finally, they must understand what the specific options are for structural change, including strategical as well as tactical alternatives. Then they must engage in sustained action to achieve these objectives. Williams has thus offered legitimate standards by which to measure any radical's intellectual and political performance. Such criteria are used here to evaluate the behavior of our three central figures.

This study is premised on the assumption that Marxists who attempt to junk the radical elements in the American intellectual tradition succeed only in cutting themselves off from our cultural existence and consequently from political reality. This is not a plea to Marxianize the American tradition or to Americanize Marx; it is simply my view that Karl Marx's ideas by themselves are not potent enough for building an adequate radical theory. Instead, his insights must be grafted onto the indigenous radical tradition as but one branch on a massive trunk from which several other limbs protrude.

Traditionally, mainline social scientists have dismissed American Marxists far too easily but have had more difficulty ignoring such figures as Dewey, Veblen, and Mills. Although it is now often overlooked, pragmatism and institutionalism once shared a relevant radical direction that placed them in fundamental opposition to main currents of American thought and practice. They were opposed to much of what has long been taken for granted in the United States, namely the dualism which pervades our existence. Dualism is evident, for example, in the false separation of production from consumption, science from values, cultural development from intellectual growth, and concentrated power from democratic control. Indeed, much of Marxism is in fundamental agreement with the pragmatic and institutionalist traditions in mutual indictment of dualism. Nevertheless, all three doctrines proved too radical, and consequently their ideas were supplanted by more formalistic and conservative notions. This was evident in the long-time dominance of positivistic epistemology and ordinary language analysis in philosophy, of neoclassicism in economics, and of narrow empiricism in political science and sociology. It is important to realize that Veblen's, Dewey's, and Mills' assault on such formalism was ultimately rooted in institutionalism and instrumentalism.

For the academic who expects every scholarly monograph to have an explicit disciplinary focus this book will be a disappointment, for it has no such parameters. Instead, it is a voyage through social and political theory, political economy, intellectual history and biography, social psychology, and modern philosophy. Given the wide-ranging interests and knowledge of Mills, Mead, Veblen, and Dewey it would be impossible to write a broad-gauged analysis of their intellectual relationship without promiscuous violation of disciplinary boundaries.

Nevertheless, I am compelled to ask what standards should be used in measuring the boundaries and delineating the substantive content of so-called "intellectual movements" or "movements of thought." Is it essential that the thinkers involved in such a movement share the same epistemology and methodology in the discipline in which they work? Is it also necessary that they have a common approach to ethics, metaphysics, and aesthetics? In addition, must they have the same politics and social philosophy? Should they employ a similar social psychology and share fundamental assumptions about political economy? Alas, I cannot answer these questions! Although it would be demanding too much to insist on all of the above, certainly some degree of commonality, convergence, or parallelism is essential before a body of thought can legitimately be called an "intellectual movement." Since a comprehensive methodological overview of intellectual history lies far beyond the scope of this study, I must show that Mead, Veblen, and Dewey all influenced Mills in their own particular ways. Mills' ultimate achievement was in coagulating the ill-woven strands of an intellectual tradition that was only in the loosest sense an "intellectual movement." Nevertheless, in many ways he exemplified what it meant to be authentically radical in America.

This book, no doubt, reflects my personal enthusiam for the work of these four original and often brilliant men. That Veblen and Dewey in particular are treated more favorably than Mills should not detract from his intellectual achievements, which make him a theorist of high stature who contributed significantly to the development of the American radical intellectual tradition. In any case I have no illusions about having avoided arbitrary personal criteria either in selecting them as topics or in forming my interpretations. By concentrating on those intellectuals who articulated the most distinctive and the most clearly indigenous twentieth-century radical approach, I attempt to summarize some of the most penetrating radical thought in the United States.

The book's main themes are intended to suggest some degree of continuity and unity in their varied and often highly individualistic thought. Still, the reader may find the unity too contrived to be convincing. For if this book has any real merit, it has to be in demonstrating Mills' creativity as a radical thinker as well as in showing the significant differences and parallels between him, Veblen, and the later Dewey.

Mills' work has not been ignored but it generally receives negative treatment from mainline social scientists, owing to the influence of behavioral methodology and centrist political bias, two related factors that are indicative of the connection between scholarly and political conventionality. Fortunately such orthodoxy is under attack, as is evidenced by the condition of the social sciences in the past fifteen years; any surviving consensus is now confined to schools or subschools of contending thought. The proper research methods, significant issues, and validity of scholarly works have all become matters of extreme controversy. Despite the continued existence of conventional social science, and the power of the Establishment in each discipline, there is much fragmenting of professional organizations and an incredible proliferation of new social-science journals. Here again Mills is central; probably no single person bears greater responsibility for this rising tide of dissent. Victimized by political and academic orthodoxy, he has greatly influenced an entire generation of dissenters in the social studies.[2]

1

C. Wright Mills and His Critics

A BIOGRAPHICAL SKETCH

C. Wright Mills was born in Waco, Texas on August 28, 1916, to a family of mixed English, Irish, and French ancestry. When Mills was a small boy his father was employed as an insurance agent and traveled a great deal. Mills was left in the company of the women in the house, who included his grandmother, his mother, and his older sister Ursula. His biographer Richard Gillam thinks this may have fostered a romantic, sensitive side to his personality. However, his prime trait as a boy was his stubbornness and ability to exert his will power. A perhaps apocryphal story is told of his refusal to attend a school he strongly disliked. One day his father took him to the school to make sure he attended class. On the way Mills broke loose from his father's grasp and wrapped his arms and legs around a telephone pole. He refused to let go and his father was forced to abandon his efforts. Such willfullness and tenacity were to become Mills' stock-in-trade throughout his career as an intellectual maverick and a relentless and inflammatory social critic.[1]

Reared as a Roman Catholic by a Catholic mother and a formerly Protestant father who apparently conformed to Catholicism without real conviction, Mills grew up in overwhelmingly Protestant communities in Texas and never practiced Catholicism after adolescence. In examining his papers I have been unable to uncover any evidence that he was intellectually influenced by his mother's religion. In fact (not discounting his avowed agnosticism), what few comments he made about religion sound Protestant in tone if not in substance. Intellectual historians trying to place Mills in the spectrum of contemporary social thought may find that radical Protestant individualism lies at the root of his social philosophy. However, it is also possible, given what little is known about the sociology of knowledge, that his Catholic upbringing in a sea of Protestantism made him a "marginal man" who became alienated from the Catholic community at an early age yet could not conform to Protestant orthodoxy however much he may have been influenced by it. Consequently, he chose the path of the dissenter and intellectual maverick.

In the 1920s the Mills family moved from Waco to Dallas, where the father had been offered a job as manager of an insurance agency. Mills spent his adolescence there and graduated from Dallas Technical High School in 1934, where he excelled at architectural studies and drafting. In the fall of 1934 he began college at Texas A&M, which at the time was an all-male institution with compulsory military training for its students. It was an unlikely place for the future radical, with its conservative rural atmosphere and militarism; Mills apparently did not like it. To make matters worse, he accidentally injured another student in a wrestling match and was socially ostracized by others who thought Mills had done it deliberately.

Consequently it was not surprising that Mills transferred to the University of Texas at Austin in the fall of 1935. He majored in sociology and impressed several professors with his powerful intellect, broad reading, and diligent study habits. The philosopher-economist Clarence Ayres, under whom Mills worked, made these penetrating comments about him:

> In some ways Mills is—or has been—a bit difficult. He is much more mature than his age and status suggest. I think he is only 22 or a little more, and I believe that some freshman requirement has hung up his B.A. Degree so that he is going to receive it in June simultaneously with his M.A. But he isn't a pale precocious bookworm. He is a big strapping fellow with an athlete's energy. He looks much older than he is. For several years he has been reading everything within his reach, and he really is prodigiously learned for his years and situation. He also has acumen, and the result of this combination of qualities has not been altogether to his advantage.[2]

Ayres went on to characterize Mills' work habits and his personality, which were to get the same mixed reception throughout his career:

The prevailing legend about him is to the effect that he takes people up and pursues them furiously until they get so tired of it they rebuff him (or until he has milked them dry and drops them). There is something in it both ways. Mills is tremendously eager and incredibly energetic. If he gets the idea that somebody has something, he goes after it like the 3 furies. I think he may have worn his welcome to shreds in some quarters. It is also undoubtedly true that he has in certain cases reached the conclusion that there is nothing there and even allowed that opinion to become known. . . . As I see it, the picture which emerges . . . is that of an unusually strong student, a youngster who may become a headliner. I think any department would be lucky to have him among its advanced students.[3]

Perhaps because of Mills' outspokenness and his sometimes brash mannerisms which apparently irritated the sociology faculty, he was refused a graduate assistantship in that department and thus decided to take his M.A. in philosophy. This decision was to have an important impact on his intellectual development—several members of the philosophy department at Texas were steeped in the ideas of George H. Mead, John Dewey, and Charles Sanders Peirce. They whetted Mills' already burgeoning interests in pragmatism to a high pitch that reached fruition in his master's thesis, in which he interpreted certain aspects of the work of Dewey and Mead from the viewpoint of the sociology of knowledge. These interests were to form the intellectual backbone of several of his early publications in major sociology journals.

The fall of 1939 found Mills enrolled in the Ph.D. program in sociology at the University of Wisconsin. Here he studied under such luminaries as sociologist Howard Becker and labor economist Selig Perlman. He also formed his long-time intellectual relationship with Hans Gerth, the German sociologist who was to co-author *Character and Social Structure* with him. Mills' years at Wisconsin had a broadening effect on him in that he became more conversant with European social thought. Nevertheless, he continued to pursue his interests in pragmatism by writing his doctoral dissertation on that subject, which he finished in 1942. Mills did not serve in the military during World War II; he failed his physical examination owing to hypertension.

His first academic position was as an associate professor at the University of Maryland, where he was more impressed by the historians than by the sociologists. Frank Freidel, Kenneth Stampp, and Richard Hofstadter, later to become three eminent American historians, were his intellectual compatriots and friends. Mills remained especially close to Hofstadter for many years afterward. However, Maryland proved to be little more than a holding pattern and in 1945 Mills took a position at Columbia University, where he remained for the rest of his life. Life in New York City suited the Texan well. He led an extremely active intellectual life and published at a prodigious rate.

The New Men of Power was his first book and it was published in 1948 when Mills was 32 years old. In it Mills attempted to come to terms with organized labor and labor leadership's changing role in American society. In 1951 he published *White Collar,* which focused on the changing composition of the middle class, its values, and its political future. In 1956 he published *The Power Elite,* a study of the new ruling elite that Mills believed had come to dominate American society. Although this study came under sustained attack by his critics, it was by far the most influential book he ever wrote.

During the 1940s and 1950s the department of sociology at Columbia had such noted sociologists as Robert Merton, Daniel Bell, Paul Lazarsfeld, and Seymour Martin Lipset. Mills did not get along well with all of his colleagues because, in addition to mutual personal animosity, he was involved in ideological and methodological disputes with them. Nevertheless, in spite of these often strained relationships, he developed an international reputation as a radical sociologist and social critic.

In the mid-1950s Mills made contacts with foreign intellectuals; doing so was easy for him since he was much admired in radical intellectual circles abroad. His travels throughout Europe occurred at the same time he began to shift his intellectual interests from the study of American society to Marxism, the post-Stalinist thaw in Eastern Europe, and the problems of the Third World. Some insight into his personality and values may be gained from an incident in the Soviet Union when he visited there:

> . . . he was entertained and honored with an official dinner as the greatest living American critic of American society. When it came his turn to raise a toast, he ingratiated himself with this diplomatic *tour de force:* "To the day when the complete works of Leon Trotsky are published in the Soviet Union!" No one, of course, can say whether this should be attributed to his crude Texas origins or simply to a nasty disposition.[4]

Mills outlined his future plans for research and writing in a letter to his parents written shortly after the onset of the heart disease that was eventually to take his life. He set forth a view of the role of the political intellectual acting as a craftsman striving to overcome the confines of his academic discipline.

> . . . lying here all these weeks and having damned near died, because this thing was pretty damned close, well it's made me much stronger and made me think about myself which I'd not had the chance to do before. I know that I have not the slightest fear of death; I know also that I have a big responsibility to thousands of people all over the world to tell the truth as I see it and tell it exactly and with drama and quit this horsing around with sociological bullshit.[5]

Those familiar with Mills' work, especially with his strictures on methodology and professional responsibility, need not inquire as to the meaning of this last sentence. However, he probably did not intend to abandon serious scholarly work in the social sciences. What he had in mind was its reorientation around more pressing political issues.

Mills' avocation was as a craftsman. He enjoyed working with tools so much that he built his own home. His admiration for skilled mechanics and craftsmen of various sorts was reflected in what he wrote on general craftsmanship as a moral and professional ideal. Mills had an air of bravado about him and was often given to unorthodox behavior. He took delight in commuting to New York City on his motorcycle in boots, leathers, and helmet, after which he deposited his paratroop boots on the podium before lecturing to his enthralled students. Mills was married three times and had children by all three of his wives. His last wife, Yaroslava, was a talented artist. Unfortunately, as Mills' home life solidified and his reputation as a radical sociologist continued to grow, his health rapidly declined. In March, 1962 he died in his sleep of a heart attack at the age of 45. America was thus deprived of its leading leftist social critic and theoretician.

MILLS' CRITICS

Political and ideological factors have played a powerful role in the interpretation of Mills' intellectual perspective and his life. Evaluation of the motives of his critics is obviously a speculative endeavor, but it is impossible to explain the writing on Mills without reference to the biases of his interpreters. For example, many of Mills' leftist critics are not impressed by eclecticism because they believe it lacks viability as a fundamental agent of social change. They find it unlikely that a blend of European social thought with American institutionalism, pragmatism, and symbolic interactionism could result in anything but acquiescence in the status quo. The belief is prevalent among radicals that these three related indigenous schools of thought are part of a larger ideological syndrome that has conservatized American social science or at least helped to divert it from a genuinely radical path.

Many who wrote for radical social-science journals such as *Politics and Society, Review of Radical Political Economics,* and *The Insurgent Sociologist,* despite their attacks on older Marxian scholarship for its dogmatism, are not eclectic in any systematic way. It is heartening to note a genuine resurgence of serious left scholarship in the American academic community. But it is disappointing to observe the conviction of many of its practioners that the non-Marxian intellectual traditions which influenced Mills are of little relevance in the development of a radical perspective. An earlier generation of Marxists and Marxist-Leninists realized that, even though Mills was a radical, he was not really one of them. They were correct in believing that Mills was not a "Marxist" except in the limited sense of being what he called a "plain Marxist." They were wrong, however, in failing to recognize the radical scholars of native birth since Veblen whom mainline social scientists have not ignored. Nevertheless, Marxists persist in their conviction that all that is valuable in Mills is either derived from Marx or else closely parallels his perspective—the same interpretation Marxists often place on the work of Veblen. To them, Mills' work is of value only when it is Marxian; its eclectic and indigenous aspects, when recognized, are viewed either as pernicious ideological dilutants or as moral and political contaminants. Perhaps this outlook explains why Marxists, as an ideological category, were more sensitive than other political groups toward Mills' intellectual pedigree and less likely to misinterpret it.

Marxists were also more prone to admire Mills' character traits and professional role. An interesting comparison of Mills and Dewey in this respect is found in a letter written by the American Marxist George Novack to Leon Trotsky's widow:

> He [Mills] has shown by his criticism of U.S. militarism and, above all, by his stance in defense of the Cuban Revolution that he is one of the most courageous and honest of all academic figures in this country today. He belongs to the same university faculty as did John Dewey, and they are of the same intellectual and moral stature, as well as of the same general trend of thought. Moreover, he is today defending the right of Trotsky's views to be presented to the public without prejudice or discrimination no less vigorously than did John Dewey in the hearings on the Moscow Trials.[6]

The left generally praised Mills' work for its focus on the "big" questions of power, wealth, and status, for its intrinsic moralism, and for its ethicization of work as "intellectual craftsmanship." But Mills was assaulted from the middle of the political spectrum by a large number of pluralists who claimed to speak in the name of an "objective" social science. They, in particular, never forgave Mills for his criticisms of their political complacency, or for his accusations that their work was essentially ideological. It is interesting to note that Arthur Schlesinger, Jr.'s "vital center," which prides itself on being "pragmatic," failed to recognize pragmatism in the American tradition in Mills' thought. One reason for this oversight is that "pragmatism" has come to mean little more than opportunism, and since Mills' politics was obviously not based on expediency the pragmatic residues in his thought have largely escaped the notice of political centrists. Yet it is well to remember that "pragmatism" has not always connoted unprincipled behavior or ad hoc politics without substantive goals.

Conservatives failed to recognize that important elements in the American intellectual tradition played a powerful role in Mills' political sociology. If conservatism exists to "conserve" our cultural and intellectual legacy, then conservatives may be advised to understand Mills' utilization of that tradition, even though they cannot accept his politics. For his is no "alien" radicalism nurtured abroad, but has roots deep in indigenous intellectual history and political practice.

It is inevitably difficult to sort out personal dislike of Mills from negative evaluations of his role as a professional sociologist. It is also hard to keep these factors separate from theoretical and ideological disagreements. But all are probably relevant considerations in explaining the attacks on Mills by such eminent sociologists as Neil Smelser, Seymour Martin Lipset, Daniel Bell, and Edward Shils, all of whom were professionally antagonistic toward Mills while closer to the center of the political spectrum.[7] In a venomous attack on Mills shortly after his death, Shils wrote that he became

> a demogogic simplifier . . . he had a singularly incurious mind . . . [he wrote] vigorous and cloudy rhetoric. Now he is dead and his rhetoric is a field of broken stones, his analysis empty, his strenuous pathos limp. He was a victim of his own vanity and of a shrivelled Marxism which will not die and which goes on requiring the sacrifice of the living.[8]

Shils' comments may reveal as much about his own ideology and his personal dislike for Mills as they do about the quality of his work, yet they are indicative of the attitude of many mainline social scientists toward Mills.

The response to Mills, especially after the publication of *The Power Elite*, often manifested the critic's ideology. Radical and left-liberal interpreters, despite their many disagreements with Mills, were more responsive to his message than those in the center and on the right. For example, contrast the sometime leftist I. L. Horowitz, who once believed Mills to be the greatest American sociologist, with the conservative H. Malcolm MacDonald, who in reviewing *The Power Elite* complained

> of the magnitude of the absurdity which emerges as its conclusion. . . .
> The sordid, vulgarized and cynical picture of American society which
> emerges from the author's personal sense of frustration leaves one won-
> dering how the organization functions at all. The overexaggeration of
> what at best are trends and tendencies in American culture places the
> author's conclusions in the realm of half truth. If his purpose in over-
> drawing his picture is to excite us to reform he again disappoints us, for
> at no stage in his narrative does he offer or propose any way out of our
> slough of vulgarity and corruption.[9]

MacDonald's review is only a few sentences in length. It is interesting to observe that one of the most widely read, often cited, and rigorously scrutinized works of political sociology published in the post-World War II era did not receive a full-length review in the leading American political-science journal! What attention it did get at the time came from a conservative who was obviously rankled at Mills' assaults on his ideological compatriots. Mills had attacked such conservative writers as Russell Kirk and Peter Viereck for their irrelevance and inconsist-ency in *The Power Elite* shortly before MacDonald praised them in his "The Revival of Conservative Thought," in the *Journal of Politics*.

That much of the criticism of his work was politically inspired did not surprise Mills, nor would it have shocked Veblen and Dewey, for they were well aware of the value-laden nature of social-science inquiry. Mills was attacked in predictable fashion from left, right and center. He was criticized by Marxist-Leninists such as Herbert Aptheker, and by independent Marxists like Paul Sweezy, for refusing to adopt the ruling-class perspective that was their stock in trade. He was de-nounced by conservatives like MacDonald for failing to realize that the United States was the land of the free and the home of the brave. The main assault, however, came through the middle from those who con-fused the politics of the center with scholarly objectivity. The moder-ates, both liberal and conservative, upon whom Mills bestowed the sobriquet of "N.A.T.O. intellectuals," have often distorted his per-spective by labeling it "Marxist." Whether intended or not, this is a traditional method of discrediting opponents by implicit association with "alien" ideology and "totalitarian" political movements. In any case such interpretations are the mark of the ideologue and indicate a gross insensitivity to indigenous radical doctrine. It is ironic that those who pride themselves on proclaiming an "end to ideology" should give ideology rebirth in their doctrinaire assaults on one of the most strenuously eclectic thinkers the United States has produced.

2

Mills' Eclectic Theory of Stratification and Power in the United States

The massive economic and social dislocation of the 1930s helped produce an environment in which the reform programs of the Roosevelt administration could flourish. It was near the waning of this period, during the winding down of the New Deal, that C. Wright Mills first reached political consciousness. He early saw himself as part of the radical tradition of protest against American capitalism. Although the ideas of this tradition were not unique to the United States, the particular formulations of them were, because they were affected by the crucial impact of an older American radicalism. The new radicalism may have reached its climax with Mills, but it was spawned earlier by the instrumentalism and institutionalism of Dewey and Veblen, which in turn drew on an older radical heritage. Academics who identified with pragmatism and institutionalism, two closely related schools of thought of native origin, provided Mills' early intellectual stimuli. Although Mills absorbed much from these intellectuals and their schools of thought, he recognized that

> My formal sociological work has been pitifully fragmentary and theoretically shallow. . . . I have been too occupied with taking courses in sociology to have read any of the important European sociologists . . . at present my acquaintance with European theory is via secondary American sources most of which, I am informed by men I believe sound, are not only inadequate, but falsifying.[1]

Mills soon remedied these shortcomings. As he did so, however, he recognized that a major deficiency in the eminent European theorists was a tendency to become absolutist in certain aspects of their work. By drawing on the contribution of the American pragmatists, Mills believed he could rid sociology of such absolutist elements and make possible "more pragmatic explorations of reality."

In striving for a new theoretical synthesis he never quite achieved, much of Mills' work had tentative and improvisatory tendencies. Had he been content to follow along the established paths of orthodox Marxism, his work would have been less eclectic, but it would not have been so closely related to the realities of American society.[2] What John Dewey said of himself in 1930—that he seemed to be "chameleon-like, yielding one after another to many diverse and even incompatible influences; struggling to assimilate something from each and yet striving to carry it forward in a way that is logically consistent with what has been learned from its predecessors"—was only slightly less true of Mills.[3] The nature of Mills' eclecticism was evident in his endorsement of Dewey as one who did not merely

> "relate" topics. He does not simply shift the meanings and shapes of two opinions so that he can "live" with both, as tends to be the rather patent case with much of William James. Dewey takes a point of sight and builds a conceptual structure within which he can grasp both the points which were being argued over; this structure is different from either of the conflicting or isolated doctrines with which it "combines." It is Deweyan.[4]

By heeding Dewey's example, Mills never let his eclecticism become the undiscriminating variety that lumps together an endless diversity of ideas into a shapeless form. In this vein Mills once complained that "a paste-pot eclectic psychology provides a rationale for . . . facile analysis. . . . That is, an eclecticism that does not analyze in any adequate way the elements and theories which it seeks to combine."[5] He also criticized this approach in a review of Gordon W. Allport's *The Nature of Prejudice:*

> Allport's own view might with justice be called dogmatic pluralism: he remains satisfied with the eclectic level of thought. This has the advantage of revealing to the reader the various results of all known viewpoints. . . . E. M. Forster's remark that "though proportion is the final secret, to espouse it at the outset is to insure sterility" [is appropriate]. One does not really need to choose between the apotheosis of one single factor and the holding still in a theoretical stalemate. Can one not "ad-

mit" all viewpoints and yet develop a structural model that containing
them all transcends them by its own creative unity?[6]

Mills opposed the improper use of an eclectic approach, not eclecticism itself. His blend of doctrinal elements thus came to include:
(1) value eclecticism, that is, the drawing together of the strands of
Western humanism from a broad spectrum of different value sources—
instrumentalism, institutionalism, Marxism, and the classical tradition
in social thought all provided material for his approach to valuation;
(2) political eclecticism, which mixed political ideas from various liberal
and radical sources; (3) methodological eclecticism, that is, his metacritique of social-science methodology as well as his own methodology,
which included the quantitative-statistical, historical-comparative,
and ideal-typical approaches; and, (4) systematic interdisciplinary eclecticism, which integrated knowledge with little regard for disciplinary lines—including aesthetics and literary criticism, philosophy,
sociology, history, psychology, economics, and political science.

But Mills' eclecticism should not mislead the reader. In his view
eclecticism should *not* be a pluralism that gives an equal weight to all
factors. Neither should it be an accommodationism from which no
transcending synthesis emerges, nor a balancing process in which conflicting elements are not modified or purged but rather remain to produce a disharmonious whole. Mills believed much "liberal" scholarship
in the social studies suffered from such faults, and that a paste-pot
eclecticism was not the way to overcome them.

The cynic may believe that ideological rigidity is an occupational
disease of Marxists, as lack of principle is characteristic of liberals, and
bad principle representative of conservatives. But Mills' work suggests, with its endorsement of a particular kind of eclecticism, a way
out of such doctrinal straitjackets. The unique quality of this eclecticism lies in its blending diverse elements of thought and contending
claims of different ideologies into a new system. It may be that Mills,
in attempting to fashion an argument that took seriously many different intellectual concerns, both juxtaposed and combined points of view
better left separate. But if fragmentation itself was a good part of the
problem, then for Mills, a disciplined eclecticism was the solution.
Although both to Marxists and behavioralists such an approach
seemed futile and iconoclastic, it was to Mills' credit that he remained
faithful to the older American radical tradition of eclecticism in terminology and perspective, method and value.

While it is evident that Mills combined various intellectual traditions, did he in fact forge a distinctively new theoretical system? It is relatively easy to be eclectic in the weaker sense by combining ideas based on ad hoc notions of theoretical significance or practical utility. But often such an approach incorporates explanations, concepts, and methodologies based on dramatically divergent assumptions. Unless such fundamental differences are reconciled, one is left with "practical theory" rather than "systematic analysis." In short, the strongest form of eclecticism is that which reconciles seemingly contradictory or at least differing thought systems within a new integrative framework. Mills clearly sought such a goal. But if in fact he accomplished such a theoretical objective, his published work does not always make this clear. Indeed, it is only with the publication of Joseph Scimecca's *The Sociological Theory of C. Wright Mills* in 1977 that Mills' achievement as a systematic theorist is finally evident.[7]

PERIODIZATION OF INFLUENCE ON MILLS

However, further clarification of the relevance of Mills' work for systematic theory is important. It is unwittingly provided by those writers who interpret Mills' intellectual development, since they disagree about which doctrinal components most influenced his thought and when they did so. For example, Darla Johnson has placed Mills' evolution in a three-phase monistic framework. The first phase, his period of social behaviorism, was concerned with the work of the pragmatists; the second phase found him under the influence of Weber; the third was dominated by Marx.[8] But Richard Peterson offered a different view:

> If Mills' early work derives its theoretical orientation from Mannheim, his middle period derives its theoretical orientation from Max Weber. . . . since 1956, the name Karl Marx comes more into the fore in Mills' writings. The underpinnings of his work, however, seem to be derived more from the Franco-Italian realists, Mosca, Michels, Pareto and Sorel.[9]

When Mills' intellectual development is phased, as Johnson and Peterson have done, by stressing the influence of a particular thinker or school, a marked discontinuity appears which distorts the actual evolution of his thought. Consequently it is essential to differentiate between one's intellectual progenitors and their ideas on the one hand and the uses to which they are actually put on the other. A theorist may employ a specific set of sources, but then develop these into an intellectual system different from the one in which they originated. Such was the case in Mills' use of Veblen and Dewey. Mills' eclecticism may best be viewed as an American foundation with a partly European superstructure, provided the analogy is not taken too literally. Looked at without regard to its evolution over time, his thought can be described as an intellectual salad, or as a marble cake (rather than a layer cake) in which it is often difficult to ascertain different intellectual sources. Nevertheless, Mills cannot be properly understood without recognizing that his eclecticism early assimilated elements from nearly every major school of social thought. For this reason periodization of his work is a risky venture, for it often ignores research and cognition in progress and pays little heed to conflicting themes. Also, it maximizes differences while minimizing continuities and often confuses publication dates with states of mind. Yet Mills' work over the years did exhibit discontinuities of subject matter and levels of abstraction. He wrote on a broad variety of topics from *both* a macro- and microsocial angle, although he felt that it was essential to relate the two and was critical of other sociologists who did not. Moreover, Mills liked to distinguish in his work between scholarly publications such as *White Collar* and *The Power Elite*, written primarily for academic social scientists, and "pamphlets" written for propagandistic purposes. In the latter category would fall *The Causes of World War III* and *Listen Yankee* which appealed to less specialized audiences. In any case, it is important to recognize that regardless of how the development of this thought is periodized with respect to external influences and irrespective of the audiences for which he wrote, his thought is essentially eclectic. But it is eclecticism with a difference, for it is originally rooted in an indigenous intellectual tradition.

Although it is difficult to make accurate estimates of the influence of intellectuals and their salient ideas, there appears to be little sustained interest in the theoretical work of American radicals like Mills. This inattention probably results from four factors. One is lack of a radical reading public of substantial size. Another is radical failure to use indigenous strains of thought that are acceptable to an audience sensitive to the American intellectual environment. A third is lack of radical recognition of the value and significance of "bourgeois" liberal political and legal institutions and practices. A fourth is covert and overt repression of radicalism by the powers-that-be. A possibility that must also be considered is that the absence of certain structural factors in American society is more important in determining the success or failure of radical movements than the ideological perspectives of its radical intellectuals. These absent structural factors include an explicit and accepted class system, the distribution of wealth and income, the efficiency and responsiveness of government to voters, and the manner in which dominant values have achieved hegemony. But it cannot be denied that insofar as the *Weltanschauung* of native intellectuals is relevant in explaining the failure of radicalism in America, the radical's doctrinal inadequacy has played a significant role.

Mills' eclecticism and his use of ideas deeply rooted in the American past are attuned to the structural realities of our political and cultural life. So is his recognition of the value of liberal political and legal institutions and processes. He thus offers a more viable radical alternative than competing perspectives that do not use the American intellectual and political tradition and attempt to function outside it. If it accomplishes nothing else, this study will demonstrate that Mills' radicalism makes massive use of American sources, and that to restrict radicalism to European versions of Marxism is thus to ignore important indigenous sources of critical social theory. "Radicalism" is all too often used to refer exclusively to Marxism by American Marxists and non-Marxists alike. Mills' own work, properly understood, is evidence that there is much more to the American Left than Marx and Marxism. Charges of theoretical poverty made against the American Left are convincing only if "left" is narrowly defined to mean "Marxist." My thesis is that the left has a rich theoretical heritage best exemplified in the work of Mills, Veblen, and Dewey. To ignore this legacy is to admit that both liberal and conservative charges of theoretical poverty made against the American left are indeed true.

STRATIFICATION AND POWER IN AMERICA

Mills' own creative role in coagulating the various strands of radical thought is important. It can best be understood by examining his work on social stratification and power. Basically, Mills' theory of stratification derives from Weber's famous class-status-power trichotomy, to which Mills added Veblen's emphasis on occupation.[10] Class is related to the amount and the source of income for "a class is a set of people who share similar life choices because of their similar class situations."[11] Mills always emphasized the unequal opportunities that accompany the various class situations. Status necessitates more than one person, for someone must claim deference or prestige and someone must honor the claim. However, power is the most basic aspect of stratification, for those who have power can exert their will over others. Usually, when we speak of power, we mean political power because the social structure is organized under the state. To the Weberian class-status-power trichotomy Mills adds the Veblenian emphasis on "occupation."

> By an occupation we understand a set of activities pursued more or less regularly as a major source of income.
>
> From the individual's standpoint, occupational activities refer to types of skills that are marketable. As specific activities, occupations thus (1) entail various types and levels of skill, and (2) their exercise fulfills certain functions within an industrial division of labor. . . .
>
> As sources of income, occupations are thus connected with class position. Since occupations also normally carry an expected quota of prestige, on and off the job, they are relevant to status position. They also involve certain degrees of power over other people directly in terms of the job, and indirectly in other social areas.[12]

Mills believed that the growth of industrial capitalism in the United States had resulted in an unprecedented concentration of power. Unlike many Marxists, however, he did not believe, after the changes brought about by the New Deal and World War II, that this country had a ruling class composed primarily of large property owners. The owners and managers of the major industrial and financial corporations were an important part of the power elite that dominated the country, perhaps the core of it. But they were not the only significant element in the power structure at the national level. Mills thought that the New Deal, for example, had greatly enhanced the power of the executive branch of the federal government. It had also given other interest groups such as organized labor and the farm bloc new access to power. Although only junior partners at best, workers and farmers had more influence on public policy than they had before the New Deal when, in Mills' view, corporate interests still held sway. Also, World War II and the Cold War had greatly increased the power of the military. The officer corps of the armed forces and the contractors of the military-industrial complex were a new and potent force in the making of United States foreign and domestic policy. Indeed, at the time Mills published the *New Men of Power* in 1948, the first volume in his trilogy on stratification, he believed that the United States was rapidly becoming a garrison state with little except organized labor standing in the way of economic slump and renewed warfare.

Mills was concerned not with power only but also with powerlessness. In keeping with the American radical intellectual tradition, in *The New Men of Power* he analyzed the inability of the labor leader to exert power while in *White Collar* he described the essential powerlessness of the middle class. In *The Power Elite*, the third volume of his trilogy on stratification, he focused on the powerlessness and apathy of mass society which included the bulk of the American people. An antidote to this powerlessness is found in *The New Men of*

Power where Mills, no longer so optimistic about the radical potential of organized labor, nevertheless advocated a program of guild socialism. His program, stated in the form of the position of the left, called for "a society in which everyone affected by a social decision, regardless of its sphere, would have a voice in the decision and a hand in its administration."[13] It would be hard to find a better example of the American radical intellectual tradition at work, for this idea of "participatory democracy" was incorporated in the Port Huron statement of Students for a Democratic Society in 1962; it is also Deweyan through and through.

THE NEW MEN OF POWER: AMERICAN LABOR

Mills' first monograph was his *The New Men of Power*, which focused on the American labor movement. It was the result of empirical studies done primarily on labor leaders. It was also a consequence of his friendship with J. B. S. Hardman, a labor intellectual whom he met in New York City, who greatly influenced his thinking about the trade-union movement and its future. Indeed, so highly did Mills think of Hardman that he dedicated *The New Men of Power* to him. In it Mills focused on the values and background of labor leaders. He contrasted the behavior of the younger leaders in the C.I.O. with that of the older men who dominated the A.F.L. and found the former more to his liking than the latter because they were further left ideologically. Later, however, he began to denounce the "labor metaphysic" of Marxism for its misperception of the future of the working class, which no longer had revolutionary socialist potential. In Mills' view the trade unions and their leaders were not politically radical at all, but instead simply wanted a larger cut of the economic pie. They were rapidly becoming integrated into the main power system as a junior partner and had thus relinquished any aspirations for structural change.

Although Mills believed that organized labor should try to halt the drift toward war and rearmament, he believed that its capacity to do so had been weakened by changes that had occurred during the New Deal and World War II. First, the unions had been partly integrated into the corporate-government complex as a junior partner due to certain structural shifts that had occurred. They now perceived their own self-interest in terms of collaborating with the powers-that-be rather than in terms of an independent, critical stance. Mills also thought that "bossism" and corruption within the unions had increased their tendency to engage in policies that were opportunistic. In short, labor's political development as an independent force had been inhibited both by external changes that integrated it into the corporate-government complex and by internal changes that weakened its capacity for independent action.

As Mills saw it, labor had been co-opted into a collaborationist policy with business and government. In *The New Men of Power* Mills voiced his uneasiness about this collaboration and pointed to the factors that had brought it about. Of prime importance was the failure of the labor movement to educate its members as to its larger aims. Mills believed that labor leaders should make massive efforts to indoctrinate the rank-and-file, which was inclined to be apathetic and inactive. But labor leaders failed to do so because their objectives were extremely short-range and narrow in scope, rarely extending beyond "bread-and-butter" issues. In keeping with his own social philosophy, Mills accused labor of not having long-range comprehensive plans for social reconstruction. These were not likely to materialize until the unions developed planning bureaus of their own. At present they were unwilling to invest sufficiently in research and theory to make long-range plans because most labor leaders had no independent vision of what the good society might be like and consequently could not plan for its achievement. Much to Mills' dismay, labor leaders were too conservative politically and too inhibited intellectually to seek the cooperative commonwealth.

He voiced his disappointment that no independent labor party existed in the United States for he felt that labor would have to lead the way if any important structural changes were to be brought about in the existing order. It could not do so as long as it was wedded to the Democratic Party and to the political framework provided by a two-party system. Unfortunately, labor leaders themselves were often blind to the realities of power. Their illusions about the distribution of power in the system were pluralistic in that they emphasized the dispersion and fragmentation of power and labor's access to policy-makers. The pluralist ideology Mills later attacked for its stultifying impact on social scientists, had already shown itself in the liberal illusions of the labor leaders.

Mills used Veblen's ideas about status emulation to explain the behavior and values of the labor movement. In his view, what labor wanted was not an egalitarian society but an emulatory one in which it could adopt the consumption patterns of those classes above it in the class structure. This meant that the main function of the labor union must be to obtain higher wages and more benefits for its members so that they could emulate the life styles of the upper middle class. One important consequence of this was the willingness of unions in collaboration with corporations, to pass unjustified wage increases on to consumers in the form of higher prices. Emulatory consumption patterns thus provided a rationale for collaboration between unions and powerful corporations, to the detriment of the common man.

Mills voiced concern in *The New Men of Power* about the growing authoritarianism and corruption in the ranks of organized labor since "bossism" and graft had made considerable inroads into trade-union politics. In part this penetration was a reaction to the authoritarianism found in the corporate structure itself. But it was also due to the passivity and disinterest of the rank-and-file, which had not been educated by the labor leaders nor encouraged by them to participate in the affairs of their unions. Mills believed that much of the bossism and opportunism of labor leaders which now impeded labor's political development had been fostered by the paternalistic policies of the New Deal. Although the Roosevelt administration had aided in the formation of unions, it had also helped to intensify some of the worst traits found in the labor movement as a whole. Since Mills prized democracy both as a means and as an end, he could not acquiesce in the oligarchic tendencies of the unions. He was dismayed by the authoritarian structure of industry and by the same tendencies in labor. Mills thought labor should formulate democratic and egalitarian goals that would result in workers' control and social ownership of the economy. However, by 1948 it was evident to him that this was unlikely to happen. Only the most progressive unions showed any inclination in this direction and their interest was slight.

Mills also faulted labor for not paying more attention to the problems of the underdogs: those who were poorly paid or unemployed and who were not members of unions nor eligible for their benefits. Again, in order to be consistent with his own egalitarian values, Mills had to insist that labor organize this underclass into unions, educate it politically, and obtain government benefits for it. Unionization of the underdog could be a way of increasing labor's social power.

WHITE COLLAR: THE AMERICAN MIDDLE CLASS

In *White Collar,* Mills' classic study of the American middle class, he examined the linkages between the various dimensions of stratification. In order to do this he found it necessary to analyze the changing composition of the middle class itself. He broke the class into two parts: an "old" middle class which consisted of small businessmen, small farmers, and independent professionals; and a "new" middle class made up of white-collar workers and professionals whose work situation was increasingly bureaucratized. The new middle class was becoming the dominant reality of American life, but the remnants of the old middle class still held antiquated values and perceptions of themselves. Because of structural changes which had occurred in the economy after the Civil War, the old middle class had declined. These changes were caused primarily by the increasing concentration of corporate power which squeezed it and simultaneously usurped employment opportunities.

Mills revered the time when America was a society of small entrepreneurs in which perhaps four-fifths of the free population who worked owned property. In this period, which was dominated by the old middle class, small property owners were so numerous and of such economic weight that it was appropriate to think of America as a middle-class society. Mills saw Jacksonian America in this light:

> At the same time the rich could easily be tolerated, they were so few. The ideal of universal small property held those without property in collective check while it lured them on as individuals. They would fight alongside those who already had it, joining with them in destroying holdovers from the previous epoch which hampered the way up for the small owners.[14]

Because he owned land or a small business, the small entrepreneur controlled his own work, and was thus independent. Consequently, there was a linkage of income, status, work, and property. Because property holding was widespread, the power distribution that emanated from it was one of dispersion and fragmentation. An invisible hand coordinated human activity in a society where individualism reigned supreme and the social bond was provided by free markets.

However, after the Civil War, Mills believed that science and technology were increasingly channeled through the corporate structure and transformed the middle class. Changes in the distribution and type of property affected the way its members lived and made the self-sustaining property owner increasingly rare. Democratic property that the owner himself worked had given way to class property that others were hired to work and manage. Property, rather than being a condition of the owners' work, had become a condition of their not having to work.

In the countryside the old middle class that consisted of small farmers had become part of what Mills called the "rural debacle." The agrarian world of the small farmer was rapidly disappearing for the industrial and agro-corporate revolutions were rapidly eliminating the family farm or leaving it stranded in an archaic subsistence economy. As large farming units engrossed more and more land, small farmers found it expedient to leave for the city. Thus in the twentieth century the ranks of the old middle class in the countryside were rapidly being depleted.

Meanwhile in urban areas, small business felt the squeeze from the new chain stores which had emerged in the 1920s and 1930s. However, even though competition with these corporate outlets made life more difficult for the small businessman, and even though business claimed to believe in the competitive way of life, competition came increasingly to mean competition between businessmen on one side and consumers on the other. For business acted collectively when it could to sabotage competition. As Mills put it:

> Both groups have made clear the locus of the big competition and have revealed the mask-like character of liberalism's rhetoric of small business and family farm.[15]

Independent professionals had also been part of the old middle class, which consisted of doctors, dentists, lawyers, and professors. These occupational groups which had hitherto enjoyed considerable autonomy were now encountering effects of bureaucratization. Institutional employment centralized direction and control, while reliance on specialization and specialists was stripping away the freedom that these professionals were accustomed to exercise.

In conclusion, Mills argued that even though remnants of the old middle class had survived, their relative numbers had diminished greatly. The effects of bureaucratization and centralization and the consolidation of property holding meant that although small businessmen, farmers, and professionals continued to believe the rhetoric of laissez-faire, social reality decreed otherwise.

THE NEW MIDDLE CLASS

Increasingly prominent were the members of the new middle class, who were essentially white-collar people drawing a salary. For them, as for wage workers, the United States had become a nation of employees for whom independent property ownership was no longer a viable option. Labor markets, not control of property, "determined their chances to receive income, exercise power, enjoy prestige, learn and use skills."[16] By 1950, it was evident to Mills that of the three broad strata composing modern society, only the new middle class had grown steadily as a proportion of the whole. During this period the old middle class increased its numbers by 135 percent, blue collar workers by 255 percent, while the new middle class increased by 1600 percent.

In *White Collar*, Mills reiterated the belief that certain psychological traits recur among individuals of the same strata. Mills' argument is based on his belief that when people have a similar mentality and ideology, they may join together for action. The probability of action will be increased the more homogenous they are with respect to class, occupation, and prestige. Mills was concerned with this homogeneity, particularly as it affects political consciousness. He found that any political ideology held by white-collar individuals arises primarily out of their occupation and is often used to set up social distinctions between them and manual laborers. The white-collar worker is thus divorced from any organizations of power since his mindset often predisposes him against joining unions. Mills asked whether white-collar workers would join with labor, support the corporations, or chart an independent political course? He hoped they would support labor and the Left, but he was not optimistic about such an outcome since political organization and political awareness were at a low ebb in the American middle class. The political future of the middle class was, in Mills' words, "up for grabs."

THE POWER ELITE: THE HIGHER CIRCLES

The central theme of *The Power Elite*, Mills' most famous and widely read book, is the existence of a ruling elite in the United States made up of "those political, economic and military circles which as an intricate set of overlapping cliques shape decisions having at least national consequences. In so far as national events are decided, the power elite are those who decide them."[17] The political part of the power elite consisted of the president, his cabinet, and about 1500 of the most important appointed officials in the executive branch of the federal government. The massive growth of the federal bureaucracy since the beginning of the New Deal in 1933, and the greatly enhanced role of the president in making foreign policy after 1939, had given the political directorate a more powerful role than it ever before possessed in United States history. Critics of Mills were quick to charge that he had been mistaken in relegating Congress to a subordinate level of power; he now believed that its role was indeed subordinate since Congress had relinquished its prerogatives to the executive branch. However, consider the often cowed and submissive behavior of Congress since

Mills' death in 1962: witness its failure to halt the Vietnam War, to develop energy policies of its own, or to act decisively on other pressing issues. Indeed, given Congress's tendency to acquiesce in the policies of whatever administration is in power, it is evident that Mills only slightly overestimated the impotence of Congress.

The second part of Mills' ruling triumvirate was the corporate elite. This consisted of top-level management, the major stockholders, and corporate lawyers representing the five or six hundred largest financial and industrial corporations in the country. It is not necessary to read between the lines of *The Power Elite* to recognize that Mills believed the corporate elite was first among equals. The corporate element was not only powerful in its own sphere—the economic—but it also had close ties with the other two parts of the ruling stratum. There was an important interchange of personnel between the military, the executive branch, and the corporations. There was also a common perception of social reality and a community of interest among the corporate elite whether it functioned within the corporate structure or served temporarily in the federal government at the top echelons as appointed officials.

The third part of Mills' ruling triumvirate was the military, especially those officers holding the rank of brigadier general or higher. Mills pointed out that since 1939 the United States had millions of men continuously under arms, that it supported a huge military bureaucracy, and that it often acted in a bellicose fashion as a consequence. Although it was not new for America to be involved in war, it was unprecedented for it to have become a militarized society. Indeed, Mills argued that Americans were now living under a military definition of reality. Mills thus claimed that "a military metaphysic" pervades American society, which meant that Americans now believed conflicts between nations can be resolved only by force or the threat of force.

The military were involved in politics simply by virtue of the fact that they have technical expertise. Mills believed that we live in a time of military secrecy, in which information is withheld from the public, and Congress is virtually subservient to the military. In short, neither the general public nor the Congress is able to effectively oversee the military. Decisions are made by the civilian secretary of defense or by the president and his civilian advisers, yet, Mills argued, these decisions are based on information given by the military.

Mills summarized the composition and the role of the economic, political, and military parts of the power elite in this manner:

The economy—once a great scatter of small productive units in autonomous balance—has become dominated by two or three hundred giant corporations, administratively and politically interrelated, which together hold the keys to economic decisions.

The political order, once a decentralized set of several dozen states with a weak spinal cord, has become a centralized, executive establishment which has taken up into itself many powers previously scattered, and now enters into each and every cranny of the social structure.

The military order, once a slim establishment in a context of distrust fed by state militia, has become the largest and most expensive feature of government, and although well versed in smiling public relations, now has all the grim and clumsy efficiency of a sprawling bureaucratic domain.

In each of these institutional areas, the means of power at the disposal of decision makers have increased enormously; their central executive powers have been enhanced; within each of them modern administrative routines have been elaborated and tightened up.

As each of these domains becomes enlarged and centralized, the consequences of its activities become greater and its traffic with others increases.[18]

Some of Mills' critics have claimed that his power elite is both conspiratorial and monolithic. They are wrong on both counts, for Mills did not succumb to what his old friend and colleague Richard Hofstadter once referred to as "the paranoid style in American politics." He did not believe that the power elite behaved in a conspiratorial manner most of the time, for that was unnecessary. Instead, consistent with the American radical intellectual tradition, he argued that a community of interests, a commonality of values, and control of basic social institutions enabled the power elite to coordinate policy without conspiring in smoke-filled rooms in the early hours of the morning. Nor did he think that their power was monolithic. Mills, himself, believed that members of the power elite were often in some tension: unified only on some points and mostly during periods of crisis.

The processes of socialization and co-optation are important in explaining why and how the power elite has the values and makes the policies that it does. In the economic realm, the cues are given by the corporate elite, and prospective recruits must perform their "proper" roles within the institution. Those who manifest "deviant" attitudes and modes of behavior will not be promoted to positions of responsibility. According to Mills, the process of socialization depends upon a network of upper-class wealth that supports private schools, elite universities, exclusive clubs, and vacation resorts through which the bulk of the corporate elite pass before they are co-opted. Naturally, most of the population can never afford to undergo this socialization process and most are thus unlikely to be eligible for co-optation into the ruling stratum. Thus the corporate elite consists of similar personality types who are predisposed to pattern their policies in certain directions because of the mind set fostered in them by their prior experiences and present institutional expectations. The military likewise produces a sameness in those who ascend its hierarchy. Education at the military academies, in particular, is the device that is used to inculcate militaristic values in the officer corps thus producing a commonalty of outlook and an uncritical adherence to the military metaphysic. Thus, Mills thought it was no accident that the three different parts of the power elite have a common perception of reality predetermined by the institutional structure of society.

Mills' trilogy on stratification provides his readers with little optimism about the future of American society. During his writing of *The New Men of Power* in 1946–1948, Mills became skeptical that labor leaders would stop the drift toward economic slump and war. Later, in *White Collar*, he portrayed the middle classes as alienated and lacking political consciousness and direction. Finally, in *The Power Elite*, Mills describes a social system in which the corporate elite, the warlords, and the political directorate are shaped by coordination and in which the possibility of democratic accountability for their actions has largely vanished. To paraphrase him, the main thrust of his trilogy, then, was that with power resting within the hierarchies of large-scale bureaucracies the individual was stripped of control over his work and his life. The "cheerful robot" was rapidly becoming characteristic of mass society and the individual was thus forced to seek what little satisfaction was open to him in his leisure life.

Whether Mills was primarily a Marxist, an institutionalist, a pragmatist, or merely an eclectic may not seem important to those who are impressed with the strength of his theory of stratification and the impact it has had on American political and social thought. But it is important to recognize that his theory cannot be fully understood without a thorough examination of its intellectual antecedents, especially those of American origin, which in the past have been so often ignored. However, before these native antecedents are analyzed, it is essential to locate Mills in regard to European social thought. It is toward this end that the next chapter is written.

3

Mills and European Social Thought: A Reappraisal

Unfortunately, many of Mills' critics do not understand the highly eclectic nature of his work and its relationship to the broad spectrum of both European and American social thought. Consequently, there is much disagreement, imprecision, and inaccuracy in the interpretation and analysis of his intellectual perspective. For example, some radical admirers have mistakenly portrayed Mills as a Marxist, while others more accurately indict him for not being a Marxist. Liberals on the other hand are often disturbed by what they perceive as a strong Marxist orientation in his work, although sometimes puzzled by the intellectually eclectic framework from which his work emerges. Finally, conservatives are repelled and angered by most of what he wrote, except perhaps for his indictment of the moral and political bankruptcy of liberalism, and consequently have made little effort to examine his intellectual background. As is evident, then, much of the analysis of his work has been acutely ideological in nature and polemical in tone.

Mills' interpreters include some of the most eminent social scientists as well as some of the most obscure. They can be placed roughly in ten categories, although it should be noted that some of the differences of interpretation stem from analysis of different parts of his work written at various stages of his career. The ten are that:

1. Mills took a Marxian position, or at least worked within the Marxian tradition;[1]

2. he was influenced by Marxism, but unfortunately never underwent complete conversion;[2]

3. he was greatly influenced by both Marx and Weber, with tension consequently existing between the two theoretical systems at certain points in his work;[3]

4. he came under the sway of institutional economics, especially the work of Thorstein Veblen, John R. Commons, and Clarence Ayres;[4]

5. he was influenced primarily by the pragmatists Peirce, James, Dewey, and Mead, and thus occupied a place in the pragmatic tradition;[5]

6. he was fundamentally swayed by the "neomachiavellians," that is, Michels, Mosca, and Pareto, particularly at the time he wrote *The Power Elite*;[6]

7. he adopted a perspective that showed the influence of Freud and the neofreudians;[7]

8. he applied Karl Mannheim's ideas to the study of power in America;[8]

9. he is difficult or impossible to neatly catalog or label;[9]

10. he had eclectic tendencies.[10]

Clearly, not all these views of Mills can be correct even though they may all contain valuable insights. Even if it is assumed that Mills was an eclectic, which is the view taken here, it is probable that some strains of thought have had significantly greater impact on his work than others. The questions are, which ones in what ways? We now turn to the claim that he was a Marxist.

MILLS, MARX, AND THE MARXISTS

Mills' association with Marxism was a developmental process which began at the University of Texas in the late 1930s and continued with varying degrees of intensity until his death in 1962. He acquired some knowledge of Marx from Professor Edward E. Hale, who taught economic theory at Austin. He read secondary source material on Marx in George H. Mead's *Movements of Thought in the Nineteenth Century*, and his master's thesis is replete with references to Marxian scholars and Marxist publications such as *Science and Society* and *The New Masses*.[11] But, according to his daughter Pamela Mills, "He did not read Marx thoroughly and first hand until 1942, at the University of Maryland, a fact which can be partially explained by the second fact that he just did not have time before then to do so."[12] Mills' Marxist library of approximately 300 volumes was begun in the late thirties.[13] Later Mills' knowledge of Marxism was deepened through interaction with the work of émigré Germans such as Horkheimer, Neumann, Marcuse, and Adorno, who had been affiliated with the Frankfurt Institute and developed their own version of neomarxism, which has since become known as "critical theory."[14] Finally, in his last years in the course of his travels, he became acquainted with other leading Marxist intellectuals in both the Communist and non-Communist world. All of these experiences had their impact on his thinking, but at no point in his work does Mills explicitly adhere to Marxism.[15]

If it were only a matter of analyzing his view of Marx our task would be simpler. However, it is also necessary to evaluate Mills' attitude toward others in the Marxian tradition, for his attitude toward Marx was naturally influenced by these interpreters. Although Mills had great respect for such leading theoreticians as Lenin and Trotsky and literally dozens of other European intellectuals and statesmen who were Marxists, he had less regard for American Marxists. Indeed, with the exceptions of Paul Sweezy, Leo Huberman, Barrington Moore, and a handful of others, his attitude toward native Marxists was largely negative. This was especially true early in his career. Revealing comments were made by Mills in 1944 when, in reviewing a book by the Marxist-Leninist Howard Selsam, he said

> As a treatise on ethics the book may be adequately reviewed in two sentences. The only ethical problem which the book raises and satisfactorily answers is whether or not it is immoral for anyone to so blur and butcher the intent of Marx. It may be important to stress that the only relation this doctrinaire series of papal-like assertions bears to the humanist ethics of Marx is the former's mechanical use of the worst jargon which can be found in the latter.[16]

In 1959 when Mills was at work on *The Marxists* he made some equally revealing remarks about Marxism. He commented that:

> . . . I'm a pretty good person to do this kind of summing up and orientation because I've never been emotionally involved with marxism or communism, never belonged in any sense to it. And yet I know the stuff pretty well. Despite that I find that I become curiously agitated when I work at it. . . .[17]

It was evident that Mills still had mixed feelings about Marx and Marxism—feelings that he had never resolved. In writing *The Marxists* he was finally forced to deal with this intellectual legacy in a more systematic and rigorous way than he ever had done before. Prior to this he had always written with reference to liberalism because that was the accepted creed of the public for which he wrote. He had not really confronted Marxism because his audience wasn't very interested in it or knowledgeable about it. So he had used what he wanted from the body of Marxian literature without really defining his relation to it. This was proving intellectually awkward now that he had ventured into the explicit realm of political philosophy.[18]

At this same time more perceptive radicals recognized that Mills was not a Marxist in any orthodox or traditional sense. One was the Trotskyite George Novack, who wrote to Leon Trotsky's widow that:

> Mills . . . is not a Marxist. He, indeed, is a critic of Marxism which, in his opinion . . . . cannot by itself answer the key problems posed by contemporary world developments. I would characterize him as a radical-liberal or liberal-radical whose basic views are in the process of development and change.[19]

The radical sociologist Barrington Moore, after reading the manuscript of *The Sociological Imagination*, wrote to the publisher that Mills

> espouses a residual and nostalgic Marxism . . . he probably has strong reservations abut Marxian economics and little belief in the Marxian metaphysics of history. . . . Were he a thorough-going Marxist he would achieve a more synthetic or integrated result at the price of wide reputation. Since he is only a residual Marxist he cannot do more than take pot-shots, some of which are excellent, at the state of sociology.[20]

Although such comments are illuminating, the claim that Mills was a Marxist, as well as his own admission that he was a "plain Marxist," must be analyzed further as they have a direct bearing on Mills' relationship to both European and American social thought. It is difficult to ascertain with any precision what is meant by many who offer such an interpretation. Is it the humanism of the young Marx, with its focus on alienation, which they see revealed in Mills' theories? Do these writers mean that Mills uses Marx's dialectical method in analyzing class structures and power systems? Are they suggesting that he believed in the labor theory of value and that he subscribed to a program of political action and social reconstruction such as that advocated by Marx? Is it meant that he viewed the state as a tool of the ruling class? Mills was not a Marxist, if such is Marxism, in any of these fundamental ways. His work can be searched in vain for a clear endorsement of these ideas. Other less explicitly "Marxist" areas of discourse must be explored to discover the influence of Marx on him.

In his well-known letter to *Commentary* in 1957, he dealt with accusations of "Marxism" by the American economist Robert Lekachman.

> Let me say explicitly: I happen never to have been what is called a "Marxist," but I believe Karl Marx one of the most astute students of society modern civilization has produced; his work is now essential equipment of any adequately trained social scientist as well as of any properly educated person. Those who say they hear Marxian echoes in my work are saying that I have trained myself well. That they do not intend this testifies to their own lack of proper education.[21]

Mills had assimilated most of the original work of Marx and Engels, much of the subsequent literature written in the Marxian traditions, and a vast amount of socialist writing of the non-Marxian variety. Certainly, aspects of Marxian doctrine were occasionally incorporated in his work. Nevertheless, it must be recognized that his analysis of classical Marxism in *The Marxists*, which was his last and presumably most authoritative statement, largely preceded the revolution in Marxian studies which has since occurred. The "new" Marx who subsequently emerged from this reevaluation of classical Marxism would probably have been more to Mills' liking. It is clear, however, that in 1957, as Mills entered the last five years of his life, he did not think of himself as ever having been a "Marxist."

The claim has also been made that Mills utilized Marx's "method." Insofar as this claim involves the formal use of dialectics, it is easy to discredit, for Mills' repudiation of dialectics is explicit. After defining dialectics—by which he means (1) quantitative changes producing qualitative changes and vice-versa, (2) the negation of the negation, and (3) the interpenetration of opposites—he says:

> the simple truth about "the laws of dialectics" as discerned in Marx, is that they are ways of talking about matters after those matters have been explained in ordinary ways of discourse and proof. . . . For us, the "dialectical method" is either a mess of platitudes, a way of double-talk, a pretentious obscurantism—or all three.[22]

In a lengthy section in *The Marxists* entitled "Critical Observations," Mills summarizes his critique of Marxism:

> Behind the labor metaphysic and the erroneous views of its supporting trends there are deficiencies in the Marxist categories of stratification; ambiguities and misjudgments about the psychological and political con-

sequences of the development of the economic base; errors concerning the supremacy of economic causes within the history of societies and the mentality of classes; inadequacies of a rationalist psychological theory; a generally erroneous theory of power; an inadequate conception of the state.[23]

In what sense, then, was Mills a Marxist? More specifically, what could he have meant when he claimed to be a "plain Marxist" as opposed to a "vulgar" or "sophisticated" Marxist? He tells us that

Plain Marxists . . . work in Marx's own tradition. They understand Marx . . . to be firmly a part of the classic tradition of sociological thinking. They treat Marx like any great nineteenth-century figure, in a scholarly way; they treat each later phase of Marxism as historically specific.[24]

Again:

Plain Marxists have stressed the humanism of Marxism, especially of the younger Marx, and the role of the superstructure in history; they have pointed out that to under-emphasize the interplay of bases and superstructures in the making of history is to transform man into that abstraction for whch Marx himself criticized Feuerbach. They have been "open" (as opposed to dogmatic) in their interpretations and their uses of Marxism. They have stressed that "economic determinism" is, after all, a matter of degree, and held that it is so used by Marx in his own writings. . . . They have emphasized the volition of men in the making of history—their freedom—in contrast to any Determinist Laws of History and, accordingly, the lack of individual responsibility.[25]

Mills summarized his own position on the inadequacies of the Marxian traditions and their potential role in the future when he comments that "if we do not develop more adequate sociological theories of the character of present-day varieties in social systems of the ways in which history is now being made and extended, then the varieties of Marxism will fill the vacuum by default.[26] In summarizing the meaning of Mills' "plain Marxism," emphasis should be on: (1) His belief that Marxism offers an admirable value system, although not a fully adequate one, by which to measure other sets of ideals, social systems, and programs of action. (2) His use of vocabulary that is partly Marxian in origin, including such terms as ideology, expropriation, false consciousness, fetish, alienation, and commodity. (3) Mills' perception of Marx as having provided a "model" that is a more or less systematic inventory of the elements to which we must pay attention if we are to understand something of significance. This concept of "model," however, is contrasted in Mills' work with a "theory," which he views as subject to empirical inquiry for purposes of proof or disproof. A theory is unlike a model, which is more or less useful but not susceptible to empirical verification. Classical Marxism has utility as a model but is very inadequate as a theory. (4) Mills' agreement with Marx in viewing history as a series of epochs separated by marked changes in the whole of society. There are close parallels between his formulation and use of such historical stages as the "fourth epoch" and the "overdeveloped society" on the one hand and Marx's "feudalism" and "capitalism" on the other hand. The similarities are evident in their mutual accentuation of particular traits that they viewed as characteristic of certain historical periods.

In light of the new interpretations of Marx now in vogue among Marxologists, Mills may have misinterpreted him. Although Mills had read the *Economic and Philosophical Manuscripts of 1844* and *The German Ideology* and had been partially exposed to the humanism and indeterminism of the young Marx, he did not live to read the major works of Avineri, Ollman, and Harrington, with their greater emphasis on these dimensions.[27] It may be that the new Marx would have had greater appeal to Mills since this Marx more closely resembles what Mills called a "plain Marxist." Indeed, Mills' own reading of Marx indicates that *The Marxists* represents a transition from traditional interpretations to the new ones now dominant among Marx scholars in the West. Nevertheless, there is little to be gained by calling Mills a Marxist since his interpretation of Marx ended in a negative appraisal of many of Marx's most basic ideas. Mills' "plain Marxism" thus amounts to little more than a willingness to use Marx's values, vocabulary, and model when they seem relevant and to ignore them when they do not. As he put it, "We are able freely to use whatever of his we felt the need of, and to reject what we do not."[28] Although this does not imply a rejection of the Marxian heritage, it is best to label Mills what he clearly was—an eclectic. Those interested in the intellectual origins of Mills' radicalism would be better advised to look to American sources such as Veblen, Dewey, and Mead, instead of focusing so narrowly on Marx.

MILLS AND THE MACHIAVELLIANS

Mills saw his work as part of the classical tradition in sociology. He believed the Franco-Italian elitists to be part of this same tradition, as is indicated by his use of selections from their work in his *Images of*

Man. However, in the normative sense he and the elitists are poles apart, for unlike Mills, the Machiavellians are prescriptive elitists. Mills believed in democracy and socialism as moral and political ideals while Mosca, Pareto, and Michels thought the institutitionalization of such values to be impossible, undesirable, or both. For them, elite rule is inevitable in both the polity and economy; for Mills, genuine democracy and socialism remain historical and political possibilities. Mills, in his more optimistic moods, believed that progress had been made toward the achievement of these goals in some societies while Pareto, in particular, cynically viewed the idea of progress as an illusion.

The difference in value position is evident in the Machiavellian thesis that it is impossible to eliminate economic inequality and hierarchy and create a classless society. Michels, like the other elitists, thought that the values prized by Mills were impossible to realize and that attempts to do so would only make the situation worse. The suppression of specifically capitalist forms of property rights would not lead to a classless social structure, but would be followed by the entrenchment of new kinds of property rights and new class divisions. Thus, Michels contended that democratic and egalitarian goals cannot be achieved because of the impact of economic institutions on sociopolitical relations. To quote Michels, himself, in a characteristically Machiavellian mode of expression:

> The law of the circulation of the elites destroys the thesis of a possibility of a society without social levels. Political theory and practice have demonstrated that, whatever be the form of government of public affairs, it is always . . . against the natural order of things that the majority rule and the minority be ruled. It is therefore necessary that the historian and economist insist on the permanence of that factor that Mosca has called the "political class. . . ."[29]

To the Machiavellians, "political formulas," "political myths," and "derivations" have normative and political significance different from what their equivalent "ideology" has for Mills. Mills advocated the undermining of such idea systems because of their politically inhibitory effect on the mass consciousness, but for Mosca and Pareto especially, such beliefs are essential for the maintenance of the integrity and stability of the social order. Mills attacks the "military metaphysic," the "American dream," and "pluralism" because they are ideologies that mask the realities of the American sociopolitical system and channel human energy into pathological activities. But the Machiavellians fear the growth of popular skepticism about dominant ideologies because it has a corrosive and disintegrative impact that undermines the existing social equilibrium. Mills' contrary view is that such skepticism may lead to the weakening of "false consciousness" and thus result in the reinvigoration of political movements favoring major structural changes. The Machiavellians are explicitly anti-utopian with regard to both ideology and programs yet—as Mills made clear in *The Causes of World War III*—utopianizing may be a condition for survival in the twentieth century.

The anti-utopianism of the Machiavellians is evident in their belief that the study of politics should be an objective science comparable in its methods to the empirical sciences. Such a science is neutral with regard to political goals. Like other science, its statements can be tested by facts available to any observer, and are in no way dependent upon the acceptance of any particular ethical aim or ideal.[30] Any reader familiar with Mills' work in the sociology of knowledge or with *The Sociological Imagination* will recognize at once his fundamentally different conception of social-science inquiry. Mills believed, as did Dewey, that facts are almost inextricably interwoven with values and that the language forms in which the two are embedded are not necessarily mutually exlusive. He also thought that the social background and position of the observer color his judgment. In any case, Mills' conception of praxis forbids the divorce of ethics from knowledge and science from norms, contrary to the main thrust of the Machiavellian analysis. The difference between Mills and the classical elitists was well summed up when Mills wrote that "I have tried to be objective but I do not claim to be detached."[31]

The similarities between Mills' political sociology and that of the classical elitists are essentially conceptual and methodological rather than normative, but even here significant differences remain. Consider, for example, the area of methodology. As Burnham put it in summarizing Pareto's main focus:

> The character of society . . . is above all the character of its elite; its accomplishments are the accomplishments of its elite; its history is . . . the history of the elite; successful predictions about its future are based upon evidence drawn from the study of the composition and structure of its elite.[32]

The Machiavellian conception of political sociology is thus a constricted one that focuses on the study of elites and on little else. For Mills, the political sociologist must also study mass society, institutional structures, interest groups, and much else as well. From Mills' perspective, it is evident that the Machiavellians concentrate too narrowly on elites, a fixation that in large measure stems from their belief in the permanent political incompetence of the masses, a value position Mills did not share.

The difference between Mills and the classical elitists is also evident in Pareto's view of elite circulation as based on biological drives or instincts in contrast with Mills' view of such change as induced by technological innovation and shifts in the cultural apparatus and institutional fabric of society. Pareto's narrow focus on the psychic traits of elites and his use of a quasi-instinctivist psychology causes him to view elites as distinct from the masses because of innate biological qualities. Mills, on the other hand, in his efforts to explain elite change emphasized the institutional position of elites and the socialization process to which they have been subjected. Elite transformation was of particular concern to Pareto, but he believed that the key to the riddles of historical change lay not in technological and institutional trends but rather in the metamorphosis of the political elite, a process largely independent from social structure. For Mills, elite change is important, but it is not a process divorced from economic and social institutions, much less one rooted in biological constants. Instead, he links the evolving character and composition of elites with technoeconomic processes and major institutional trends—factors to which Pareto paid far less attention.

A comparison of Pareto's theory of elite transformation with Mills' shows it to be different in still another way. Pareto, by blurring the differences between the rise and fall of individuals and the rise and fall of social classes obscures a critical distinction that is implicit in Mills' analysis between two very different types of elite circulation. Individual turnover is obviously an important issue, but if incumbent and successor are fundamentally similar, indicating that the social composition of the elite remains the same, elite transformation of the sort Mills discusses in *The Power Elite* can hardly be said to have occurred.[33]

Mills' thesis in *The Power Elite* also differs in fundamental ways from Mosca's theory of the ruling class. As Mills once put it:

> It is not my thesis that for all epochs of human history and in all nations, a creative minority, a ruling class, an omnipotent elite, share all historical events. Such statements, upon careful examination, usually turn out to be mere tautologies, and even when they are not, they are so entirely general as to be useless in the attempt to understand the history of the present.[34]

He adds in a footnote, "As in the case, quite notably, of Gaetano Mosca, *The Ruling Class*."[35] Mills elaborates on this difference with

Mosca when he says, "Our definition of the power elite cannot properly contain dogma concerning the degree and kind of power that ruling groups everywhere have. Much less should it permit us to smuggle into our discussion a theory of history."[36]

While Mosca bases his thesis of the ruling class on the unique personal qualities of the elite, he is forced to concede the efficacy of "social forces" both in producing the traits of a particular elite and in the transformation of elites within a system. To Mills, the power elite has no unusual biological qualities. It is the institutional fabric and the opportunities for power and privilege, not any gene pool they inherit, that make the higher circles what they are.[37] In the nature vs. nurture controversy, Mills comes out firmly on the side of nurture; whereas Mosca, and to a greater extent Pareto, never rid themselves of the conviction that societies are dominated by biologically superior ruling classes and elites.

Mosca was not "historically specific" in the Millsian sense for he claims that his concept of the ruling class applies to all regimes—to those based on the doctrine of popular sovereignty as well as to aristocracies and monarchies. Mosca insists that the contest for control is not between the many and the few, but between one elite and another, while Mills emphasizes the disharmony that exists between the power elite and the masses. As Meisel puts it:

> Mosca's predicament is that he treats the ruling class as basically representative of the totality of social forces, that is, the majority. If it is not, that must be due to aberrations and anomalies and not, as Mills might insist, to the essential incompatibility of the two classes.[38]

Further, Mosca pointed to the danger that representative government may deteriorate into tyranny. To offset the weaknesses of democracy, he wanted the suffrage to favor those with education and property. He also wanted an increase in the powers of appointed officials. Mosca's ideal was genuine rejuvenation of the entire political class on the basis of individual merit and technical competence; but Mills' ideal, while it includes such traits, focuses on the creation of genuine publics to whom elected and appointed officials are truly responsible and accountable.

These differences also separated Mills from Robert Michels, another of the classical elitists, although Mills claimed Michels' work was

> first-rate; much of the value that is often found in Pareto has been better incorporated by Michels—and by Pareto's academic rival, Gaetano Mosca. Michel's point I think relevant not only against social

unions and parties . . . I think it holds generally against liberalism! At least, that interpretation does lead to a very fruitful reading of his *Political Parties*.[39]

Despite his praise of Michels in this passage, Mills did not find his most important theoretical contribution, "the iron law of oligarchy," to have the universal validity Michels claimed for it. Instead, in an analysis of American pressure groups and parties he wrote that:

> The gap between speaker and listener, between power and public, leads less to any iron law of oligarchy than to the law of spokesmanship: as the pressure group expands, its leaders come to organize the opinions they "represent." So elections, as we have seen, become contests between two giant and unwieldy parties, neither of which the individual can truly feel that he influences and neither of which is capable of winning psychologically impressive or politically decisive majorities. And, in all this, the parties are of the same general form as other mass associations.[40]

From the foregoing it can be seen that Mills is not a Machiavellian, if that term implies a direct intellectual linkage between his thesis in *The Power Elite* and the elite or ruling-class theory of the classical elitists. Interpreting Mills as Machiavellian is vague, ignores the differences that exist between Mosca, Pareto, and Michels, and deprives Mills' thesis of the originality it is entitled to claim. It may be conceded, however, that even though his power-elite thesis was fundamentally different, it was developed in part out of dialogue with the major works of the Machiavellians.

It is apparent that those who advance the claim that Mills was a Machiavellian are misled about Mills' use of elites. They confuse his analysis of elites with his use of a particular theory of elites. As he put it in response to his critics:

> I don't really understand what is meant by "the elite theory." There is no such thing. Merely to study elite groups is not automatically to accept some one definite theory of elites. Do the critics mean Pareto's theory of the circulation of the elite? I don't accept that. . . . Do they mean only that "elite theory" reduces power to "conquest theory of politics?" If so, then certainly I do not hold "the elite theory."[41]

Mills explained what he found relevant in the theory of elites, but little in his explanation will give comfort to those who pin the Machiavellian label on him. His point was that the "structural mechanics" and the shape of modern institutions made them unusually vulnerable to extreme centralizations of power and thus to elite domination.[42]

Mills' interpreters have largely ignored the new American elite theories that were circulating in the 1930s and early 1940s as intellectual components in his power elite theory. For example, in James Burnham's emerging managerial state the ruling elite were the managers; in Harold Lasswell's "garrison state," the military; and in Ferdinand Lundberg's "America," it was the 60 richest families.[43] Thus a viable theory of power would have to evaluate the role of the managers, the military and the super rich. Mills had to come to grips with these theories because they were among the leading alternatives to the prevailing liberal theory of power. Although he did not believe any of them adequate, each focused on potential or actual elites the dominant theory tended to ignore. It must be acknowledged, however, that both Lasswell and Burnham were influenced by the Machiavellians. The scholarly appendage to Lasswell's *Politics: Who Gets What, When, How* (1936) refers the reader to the major works of Michels, Mosca, and Pareto, while Burnham's *The Managerial Revolution* (1941) was followed shortly thereafter by his well-known study of *The Machiavellians*. Thus while the Machiavellian influence on Mills may be traced indirectly through the American elite theorists, this native filter diluted its impact even further.

MILLS AND MAX WEBER:
INFLUENCE AND DISCONTINUITY

In *Images of Man* Mills indicated his belief that one of the two most important intellectual figures in the history of Western sociology was Max Weber.[44] Mills valued Weber's work because it did not fit within any one academic discipline, and because like Marx, he held certain moral values passionately but critically.[45] In fact Mills sometimes referred to Weber as a "sophisticated revisionist of classic Marxism."[46] Mills explained that to Marx's "class" as an economic category, Weber added "status" or "prestige" because they supplied a better clue to understanding the psychology of classes. Weber had thus finished the uncompleted work of Marx by making the idea of class more sophisticated. Indeed, Weber's work on class, status, and party had become the definitive work on stratification. But Mills asserted that Weber differed from Marx because he did not keep class struggle at the center of his analysis but instead shifted to bureaucracy and the fact of large-scale organizational rationalization.[47]

Mills acknowledged his debt to Weber in *White Collar* when he wrote "The technical vocabulary used, and hence in many ways the general perspective of this volume, is derived from Max Weber. Such concepts as class, occupation, status, power, authority, manipulation, bureaucracy, profession are basically his."[48] For Mills, Weber's vocabulary had the advantage of flexibility and heuristic openness, and furthermore, it cut across disciplinary boundaries. It was flexible because in it the relationships among status, power, and class were not placed within predetermined limits. It was heuristically open because it permitted empirical study of particular societies without a priori assumption, and it was interdisciplinary because it included anthropological, psychological, sociological, and economic variables.[49] These aspects of Weber's vocabulary are all essential elements in an eclectic perspective which is, no doubt, why they appealed to Mills. Mills employed ideal types as a methodological device in the grand Weberian manner. Examples of this are his accentuation of certain character traits to produce the "cheerful robot," exaggeration of methodological tendencies to produce "abstracted empiricism" and "grand theory," and intensification of certain structural changes to produce the "Fourth Epoch" and the "overdeveloped society." Weber's methodological influence is also evident in Mills' use of the historical-comparative methods.

Not only does Mills use Weber's vocabulary in *White Collar* and other important works, he probes various Weberian themes in the book. Its organization follows the structure of Weber's essay "Class, Status, Party." Parts One and Two, "Old Middle Classes" and "White Collar Worlds," are concerned with issues of class—the weakening of the old middle classes, the advent of the new middle classes, and the kinds of people chosen and shaped by white collar work. Part Three, "Styles of Life," deals with status—including status panic, the significance of work, and patterns and ideologies of success. Part Four, "Ways of Power," focuses on power—the organization and power of the new middle class and its political mentality. When it is remembered that Mills aided Gerth in the translation of Weber's work, and that he was involved in this project while writing *White Collar*, it is not surprising that the latter bears a close structural resemblance to Weber's "Class, Status, Party." But those who stress the Weberian origins of Mills' analysis often neglect to mention that Mills adds Veblenian notions of the impact of occupational discipline and the role of status emulation to the Weber triad of power, wealth, and status. Nevertheless, it is in *White Collar* that Weber's influence on Mills reached its zenith.

Mills later stated that his definitions of key sociological terms were "loose formulations of Max Weber's terms" and that in *Character and Social Structure* he intended to make them "more elaborate and precise."[50] He then defined these terms in the following way:

> *Class* situation, in its simplest objective sense, has to do with the amount and source (property or work) of income as these affect the chances of people to obtain other available values.
> *Status* involves the successful realization of claims to prestige; it refers to the distribution of deference in a society.
> *Power* refers to the realization of one's will, even if this involves the resistance of others.[51]

Unlike some Marxists, Mills refuses to reduce status and power to a function of class, for he believes the contemporary social structure is more complex. On the other hand, unlike many liberals, he refuses to sever power, class, and status from each other except for analytic and conceptual purposes, for like Weber he believes that they are often linked with each other in reality. As he once put it:

> The power position of institutions and individuals typically depends upon factors of class, status, and occupation, often in intricate interrelation.[52]

Mills then proceeds to develop a series of arguments and historical examples that purport to show that power, class, and status (prestige) are closely linked together in the contemporary setting of advanced industrial society. In his words:

> Power over the political and military, the economic and the religious community brings prestige to those who legitimately make or pronounce the key decisions, or to those to whom the key decisions are ascribed by the community. . . Big power carries in its train big prestige.[53]

Perhaps Mills' most definitive statement on power-class-status relationships is found in his claim that

> Status may be said to "overlay" class structures. Each has its peculiarities and its relative autonomy, yet the first is dependent upon the second as a conditioning and limiting factor. . . . This of course does not mean the doing away with status groups, nor with all grounds upon which status distinctions rest. But it does mean that status dimensions are more closely tied to the economic order and that class dynamics are automatically transformed into status dynamics.[54]

Mills thought force was a factor in all social orders, but like Weber he did not think it was always a monopoly of the ruling class. Mills claimed that the Marxist definition of the state, as rule by the dominant class, assumed a connection between class and rule, whereas the relationship should not be assumed but should be left open for empirical investigation.[55] He thus opposed the Marxist definition of the state because it unduly narrowed the relationships studied. Mills is closer to Weber than Marx because of his insistence that class and power be kept separate from one another for analytical purposes, even though Mills concedes there is often a link between class position and the exercise of power. Mills also differentiated between class and status on the basis of Weber's distinction between the two, which Marx had failed to adequately recognize. Mills identified class with property and status with the claim for, and recognition of, prestige. Basing his ideas on Weber, he dealt with stratification in terms of class, status, and power. These relationships were often the basis for Mills' investigations in political sociology and they provided the conceptual foundation for his models.

The meaning of power, class, and status and the linkages that existed between them in various kinds of societies was a problem that fascinated Weber. His work in this area was incomplete, left unfinished at his death. Nevertheless, it is extraordinarily rich and suggestive. A characteristically American interpretation of his conceptualization of power, class, and status relationships is that he separated them from each other conceptually and analytically and that he did not believe them to be closely linked in advanced industrial societies like our own. Consequently, American political scientists like Nelson Polsby argue that political notables, social notables, and economic notables are different people and that the institutional linkages between them are weak or nonexistent.[56] Although Polsby's analysis may not be explicitly Weberian it is probably in part a result of the way Weber's ideas on stratification have characteristically been used in the American environment: namely, to buttress pluralist political theory.

It is interesting to note, however, that Mills reached opposite conclusions regarding the American national power system and that he did so in part by using Weber's analytic and conceptual apparatus. It is equally interesting to observe that even though Weber often separated considerations of class, power, and status for analytic and conceptual purposes, many of the historical examples he gave to illustrate his points show that class, power, and status overlap with each other. Mills was thus correct in his appraisal of Weber as a scholar who revised and improved upon Marx's original work, for he saw radical implications in the analysis that he put to good use in *Character and Social Structure, White Collar,* and *The Power Elite.*

Mills drew from Weber, as well as from Mannheim and Veblen, the idea that class position does not always correspond to a particular state of mind. He often claimed that what people are interested in may not be to their interest. Mills believed there was an empirically ascertainable difference between one's objective position in society and one's subjective state of mind about this position. Classes could have common economic interests and yet no common mind set or shared values might evolve from these. As Mills put it:

> To understand the occupation, class, and status positions of a set of people is not necessarily to know whether or not they (1) will become class conscious, feeling that they belong together or that they can best realize their rational interests by combining; (2) will have "collective attitudes" of any sort, including those toward themselves, their common situation; (3) will organize themselves, or be open to organization by others, into associations, movements or political parties; or (4) will become hostile toward other strata and struggle against them. These social, political, and psychological characteristics may or may not occur on the basis of similar objective situations. In any given case, such possibilities must be explored, and "subjective" attributes must not be used as criteria for class inclusion, but rather, as Max Weber has made clear, stated as probabilities on the basis of objectively defined situations.[57]

Unlike many of his pluralist critics, Mills did not rest content with demonstrating that there was often a disparity between the way a class perceived itself and that class's objective position in society. Instead, he sought to understand why this discrepancy existed. Furthermore, he made inquiry as to what political action might be taken to narrow the gap between what people are interested in and what is actually to their interest.

In *Character and Social Structure* Mills relied heavily on Weber's interpretation of early Protestantism. The influence of Weber's famous *The Protestant Ethic and the Spirit of Capitalism* is clearly apparent in Mills' efforts to understand the subtle interaction between religion and economics in early modern Europe. For example, Weber's idea of "inner-worldly asceticism" is viewed by Mills as having contributed to the personality formation of the entrepreneurial middle classes. The systematic following of a vocation was religiously sanctioned by many of the early Calvinist sects who, Weber argued, attempted to reassure themselves through hard work, self-mastery, and the conquest of nature that they were among the elect predestined for salvation. The Puritan, for example, was no medieval monk retreating from the world into a monastery, but a soldier of Christ striving relentlessly to fulfill his vocation in the here and now. A new morality and a new historical type had thus come upon the scene and was linked with the historical development of capitalism. For in order to serve God, the Protestant must avoid ostentatious consumption and invest his surplus capital in economic growth. To follow through this program required the methodical and systematic observation of self and an ever-renewed self-discipline; the Calvinist was the steward of his own wealth, which must be used for God's greater glory and to serve the community. In spite of a vast outpouring of scholarly criticism of the Weber thesis, Mills uncritically used Weber's central ideas to explain the relationship between the emergence of a new character type (the Protestant entrepreneur) and a new economic system (capitalism).[58]

Weber had distinguished three main types of legal administrations and staffs, which parallel his types of political authority and his types of education: charismatic, traditionalist, and rationally bureaucratic. Mills was particularly prone to use this typology to explain the role of leadership and the function of various kinds of authority in different historical and cultural settings. The question of leadership, according to Mills' understanding of Weber, was the question of why the led follow. Weber answered the question in terms of three types of legitimation: charismatic, traditional, and legal. These represented formal reasons for more or less voluntary obedience: the first, charismatic, because the led impute to the leader extraordinary personal qualities; the second, traditional, because they feel that the leader has always been followed and rightly so; and the last, legal, because they feel that the leader has attained his position according to legal rules which the led accept. Mills commented that "This classification is quite useful; but as an overall model it is, of necessity, highly formal and leaves untouched many aspects or dimensions of leadership to which we should like to pay systematic attention."[59]

Seeing the pervasive bureaucratic character of industrial society, Mills found Weber's definition and analysis of bureaucracy particularly useful. As Weber noted, bureaucratic structures bring about a concentration of the means of administration and violence. Taking his cues from Weber, Mills' "Fourth Epoch" centralized control of production, administration, and violence within the bureaucracy itself. Consequently, the blue-collar worker was not alone in losing control over the work process and workplace. His situation was shared by the white-collar worker, similarly separated from the tools of administration, and by the soldier, comparably denied control of the means of violence. But Mills realized that Weber's ideal-type definitions of bureaucracy must not be taken literally as adequate characterizations. For example, he thought most businesses were mixtures of bureaucratic and entrepreneurial forms of organization. Foremost among them was a type which Mills called "the New Entrepreneur." This new type of manager was an entrepreneurial adaptation who operated in the unroutinized parts of the economy—public relations, commercial research, advertising, labor relations, and mass communications among others. The new entrepreneur was a "fixer" who used his expertise to sidestep red tape in solving new kinds of problems. In selling his services to the powers-that-be, his success was dependent upon their ignorance and anxiety. His career, rather than following the ideal-typical Weberian bureaucratic path upward, moved back and forth at the same level among private enterprises, business, and government.

Mills was heavily influenced by Weber's understanding of the legitimation functions of master symbols. In a strikingly eclectic passage Mills once wrote that:

> Various thinkers have used different terms to refer to this phenomenon: Mosca's "political formula" or "great superstitions," Locke's "principle of sovereignty," Sorel's "ruling myth," Thurman Arnold's "folklore," Weber's "legitimations," Durkheim's "collective representations," Marx's "dominant ideas," Rousseau's "general will," Lasswell's "symbols of authority," or "symbols of justification," Mannheim's "ideology," Herbert Spencer's "public sentiments"—all testify the central place of master symbols in social analysis.[60]

As a radical social scientist interested in fomenting structural change, Mills was particularly concerned about the rise of competing symbols of protest and their interplay with symbols of justification. His more polemical work represented a deliberate effort on his part to undermine the master symbols of his own time and to substitute for them counter-symbols which would convincingly demonstrate that the Emperor wears no clothes.

Mills also found Weber's work valuable for understanding human motivation. Mills endorsed Weber's definition of motive as a complex of meaning, that appears to the actor himself or to the observer to be an adequate ground for his conduct. Mills was impressed with this definition because of its intrinsically social character. A satisfactory or adequate motive was one that satisfied the questioners of an act or program, whether others' or actors'. As a word, a motive tends to be one which is to the actor and to the other members of a situation an unquestioned answer to questions concerning social and lingual conduct. Stress on this idea would lead to investigations of the compartmentalization of operative motives in personalities according to situation. It would also lead to inquiry into the general types and conditions of vocabularies of motives in various types of societies. The motivational structures of individuals and the patterns of their purposes were thus relative to societal frames.[61]

The Weberian origins of Mills' thought may seem apparent in the view that his conception of praxis is a matter of balancing or reconciling Weber's "ethic of responsibility" with his "ethic of conscience." But this delineation of Mills' intellectual pedigree misrepresents his conception of praxis by deradicalizing it. Mills was more committed to an ethic of conscience and fixed social ends than was Weber. Unfortunately, Mills' critics are prone to make a rigid distinction between Weber's ethic of responsibility and his ethic of conscience, thus making it difficult for themselves to recognize as legitimate any form of politics that goes beyond the first to embrace the second. For this consequence, Weber himself is not without blame, because as Gerth and Mills point out: "Although he was passionately concerned with the course of German policy, in theory he rigidly segregated his role as professor and scientist from that of a publicist."[62] Although there has been much disagreement over the meaning of Weber's famous essay *Politics as a Vocation*, one as steeped in Deweyian instrumentalism as Mills would be unlikely to accept such a separation of facts and values, of theory and advocacy, and of creed and action as Weber seems to endorse. In Weber's scenario, despite both his political preferences and the political consequences of his research, the social scientist cannot play an active role in political life if he is truly committed to objective knowledge.[63] In view of this questionable separation of politics from social-science inquiry, Weber's impact on Mills' view of praxis must be regarded as marginal at best and other intellectual sources must be scrutinized for a more convincing explanation of its origins. One of the most important of these sources was Dewey's *The Quest for Certainty*, which will be dealt with later.

Gerth and Mills, in their introduction to *From Max Weber*, stress the pragmatic qualities of Weber as though there were strong affinities between Weber and the American pragmatists Dewey, Mead, and Peirce. Since they are introducing Weber to much of the English-speaking world, it is not surprising that they do so by using a philosophic tradition familiar to their readers. Nevertheless, this stress is another manifestation of Mills' early training in pragmatism.

It is also indicative of his tendency to interpret other theorists from an intellectual perspective initially constructed from a critical analysis of the most distinctively American philosophy. But given the similarities between the pragmatic and the Weberian it is not always easy to separate the influences of the two on Mills. Indeed, as Joseph Scimecca has shown, Mills' notions of social structure were borrowed in part from Weber and fused with pragmatic ideas of personality formation to form a radical social psychology.[64] Mills' interpreters have been on firm ground in seeing Weberian strains in his thought, although in view of his eclecticism they are stretching the perception to extreme lengths when they interpret Mills as a "disciple" of Weber or as a member of the "Weber School."

Mead, Freud, and the Neofreudians

Another example of unjustifiable emphasis on European influence are the interpreters of Mills who stress the influence of Freud and the neofreudians while ignoring the fact that Mills filtered Freud through the work of George Herbert Mead. Mills and Gerth indicate in their preface to *Character and Social Structure* that social psychology can benefit from an appropriate integration of Freud with Mead.[65] They point to shortcomings in the work of each man that could be remedied by drawing insights from the other. Yet much of the analysis is a synthesis of Mead with sources other than Freud, rather than a selective fusion of symbolic interactionism with the psychoanalytic tradition. Mills was critical of Mead and of Freud for different reasons: Mead had no concept of passion or emotion to use in his analysis of psychic structure, while Freud was weak on the social aspect of personality formation. To these criticisms Mills added his belief that neither man had an adequate conception of social structure. While both had a view of the small-scale setting of interpersonal relations, the broader context in which these relations were situated was neglected. They needed to be systematized into a general concept of social structure in which the various institutional orders were articulated with each other. Mills was particularly critical of Freud because he believed that for Freud the process of character formation was at least "quasi-biologically" set, hence "a universal occurrence" that overgeneralized the psychic impact of a particular type of kinship organization, that of the Western patriarchal family.[66] Mills preferred the Meadian perspective, however inadequate, because Freud and most of his disciples relied far too heavily on the instinctual basis of human behavior and the formative impact of childhood sexual experiences. Instead, Mills

believed that instinctual drives take on significance only when channeled by the social environment, which in Mills' perspective involved
various "significant" and "generalized" others, not just the parents.
Consequently, for Mills human sexuality had more diverse and varied
ways of manifesting itself. It was not simply an artifact of the Western
patriarchal family structure.[67] Mills further illustrated this flaw in
Freud when he wrote that:

> The idea of some constant, lying back of conduct and in man's universal
> nature, has been the most frequent and persistent error of psychology,
> including that of Freud. It is as if this quest for some constant element
> has served as a compensation for the enormous relativity of human
> nature which anthropology and world history make so evident. . . .
> Nowadays, however, the idea of immutable biological elements recedes
> and is no longer a problem engaging all our energies. We did not solve
> the problem, we outgrew it. . . . The establishment of the reality of the
> social and plastic nature of man is a major accomplishment of U.S. social
> psychology.[68]

Once again the influence of Mead and Dewey on Mills is evident, illus-
trating the impossibility of correctly interpreting Mills without recognizing his roots in the American intellectual tradition. Mills showed
Mead's superiority over Freud in two respects by attacking Freud at
his weakest points—his instinctual-drive theory of motivation and his
narrow conception of the social environment as the family. As Mills
interprets Freud, only when social influences remain properly within
their assigned realm and follow the path sketched for them by the
organic determinant are they to be considered.[69] Mills' willingness to
substitute Mead for Freud can be attributed to his recognition of
Freud's neglect of the historical and social nature of the self.[70] Mills
attacked Freud for his attempts to restrict the status of significant
others to one or two persons and locate these in the childhood of the
person. The significant other was thus believed by Freud to be the
forbidding or authoritarian parent. Thus Freud excluded bases of the
superego that Mills felt were too important to neglect.

In his early work on the sociology of knowledge, Mills called for a
terminology of motives culled from the vocabularies of motives actually verbalized by actors in particular situations. The only method of
determining what an actor's actual motives were, in a given situation,
was to examine the vocabulary of motives used by the actor.[71] Here
Mills rejected the Freudian view of "unconscious motives," which to
him were simply motives not explicitly verbalized. Mills saw the quest
for "real" motives as part of a metaphysical view that the "real" mo-

tives are in some major part biological or innate. Behind a quest for something "more real" was the belief of those who held that language was an external manifestation of something more genuine, or deeper, in the individual. The net result of holding a person's "real attitudes" over against what was "mere rationalization" is that we are merely inferring from an individual's language what "really" is his attitude or motive.[72]

Freud thought that the psychic drives may be socially canalized, but Mills believed that in the Freudian theory they were not themselves subject to basic social modifications. For example, the concept of sublimation implied that role-conditioned forms of psychic drives are epiphenomena of the basic drives. These "real drives" were assumed to lie in the psychic structure or in the constitution of the organism. In Freud's theory the split between man's biological nature and his socially conditioned personality was kept, and according to Mills a metaphysical accent was placed upon it at the biological-psychic level.[73]

Early in *Character and Social Structure* Gerth and Mills make the claim that

> ... from the side of depth psychology and of the mechanisms of personality formation and change, enormous advances have been made. Freud and George Mead, when appropriately integrated and systematized, provide a well-articulated model of character structure, and one of the most fruitful sets of ideas available in modern social science. It is our aim, ... to construct a model of character structure that enables us to systematize some of these ideas and make them available for more sociologically relevant use.[74]

Both writers were knowledgeable regarding Freud and later neofreudian literature. But they largely fail to bring off the integration and systematization of Freud and Mead that they suggest at the outset of their joint project. Nor have more recent writers been more successful in this venture. Perhaps Freudian psychoanalytic theory and Meadian symbolic interactionist social theory are not as easy to integrate and synthesize as Gerth and Mills imagined.

Generally, *Character and Social Structure* represents a significant intellectual achievement and was widely praised at the time of its publication in 1953. But in hoping to achieve the synthesis and integration of Mead and Freud the two authors promised far more than they were able to deliver. In fact much of Mills' limited use of Freudian and neofreudian doctrine is probably motivated by Mills' desire to show that it parallels features of Mead's thought or contains language that is in commonplace usage. Only rarely in Mills' work does he actually attempt to integrate or synthesize Freudian insights with either Meadian or structural sociology. Instead, he is more likely to briefly show how Freudian doctrine or vocabulary parallels or converges with Meadian theory and then turn to some other topic. For example, he once wrote that "Our conscience—the generalized other or superego—is the product of all expectations of significant others in our life history."[75] Here his use of Freudian jargon contributed little or nothing to the actual analysis. It is likely that he uses it only because the reader is more likely to be familiar with the Freudian term "superego" than with Mills' "generalized other."

While the impact of Freud is of little consequence in explaining Mills' intellectual pedigree except in a negative way, the neofreudians Harry Stack Sullivan, Karen Horney, and Erich Fromm had a little more influence on him. Even so, Mills' perspective more closely resembles that of Dewey and Mead than that of the neofreudians:

> Both Fromm and Horney attempt to resolve the problem by invoking components of the psychic structure as "the real self." This does not seem to us an adequate solution: the psychic structure, if it is to operate in a manner harmonious to a social order, must itself be quite socialized in specific directions, even stereotyped in some. The answer to the "façade self" and the "real self" dichotomy is found not by trying to jump past the socialized portions of the personality and finding something more "genuine" in the psychic or organic "foundations," but by viewing the social process of the self in a longitudinal way, and "finding" a "genuine self" that is buried by later socializations.[76]

Once more Mills' interpreters fail to establish anything more than a vague linkage between the salient ideas of a particular European theorist and Mills' intellectual heritage. The affinities between Freud and Mills are tenuous at best and although the linkage with the neofreudians is stronger, Mills remained critical of Horney and Fromm because they had "not succeeded in entirely overcoming Freud's biological metaphysic."[77]

MILLS AND MANNHEIM: PARALLELS AND CONFLICTS

Those wishing to assess the influence of European social theory on Mills ought to consider Karl Mannheim as a source nearly equal to Marx and Weber. This has escaped the notice of most who stress other aspects of European thought as the main component in Mills' social theory. But Mills' early impression of Mannheim as a social theorist was less favorable than it later became. This was evident in a letter Mills wrote to Robert Merton in 1941:

> Now you can find a lot of things in this guy Mannheim and I don't value him as highly as certain sociologists of knowledge in very high circles do. Since there are many things in the man's writing I suppose it best to select all that one can agree with, all that appears usable and systematize it for research, rather than compile all the inconsistencies and learnedly stick out our tongue at him. Why should we shovel up inconsistencies all the time with a great philosophical shovel? Hell, we want a parade, not a street cleaner. . . . I share your feelings fully that he is very equivocal, vague and unfinished. Everyone with even elementary philosophical training can see that.[78]

Mills' later and more positive appraisal of Mannheim may have come via his close intellectual relationship with Hans Gerth, who had been a student of Mannheim before coming to the United States. Whatever the case, by 1960, Mills included in his *Images of Man* a section from Mannheim's *Man and Society in An Age of Reconstruction* and referred to him as "one of the two or three most vital and important sociologists of the interwar period."[79] Nevertheless, in spite of Mills' more favorable view of Mannheim's work in later years, it is evident when he uses Mannheim's ideas that he does so in his characteristically eclectic manner, not as a disciple of any single thinker or school of thought.[80]

It is argued that Mills "made the most serious application of Mannheim's perspective in his analysis of power in America."[81] The proponents of this claim emphasize Mills' interpretation of the power system as dominated by elites manipulating a mass society. Elite control and domination of the American system is facilitated by the growth of false consciousness within mass society. Mills' particular way of analyzing the idea of false consciousness is based on a dichotomy between "objective" and "subjective" interests. It rests on the distinction between what men are actually interested *in* and what is *to* their best interest. Although the concept is found in Marx and in altered form in Veblen's ceremonial-technological dichotomy, the version evident in Mills is probably derived from Mannheim, who once wrote that "Class position is an objective fact whether the individual in question knows his class position or not, and whether he acknowledges it or not."[82] As Mills noted, "class consciousness" does not necessarily accompany membership in a class and its failure to evolve is a matter for serious investigation.

Mills uses Mannheim's distinction between substantial and functional rationality with telling effect in his penetrating commentaries on the robotizing effects of bureaucracy. Substantial rationality signifies an understanding of the interrelation of events in complex social institutions and an ability to transcend immediate environment and thus comprehend relationships in the social structure itself. It involves the capacity for independent judgment and the ability to make intelligent decisions based on the available evidence.[83] On the other hand, functional rationality means that a series of actions is organized to lead to a previously defined goal. It signifies means-ends congruence and mastery of technical detail.

Mills believed that in a society based on widespread property-holding where each man is an owner and manager of his own property, substantial rationality had flourished because the institutional preconditions necessary for its existence were present. For example, the liberal social order of the Jacksonian United States offered a much better chance of providing the individual with psychological preparation for the growth of substantial rationality. The yeoman farmer and the small businessman were independent in their judgments and had to direct and organize economic units according to their own more or less rational interpretation of the course of events. But, with the growth of industrialization and bureaucratization, and with a decline in the relative numbers owning and managing their own property, functional rationality became more prevalent and substantial rationality increasingly rare. Mannheim viewed this change as the cause of the growing distance between the elite and the masses and of irrational appeals to the "leader" which had become widespread. Mills agreed with Mannheim that industrialization and bureaucratization had caused a decline in the amount of substantive rationality, but he did not share Mannheim's view that elites were now more likely to possess substantial rationality. As Mills asserts:

> By the mindlessness and mediocrity of men of affairs I do not, of course, mean that these men are not sometimes intelligent men, although that is by no means automatically the case. It is not, however, primarily a matter of the distribution of "intelligence." . . . It is rather a matter of the quality of mind, a quality which requires the evaluation of substantive rationality as the key value in a man's life and character and conduct. That evaluation is what is lacking from the American power elite.[84]

Like Mannheim, Mills focused on the increasing interdependence of society, with the implications this had for the development of a mass society subject to elite control and domination. The process of growing interdependence meant that to an ever-increasing degree individual activities were being linked up with one another into larger wholes. This facilitated centralized control over social institutions and was an important step in the evolution toward mass society. Mills thus adopted Mannheim's view of the increasing centralization and interdependence of social institutions with the breakdown of communities as primary groups. To this he added the growth of functional rationality divorced from substantial rationality within a bureaucratic society and simultaneously included the several meanings of Marxian alienation and Durkheimian anomie. These are the European sources of "massification" that play a significant role in *The Power Elite*. Nevertheless, Mills was critical of certain aspects of Mannheim's theory of mass society.

> The transition from a "democracy of the few" to a mass society explains another set of changes. The [mass] "society" is one of the least substantiated notions in the book. One wishes Mannheim had characterized it less with words like "emotional" and "irrational" and more with such indices as voting trends. It should also be related more precisely and rigorously to his "fundamental democratization," the trend in bureaucratic organization, "functional and substantial rationality," and the sociopolitical incidences of industrialization.[85]

Mannheim was more willing to acquiesce in elite hegemony, provided it was the right kind, than Mills, who remained committed to egalitarian-participationist values. Even though Mills tempered his views with the realization that structural changes had antiquated the Jeffersonian ideals, unless basic changes in the institutional framework occurred to make those ideals once again realizable, he steadfastly urged the pursuit of goals compatible with both the Jeffersonian tradition and that of guild socialism. But there are two ways of interpreting this position. One is that he wanted, like Mannheim, to make the power elite responsible and accountable for its behavior to the electorate without any substantial decentralization of power. The other is that he favored massive structural changes that would result in democratic socialism based on workers' control and social ownership of industrial property. Both views are probably correct, but the first was a short-term prescription, while the latter remained a long-range goal. Mills was committed to both.

Mannheim was more optimistic than Mills that elites would reconcile their class interests with the human needs of the downtrodden and impoverished. Mills, a few years later in the United States, found the

American elites less adaptable and influential than those that Mannheim had observed in Britain. Related to this divergence was Mills' criticism of Mannheim for his inadequate handling of the role of private property in a corporate economy. He linked this deficiency with Mannheim's failure to be concrete about which specific groups or types of groups he thought were likely to obtain power in the democracies. Mannheim was also faulted for failing to indicate which power blocs "would like to attempt actualization of his type of planning."[86] In short, he was accused of failing to adequately relate class structure to elite power and of failing to link both to the problems of planning.

Much of Mills published work from 1939 to 1943 was in the sociology of knowledge, both as matter and as methodology. Written when he was in his mid-twenties, it consisted of four articles in the two leading American journals of sociology.[87] But, due to the similarity between the intellectual style and content of Mannheim's work and that of the American pragmatists, it is not easy to separate their influence on Mills in any precise way. Mills himself well-recognized the parallels that existed between Dewey and Mannheim. One of these was epistemological, for Mills believed Dewey to have the same epistemological basis as Mannheim. He put it this way:

> . . . the guy has a very *suggestive* idea (admit it?), which . . . although blurred and loose and all becomes really fine when one weds it to, interprets it not from the neo-Kantian view, but from the standpoint of American pragmatism. To my own knowledge, Mannheim has stated that he considers pragmatism his own basis as far as epistemology goes.[88]

Another similarity lay in the fact that both Mannheim and Dewey believed that criteria of evaluation are largely situational; that is, they are derived from problems that emerge in a particular social circumstance. Thus in their major work they share a pragmatic criterion of validity. For both men, practice or action is the test of a theory's truth. An ethical attitude is invalid if it is oriented to norms with which action in a given historical setting cannot comply. A theory is incorrect if in a given practical situation it uses concepts and categories which, if taken seriously, would prevent man from properly adjusting himself in a particular circumstance.[89] It is evident that Mannheim's, Dewey's, and Mills' conceptions of praxis converge in their opposition to the separation of thought from action. The unity of theory and action must be recognized and restored in practice so men may gain a fuller consciousness of the consequences of their acts. For Dewey and Mills the function of theory was to guide men in changing the world; likewise for

Mannheim the rationale of his sociology of knowledge was to provide scientific guidance for action directed toward social change.[90]

Mannheim, like Marx, emphasized the relationship between class structure, class interests, and social ideology. In fact it was one of Mannheim's seminal contributions to have developed this relationship in his sociology of knowledge more fully than Marx himself. In turn, Mills probably analyzed the relationship in the American system more provocatively than any other scholar of his time. He had the temerity to suggest that academicians have material interests and that these affect their political ideology and scholarly work. For his efforts in this vein Mills was rewarded with the hostility of much of the social-science profession. Their negative reaction may also have been due to the commonly held belief that in the physical sciences the social position of the scientist and his value orientations do not penetrate the scientific content of his work. But for Mills and Mannheim "penetrate less" would be a more accurate description of what occurs, for both men saw a qualitative difference between the impact of individual values on the physical sciences as compared with the social sciences, although the difference was less pronounced in Mills' analysis. As Mannheim put it:

> the type of knowledge conveyed by natural science differs fundamentally from historical knowledge—we should try to grasp the meaning and structure of historical understanding in its specificity, rather than reject it merely because it is not in conformity with the positivist truth-criteria sanctioned by natural science.[91]

Both Mills and Mannheim believed that the imposition of mathematical and statistical techniques had led to a situation in which many social scientists no longer asked what was worth inquiring about, but regarded as worth knowing only what was measurable. Both were convinced that the way to counter this narrow scientistic trend was to recognize that the total social-science domain could be grasped only through qualitative analysis. Mannheim complained that "many empirical investigations in the social sciences are made merely because the data are at hand, and not because the investigators are faced with problems which they are seeking to solve."[92] As an antidote to this Mills approved of Mannheim urging social thinkers to take up again the comprehensive themes of the Enlightenment instead of specializing themselves away from the great problems. As Mills put it, "we could break up big themes for empirical solution without losing our grasp upon them as central wholes and being engulfed in speculative phrasemaking."[93] Later, Mills was to urge other social scientists to ask the "big questions" and to relate smaller parts to larger structural wholes. This direction reflected the intellectual legacy of Mannheim and was in keeping with the classical tradition in social thought that Mills analyzed in his *Images of Man.*

Finally, Mills' notion of a "working model" may also have been derived from Mannheim. A working model attempts to cope with "various social structures in their totality" and "typological models into which specific researches may be fitted."[94] Mills distinguished between a "theory" and a "working model." A theory is a statement that can be proved true or false, while a model focuses on the causal weight and the relations of its various elements and is thus an inventory of salient features we must pay attention to if we are to understand something of social significance.[95] It is impossible to understand much of Mills' work unless it is realized that it is a "working model" rather than a "theory."

Much misinterpretation of Mills' use of the Western intellectual legacy must venture beyond Mannheim and other European sources. There are, to be sure, certain important parallels between Mannheim and Mills; there are also very explicit statements by Mills that he read Mannheim while an undergraduate. Nevertheless, Mills' early work in the sociology of knowledge was heavily influenced by the symbolic interactionism of George H. Mead, the pragmatism of Dewey and Peirce, and the institutionalism of Veblen. Mills' published and unpublished writing in the late 1930s and early 1940s is studded with references to these sources and with manifestations of their influence.

CONCLUSION

After this substantial analysis of Mills' relationship to European social thought, a fundamental question still remains unanswered. What are the reasons for the erroneous views among social scientists as to the prime influences on Mills? Why have they been so prone to overemphasize European intellectuals and ignore the eclectic and indigenous aspects of his work? Certain answers suggest themselves although not all carry equal weight. First, many of his interpreters have overemphasized *The Power Elite*, where they believed European influence to be the strongest, to the neglect of the rest of Mills' theoretical work. Because of this narrow focus on one book, Mills' eclecticism had not received its just due. Moreover, his intellectual background and ideological genesis make a tangled web that synthesized various schools of thought without always showing clarity of origin. As a result, the ideational strands of his work are difficult to separate and misinterpretation has resulted. Also, his premature death may have prevented him from achieving a theoretical approach in which conflicting intellectual crosscurrents were more systematically and explicitly integrated with each other; had this integration occurred, his critics would be less inclined to single out one influence as dominant. Nor can one ignore the fact that many of his interpreters lack familiarity with institutional economics and instrumentalism, hence are prone to stress the influence of other theorists about whom they are more knowledgeable, such as Marx and Weber. It is ironic that many of his American critics are so indifferent to their own intellectual heritage that they believe the prime influences on Mills are European in origin. Consequently we must now turn to an analysis of the indigenous roots of his thought.

4

Veblen and the Institutionalist Influence on Mills

BIOGRAPHICAL SKETCH

Born in 1857, Thorstein Veblen was reared in a Scandinavian-Lutheran environment in the Midwest. He was the fourth son of Norwegian immigrant farmers who raised a large family. Several of the Veblen children went to Carleton College in Northfield, Minnesota, where Thorstein was trained in economics under the tutelage of John Bates Clark, who later became a prominent neoclassical economist. After receiving his bachelor's degree at Carleton, Veblen taught for a year and then enrolled at Johns Hopkins for his doctorate. After a short stay there he transferred to Yale, where he obtained his degree in philosophy in 1884, while studying under such noted academicians as Noah Porter and William Graham Sumner.

He was then idle for seven years, most of them spent on the farms of relatives or in-laws in the Midwest—largely because Veblen's agnosticism made him unemployable in schools with religious affiliations and because he had not yet established a reputation in economics. Finally, in 1890 he obtained a graduate position at Cornell University, where he became a Ph.D. candidate in economics. The economist J. Laurence Laughlin was impressed by him and in 1892, when Laughlin moved to the newly founded University of Chicago, he took Veblen with him.

It was probably there that Veblen first came to know John Dewey personally and intellectually. Although no correspondence between Veblen and Dewey has ever been found, a mutual intellectual influence was probable. Dewey once commented that "I have always found Veblen's own articles very stimulating and some of his distinctions, like that between the technological side of industry and its 'business' aspects, have been quite fundamental in thinking ever since I became acquainted with them."[1] Veblen once remarked after hearing an attack on Dewey and James by a leader of behavioristic psychology, "he will never know as much as Dewey and James forgot."[2] After Veblen's *The Theory of the Leisure Class* won him fame, if not fortune, Dewey commented to the effect that its terminology would survive the book.[3]

At Chicago, Veblen edited *The Journal of Political Economy* and began publishing in the field of economics. In 1899 his most famous book, *The Theory of the Leisure Class*, appeared and achieved a notoriety all of its own. Veblen's personal idiosyncrasies and his failure to properly "advertise" the University, however, offended the administration at Chicago and he was forced to move. His next job was at Stanford, where in a few short years he encountered similar difficulties which were exacerbated by his "womanizing." He was compelled to move again, this time to the University of Missouri.

World War I found Veblen briefly in Washington as an employee of the Food Administration. After the war he served for a short time as one of the editors of *The Dial*, a journal of literary and political opinion, and as a member of the faculty at the recently founded New School for Social Research in New York City. By then, even though his reputation as a scholar and author was at its peak, his academic career was at an end. Veblen retired and moved to California, where he lived an isolated existence in a cabin in the woods; he had divorced his first wife in 1911 and his second wife had been committed to an asylum. He died in August, 1929, shortly before the onset of the Depression. Today he is best known for his iconoclasm, mordant wit, and sardonic world view, traits readily evident in his writing.

VEBLEN, AYRES, AND MILLS

Veblen was the leading intellectual figure of institutional economics, and, of the institutionalists, it was he who had the greatest influence on C. Wright Mills. Indeed, Veblen probably had a greater impact on Mills' analysis of American society than any other thinker; Mills viewed Veblen as "the best critic of America that America had produced," and contended that "his biases are the most fruitful that have appeared in the literature of American social protest."[4]

> His language is part of the vocabulary of every literate American; his works are the most conspicuous contribution of any American to Ameri-

can studies; his style, which makes him the only comic writer among modern social scientists, is an established style of the society he dissected. Even the leisure class which has now been reading Veblen for more than a generation talks a little like him. . . . There is no better set of books written by a single individual about American society. There is no better inheritance available to those who can still choose their own ancestors.[5]

A few years later he exceeded his earlier praise in writing that "Veblen . . . is the best social scientist America has produced."[6]

Mills was one of the few American radicals to adequately grasp Veblen's importance and at the same time incorporate Veblenian ideas in a novel way in his work. In recent years, despite the resurgence of radical scholarship and the formation of various radical social-science associations, leftist social scientists continue to rely on Marx and the Marxian traditions. They largely ignore the existence of an American radical legacy. Indeed, a survey of leading radical social-science journals such as *Politics and Society, Review of Radical Political Economics,* and *The Insurgent Sociologist* show little interest in Veblen and his work.[7] Thus, it is not surprising that there is little radical recognition of Veblen's influence on Mills and of the important structural parallels in their work. Nevertheless, significant similarities exist between Mills and Veblen; these include their independent intellectual and political stance, their common critique of the social science establishment, and their alienation from mainstream American culture.[8] Furthermore, they were alike in their mutual emphasis on such values as workmanship, equality, peace, rationality, and participation. Mills obtained the use of evolutionary institutional analysis from Veblen, as well his historically rooted macrosociological perspective. As the American Marxist Leo Huberman once wrote in a letter to Mills, "You are saying what needs to be said in a way that has not been done since Veblen. You are, in fact, our current Veblen. I respect you for it—and so, I think, will history."[9]

To understand the impact of Veblen on Mills it is necessary to briefly consider the intellectual influence of Professor Clarence Ayres, under whom Mills worked at the University of Texas in the late 1930s. Ayres held a doctorate from the University of Chicago in philosophy, but taught in the economics department at Austin. His main scholarly achievement was to incorporate instrumentalism into Veblenian economics for Ayres believed Dewey's principal ideas closely paralleled those of Veblen.[10] He is largely responsible for the prevalent view that institutionalism is an extension of instrumentalism in the discipline of economics. Ayres introduced Mills to Veblen's work through courses on economic theory and economic history, and Mills regarded Ayres as "probably the foremost authority on Veblen."[11] He also had considerable informal contact with him. As Richard Gillam reveals:

> Ayres may have taken a certain personal interest in Mills; he was apparently conscious of his student's self-styled rebellion and once told him with indulgent good humor "if I felt that way good, but by all means to 'keep my pants pressed . . .' ." Yet the professor of economics probably exercised more of an intellectual than a personal influence.[12]

The nature of Ayres' influence is evident in a letter of recommendation he wrote for Mills in 1939 which reveals his admiration for Mills but also indicates his contentiousness as a student.

> . . . Mills had been saying that I dodged his questions, failed to meet the issues he brought up, and that he had concluded there was nothing in my stuff. However, this story has a sequel which may explain Mills. . . . Early last winter Mills came up and said that he had been exploring C. S. Peirce's logic and that he felt he was beginning to understand what I am driving at in my emphasis on the principle of technological continuity in economic development. We talked about it and I agreed with him that the principle Peirce and Dewey were developing was in fact the same as the one I had been pointing out in Veblen. He began visiting again and is now registered in my advanced theory course. My conclusion is that his early adverse judgment was honest and was justified in terms of the ideas he was then playing with (chiefly Mead).[13]

The "technological continuity in economic development" and the instrumental logic which grew out of it that became an important part of Mills' intellectual development and a major focus of his early publications. These closely related facets of indigenous thought tied him irrevocably to the pragmatic and institutionalist schools of thought, although as the years passed his ties with both loosened.[14]

But, given these ties, a short explanation as to what it means to be an "institutionalist" is perhaps in order. Allan Gruchy, in his study of neoinstitutionalism, distinguishes between the institutional economists like Thorstein Veblen, John Commons, and Wesley Mitchell, who did the bulk of their work before 1939, and the neo-institutionalists such as Clarence Ayres, Gardiner Means, and J. K. Galbraith, who have published their major work since then.[15] The term "institutionalism" was first coined by Walton Hamilton, who was impressed by the emphasis Veblen and others laid on the interaction of technology with institutions, and by stress they laid on the contrast between the dynamism of modern technology and the static ceremonialism of the institutional fabric. This focus is fundamentally different from that of neoclassical economics, where the main emphasis is on the price system and the market mechanism, even after the Keynesian Revolution focused attention on macroeconomics—so different, in fact, as to cause neoclassical critics of the institutional school to refer to it as "sociological economics."

A second primary difference between neoclassicism and institutionalism lay in the rejection of hedonistic psychology by Veblen and his disciples. They repudiated the neoclassical view of the human psyche as a maximizer of utilities and a rational calculator of pleasure versus pain, favoring instead a view of man as a creature of habit and custom and as a product of environmental conditioning. A third distinction is the area of policy prescription, where most institutionalists developed a bias in favor of welfare and regulatory state collectivism, economic planning, and income redistribution—attitudes that put them to the political left of orthodox economists.[16] A fourth difference is the adoption by institutionalists of Dewey's instrumentalist theory of value as opposed to the utility value theory adhered to by neoclassicists. Finally, there is the tendency on the part of institutionalists, and certainly of Mills, to view capitalism as a power system that constrains choice and allocates resources in a biased manner rather than as a system that maximizes freedom of choice and efficiency of resource allocation.[17]

Much of Mills' work contains commentaries on the relevance of Veblen's theoretical insights and those of other institutionalists.[18] So evident is his knowledge of Veblen and so pervasive is Mills' use of his ideas that some explanation must be offered as to why these are so often overlooked. Typical of such oversight is the comment by Immanuel Wallerstein to the effect that "Mills . . . found the substance of his work less useful than the style. It is indeed in style and populist bias that Mills most resembles Veblen."[19]

This characteristic comment, perhaps more than anything else, reflects the lack of knowledge of Veblen on the part of American social scientists. Indeed, outside the neoinstitutionalist movement, only a few historians and an occasional aesthetician now pay much attention to him. But the difficulties scholars have in understanding the intellectual origins of Mills' work are evidently due as much to their political obtuseness and ideological bias as to their lack of familiarity with Veblen. Nevertheless, it is also Mills' fault, for the original intellectual influences on him are often confused by his tendency to attribute certain core ideas to different sources. With this in mind, it should be evident why it is important to clarify Mills' Veblenian roots or else relocate his primary ideological sources. Given the similarities between Marx and Veblen, it is essential to examine Mills' understanding of the parallels between them.

MILLS ON THE RELATIONSHIP
BETWEEN VEBLEN AND MARX

On several occasions Mills wrote that Veblen was heavily influenced by Karl Marx. In fact, in one of his unpublished writings he claimed Veblen was "generally a Marxist."[20] However, with the exception of this one aberration, he stressed the relative influence of Marx on Veblen, not an extreme dominance of Marx's impact on him. Mills' more characteristic interpretation was that Veblen's "'business' and 'industrial' employments . . . are a kind of translation of Marx for the academic public." Mills also wrote "of the several Marxist overtones in Veblen."[21] Veblen was one of the few American social scientists of his time who actually read Marx, treated his writing as serious scholarly contributions, and incorporated them into his own work. Nevertheless, though just as critical of the main features of capitalism as was Marx, he was too creative a thinker and too much an iconoclast to be regarded as a Marxist.[22]

Although Mills went too far in his interpretation of Veblen as a follower of Marx, certain of Veblen's core ideas were similar. Perhaps because of these similarities Mills viewed Veblen primarily as an elaborator and translator of Marx.[23] But Mills suggested that Veblen's role as a Marx scholar was an innovative one when he wrote that "To Marx's class as an economic category both Weber and Veblen add status or prestige, and both realize that it is often prestige that is the readier clue to understanding the psychology of classes. . . ."[24] To this Mills added his conviction that Veblen had Americanized Marx:

> The master clue to Veblen's work as a whole is undoubtedly the distinc-
> tion between pecuniary and industrial employment, business and indus-
> try, institutions and technology. This distinction is in many ways a
> parallel and an extension of Marx's proletariat and bourgeoisie. But it is
> camouflaged or if you like adapted, for an American academic audience,
> and it does tend to be more convincingly applicable to the American
> case.[25]

Mills' peculiar analysis of the Marx-Veblen relationship overemphasized Veblen's intellectual debts to Marx.[26] His own extensive use of Veblen demands that we ask why he devoted so much time to a theorist whom he deemed a mere translator of Marx for American academics? There is a real inconsistency in Mills' relegation of Veblen to this role on the one hand and his persistent use of Veblenian ideas on the other. Perhaps he did not fully recognize the extent of his own indebtedness to Veblen. In any case, it is to this influence that we must now turn.

TECHNOLOGY AND THE INDUSTRIAL ARTS

There is considerable evidence of institutionalist influence on Mills' view of the role of technology in industrial society. For example, his broad definition of the "technological sphere" closely parallels Veblen's definition of the "state of the industrial arts." As Mills explains:

> By the "technological sphere" we refer to tools and machines as well as to the ways in which they are used. In this sphere we find wheelbarrows and prayer wheels, flint knives and rosaries, bulldozers, carbide tipped lathe chisels, plywood, and atom bombs. But beyond these material objects, the term also covers the implementation of human conduct by such tools and machines, which means that it refers to the various skills required of those using such artifacts.[27]

Mills, Ayres and Veblen use the term "technology" to mean both tools and tool skills. This is in keeping with the institutionalist tradition of defining technology broadly as "the state of the industrial arts." It includes the existing level of understanding and technique as well as the tools and equipment used by a community. The technology of a society is viewed as a common stock, collectively held and improved by a culture. Since the state of the industrial arts is the result of group endeavor, progress is due to the opportunity of scientists and inventors to tap the reservoir of science and technology that is the collective legacy of the community. Consequently, there is no such thing as an individual "genius." What Mills shares with the institutionalists is a belief that the production of goods and services and the art of invention are the results of the joint efforts of the community, since the state of the industrial arts is itself a social heritage.

CULTURAL LAG

According to Veblen and Ayres, human behavior consists of two parts, the ceremonial (institutional) aspect and the technological (instrumental). The ceremonial includes all the institutions based on legend, inherited beliefs, mores, status, and the hierarchical ordering of society. This part of human culture is inhibitory in nature. It is resistant to change and acts to preserve existing class arrangements and constraints. On the other hand, the technological aspects of human culture include scientific knowledge and tool skills. What Ayres calls the "tool combination-tool accumulation principle" is accelerative in nature and exerts constant pressure against the charge-resistant ceremonial qualities of major institutions. Since the institutional structure is resistant to change, the adaptation of institutions to the changing technoeconomic base is slow. It is associated with conflict between those groups and classes whose status is threatened by technological change and those who stand to gain from new institutional arrangements. The lag between institutional and technological change thus continuously impacts on the social order.[28]

Mills' own conception of cultural lag has close affinities with this view. He has been interpreted as a "conflict" theorist, correctly. But the conflict he focuses on arises from the dichotomous view of society he inherited from the institutionalists rather than from Marx's dialectical view of social change, although this undoubtedly influenced him later. It has often been noted that the Veblen ceremonial-technological dichotomy resembles Marx's contradiction between the relations and forces of production which is true in certain respects. But Mills' position is closer to Veblen than to Marx because of his greater emphasis on the change-resistant (ceremonial) qualities of social institutions and the cultural apparatus. For Marx, the time lag in the adjustment between base and superstructure is generally shorter and the adjustment more certain to occur. But, for Veblen and Mills, cultural lag is an uncertain, time-consuming process where numerous intervening variables are likely to prolong the maladjustment between technoeconomic base and superstructure. For example, there is no expectation in the later work of either Mills or Veblen that the labor force will develop socialist consciousness, much less a belief that a proletarian uprising will occur.

But this absence does not imply a strictly evolutionary perspective in which social change is reduced to small increments, being advanced by pressures generated by new technology and then retarded by tradition. Mills and Veblen both recognized the occurrence of sharp social discontinuities. Nor does it imply to Mills that the making of history is an anonymous development driven forward by the inexorable march of the machine process. Clearly, the individual-volitional element intrudes in Mills' epochal view of history, with epochs being defined by *who* is in power as well as by the social source of the power.

The concept of cultural lag that Veblen used to analyze social processes is used by American sociologists to account both for social change and social problems. In their view, change stems from science and technology, and problems result from the failure of institutions and organizations to keep pace. Veblen himself often contrasted the old institutional framework based on private property with the new machine process of industrial production, which was severely restricted, he argued, by its archaic institutions. Veblen frequently spoke of the "triumph of imbecile institutions," for the forces of technological change had taken direct effect in the industrial arts, yet touched matters of law and custom only indirectly. The principles that controlled knowledge and belief, law and morals, had lagged behind in contrast with the forward drive that occurred in industry and in the "workday conditions of living."[29] Much of Mills' work on cultural lag was thus based on certain issues raised by Veblen and it was from this problematic that he attacked the characteristic use of the cultural-lag concept. He praised Veblen's use of the concept in these words:

> Veblen's use of "lag, lead and friction" is a structural analysis of industry versus business enterprise. He focused on where "the lag" seemed to pinch; he attempted to show how the trained incapacity of legitimate businessmen acting within entrepreneurial canons would result in a commercial sabotage of production and efficiency in order to augment profits within a system of price and ownership.[30]

But Mills complained that in contemporary sociology the idea of cultural lag had lost its "specific and structural anchorage." It had become so generalized that it was applied to everything fragmentarily. This depreciation of meaning had been accomplished with the aid of such sponge words as "adaptive culture" and "material culture." Consequently, this conception of cultural lag was useless as the basis for a program of action.[31] The clear implication of Mills' analysis is that the concept was too apolitical and unfocused to serve as the basis of programatic or ideological anticapitalism.

Mills characterized the professional ideology of mainstream sociology as the ideology of "liberal practicality." The emphasis on practical problems of everyday life and the notion of orderly change were typical of the liberal model of society. Thus the cultural-lag model was tacitly oriented in "utopian" and progressive manner toward changing some culture and institutions so as to "integrate" them with the present state of technology.[32] Mills thought this this model uncritically endorsed both the natural sciences and orderly, incremental, progressive change. It was rooted in the ideology of the Enlightenment and was therefore rationalistic, messianic, and politically naive.[33] Mills believed that the cultural-lag concept was manipulated for ideological purposes by advocates of liberal ameliorism who wrote most textbooks and dominated the major departments and professional organizations in sociology. It was Veblen's radical use of the concept, and his use alone, that won Mills' praise. Veblen gave the concept a specific structural anchorage that would permit it to be used for an anticapitalist program of action. In the meantime, Mills, in his typical fashion, warned that sociologists could not avoid making value judgments, but that they should be aware of them regardless of who made them.[34] Perhaps he should also have commented on Veblen's propensity for placing value judgments behind massive barrages of satire and irony. In any case, the impact of Veblen's cultural-lag concept was evident in Mills' refusal to accept mainline sociology's use of it.

THE CEREMONIAL-TECHNOLOGICAL DICHOTOMY

Veblen's distinction between business and industrial pursuits was refined by Ayres into the ceremonial-technological dichotomy that is its generalized form when employed by institutional economists. Both Veblen and Ayres use ideal types as polar opposites in this method of analysis and valuation. Thus business pursuits are contrasted with industrial pursuits, pecuniary capital with physical capital, making money with making goods, and vendibility with serviceability. Although Mills was aware of the simplistic nature of the categories of the ceremonial and technological,[35] he praised Veblen for his use of the dichotomy[36] and he used it as a polemical tool in his attacks on the corporate structure. This is evident in Mills' contrast of corporate managers who understand the industrial process with those who do not because their primary function is financial (ceremonial).[37] It is also found in his claim that "The truth, known to any close observer of the higher circles in America, is that most high-up American businessmen are more often than not industrially incompetent and scientifically ignorant."[38] Veblen thought that most businessmen had the characteristic of "technological unfitness" and Mills shared his view. But Mills was not as consistent on this point as Veblen because he seemed to believe that some purely "business" functions have instrumental value and are oriented toward community serviceability.

Mills used the ceremonial-technological dichotomy as an undergraduate and continued to use it for the rest of his career although he was not always explicit. For example, in 1938, he argued that the growth of science and technology has been impeded by institutional restraints of a ceremonial nature although he believed this was less true of theoretical science than of applied science and technology.[39] In using the dichotomy Mills also commented that, if the social autonomy of science were not possible, he doubted that the physical sciences would have developed to the point they had. "We would still be listening to the croak of the alchemist and the chant of the priest."[40] Years later in a very different context Mills complained that

> there seems to be a technization of the manager, and a sentimentalization of the employee. In this connection, Veblen's distinction between industry and business seems to be absent from this literature—in fact, without explicit consideration, denied. The problem is thus put in terms of technological advancement, as a problem of the engineer and the human being rather than in terms of human beings in power and economic relations. The issue between manager and worker is thus seen as a vast misunderstanding, which perhaps accounts for the great emphasis upon "open channels of communication."[41]

Mills' point is that the role of industrial managers in their dealings with employees is not viewed, as Veblen saw it, as the ceremonial manifestations of a power system, but simply as a technical problem of improving communications. Indeed, much of the writing Mills did in organization theory focused on the ceremonial aspects of industrial management with particular emphasis on its manipulativeness and its authoritarianism.

POWER, SOCIAL CHANGE, AND CONTROL OF TECHNOLOGY

A primary focus in the work of Veblen, Ayres, and the institutional school was on the role of science and technology in promoting social change, and on the effect of institutions in retarding it. Their view is often mistakenly portrayed as turning technology into an irresistible force with an inner developmental logic of its own that makes it the forcing bed of social change. It is thus imbued with a capacity for automatic progress that puts it beyond human control. An opposite point of view is that human institutions can be restructured to control technological change. Men will master machines instead of being enslaved by them. However, a characteristic Mills' statement was that

> technology does not advance automatically, of its own force. . . . Before technology can effect historical changes, institutions must raise effective demands to incorporate it. . . . Institutional orders vary in this respect; and hence . . . the technological spheres of societies are differently anchored. Nevertheless, does not technology have some causal autonomy? . . . These are the rhetorical questions of "technological determinism," perhaps nowadays the leading theory of social

change. . . .The most fargoing statement of this theory has been presented as an interpretation of Veblen's work by C. E. Ayres.[42]

Although Mills exaggerates the degree to which Ayres and Veblen were technological determinists, this is understandable, for part of their work lends itself to this interpretation. On balance, however, both Veblen and Ayres were aware of the effect of institutional restraints on scientific and technological progress. But, in their enthusiasm for the gospel of technology, they sometimes forgot the powerful and pervasive restraints that social institutions can impose. Veblen and Ayres laid great stress on the view that "invention is the mother of necessity." They believed there was an immanent logic of progress present in existing tool patterns which caused the random pursuit of idle curiosity to result in invention. Mills tried to balance their view that "invention is the mother of necessity" against its opposite ("necessity is the mother of invention") when he wrote that "Necessity or purpose is the mother of adaptive inventions; but invention is also the mother of necessity."[43]

The institutionalist origin of Mills' ideas on the relationship between science, technology, and invention is also evident in his comment that:

> One aspect of the conception of technological development as autonomous deserves particular attention: Many discoveries have not been made out of regard for any usefulness. Of course, they have been adapted with great ingenuity to given demands, but the discoveries themselves were the results of combinations playfully made out of the existing stock of technologies and ideas. . . . It is the "immanent logic" of playful or systematic combinations that is concretely meant by the "idle curiosity" (Veblen's phrase) of the scientist, or the pursuit of science for science's own sake.[44]

Mills' analysis combines Ayres' view of the development of the tool continuum through the tool-combination-tool-accumulation process with Veblen's "instincts" of workmanship and idle curiosity to explain the evolution of the industrial economy.

Like Veblen and Ayres, Mills is concerned about the use of technology by institutionally dominant groups for their own selfish ends. His view is that those who control institutions decide which scientific discoveries to ignore and which to use. The technological application of science is thus controlled through institutions and does not "automatically" serve the best interests of mankind. Whether an institution uses a given discovery depends not only on technical feasibility, but on the value the institution attaches to achieving a particular end. Elites select the contents of their respective technological spheres in order to better achieve their own goals. The sheer availability of a new technology was only one factor in determining whether it would be implemented or not. In this sense, technology is not autonomous.[45]

MORAL ASPECTS OF TECHNOLOGY

Mills believed that America had for too long substituted technical solutions for problems that were political or moral in nature. This was what he meant when he wrote "If one continues to focus upon technology as a *means* and yet as *the key good*, assimilating questions of ends to questions of means, then politically one should expect an implemented aimlessness."[46] His point was that technology as means usurps moral and political values as ends. Nevertheless, he earlier had begun to evolve what he called a "gospel of technology."

> We need . . . a gospel of technology and a philosophy of human work . . . [T]his phrase I steal from my old teacher, C. E. Ayres, who has used it for other purposes with which I do not hold. In order to regain our capacity for radical imagination and the political use of it, we first need to dethrone the current run of tehnological projectors. To do this we have got first to reappraise the place of physical science itself, and as well of art and reason; second to work out a morally grounded view of the role of technology in various kinds of society.[47]

Mills was less optimistic than Ayres that science and technology would be used in the common interest.[48] He was committed to the view that because they are value neutral their utilization depends on who controls institutional access to them. For both he and Veblen it was not technology *per se* that counted, but serviceability to the community as a whole—measured without regard to invidious comparisons, status rankings, and power differentials among individuals.[49] Mills' focus was on the power system and institutional matrix that determined how technology was used and to what ends it was put rather than on the values it fostered. (In this respect he differed from his institutionalist mentors who gave more emphasis to the dissemination of technological values, although they were also concerned as to how power configurations affect the use of technology.)[50] Mills once wrote that "in and of itself, the technological continuum is socially, economically and morally blind; it is no Messiah; it has no other aim than to allow man to implement any given end he may have with less physical effort in a shorter time." Unlike the early Veblen in particular, Mills did not assume that technology produces technological values in those who interact with it. Mills' view was that although technology fosters functional rationality in the labor force in terms of understanding means-ends congruence, it does not inculcate substantial rationality in the sense of ability to understand complex sets of social relationships.

Craftsmanship

Mills' craftsmanslike abilities in mechanics and carpentry were biographically related to both his family background and his own theory of craftsmanship. In a letter to his parents in 1939 he put it this way:

> From my father I absorbed the gospel and character of work, determination with both eyes always ahead. That is part of the America he knows, and it is part of him too. There was a time when I thought he did not possess a feeling of craftmanship. But I was wrong. It is merely that his line of effort is one I did not understand. Looking back, I see he always did a good job, that he never quit until it was finished. So from both of you I have gotten a living craftsmanship.[51]

This is an interesting comment by Mills since his father was an insurance agent, a profession for which Mills probably had little respect. In any event, Mills did thus summarize the impact of his parents on his attitude toward work, and the seeds of his theory of craftsmanship are present in it. For him, as for Dewey and Veblen, work was to become an ethical imperative. Indeed, the ethicization of work is theoretically important for all three.

When Mills uses the term "craftsmanship" he is referring both to a style of work and to a way of life in which individuals obtain pride from what they produce. They must understand the relationships that exist between the work process and the completed product, in order to obtain the satisfaction that comes from successful completion of it. As Mills once put it, "Craftmanship as a fully idealized model of work gratification involves no ulterior motive for work other than the product being made and the processes of its creation . . . the details of the craftsman's daily work are meaningful because they are not detached in his mind from the product of the work."[52] There should not be an artificial separation of work from leisure activity. Instead, work must become central to the individual so that a unity exists between it and leisure. Thus the craftsman's way of livelihood both determines and permeates his entire mode of living. Consequently he is at work and play in the same act and does not try to escape from work into the sphere of leisure.[53] Also, to paraphrase Mills, the craftsman must be able to learn from his work because it is part of a developmental process of self-cultivation. His work must be a means of developing himself as a person as well as enhancing his skill. This self-development is not a separate goal, but a cumulative result of devotion to and practice of his craft. It is essential that the craftsman recognize the broader social meaning that his work possesses by grasping the moral and political implications of his work for the society in which he lives. As a craftsman the worker must be free to control his own work according to his own plan and be free during the work activity to modify its course.[54] Plan and performance are thus unified and in both the craftsman is master of the activity and of himself in the process. This joining of plan and activity brings firmly together the consummation of work and its instrumental activities by infusing the latter with the joy of the former.[55]

THE DISINTEGRATION OF CRAFTSMANSHIP

Mills once wrote that the contemporary white-collar worker had "neither Calvin nor craftsmanship." He meant that the moral and spiritual underpinnings of the Protestant work ethic had largely disappeared along with the dignity and self-respect they lent to the worker. This loss had occurred without a subsequent development of craftsmanship. Mills examined the absence of each of the elements of craftsmanship in the modern organization of work. He found that the large-scale working unit and the minute division of labor detach the worker from his product and drastically limit his view of the rest of the process of production. To the worker the traditional meaning of work had withered away. Mills quoted George Herbert Mead to the effect that:

> When the goal is too far removed in time and method of approach, the imagination leaps to the ultimate satisfactions which cannot be fused with the uninteresting detail of preparation, and daydreaming supervenes and cuts the nerve of action. . . . In daydreaming it is the very lack of connection between means and the end that leads one to the Barmecide feast of an end that is not expressed in terms of means.[56]

Mills argued that the routinization of work can foster formal but not substantial rationality. This means that it produces an understanding of means-ends congruence without any comprehension of complex sets of social relationships. He discovered that power over the technical aspects of work had been stripped from the individual, first by the development of the market that determines how and when he works, second by bureaucratization that subjects the work process to discipline. This environment deprived the individual of control over his own work life. Mills believed the centralization of decision-making and the formal rationality of bureaucratic hierarchies of work expropriate the individual's substantial rationality. Consequently, the worker is no longer free to plan his work, or to modify the plans of others who have control over him. The worker is deprived of the chance to develop in a free manner, and self-cultivation thus becomes impossible as work loses its developmental potential. As a result work is split from the rest of life, especially from the spheres of conscious enjoyment. Because work is unsatisfactory, leisure is seen as containing all that is enjoyable.

In summation, Mills concludes that the individual workman should be self-cultivating in terms of improving his capacity for analysis and cultural development. He should be rational in the sense of able and willing to judge his environment, and he should be participant in the sense of ability to take part in controlling his environment. Unfortunately structural constraints in his work environment make realizing all these impossible. Given this unsatisfactory state of affairs, it is not surprising that Mills would suggest ways to change the existing situation in the workplace. Although these ways may not have been adequate, they were more explicit than those recommended by Veblen, who in spite of his critical stance failed to prescribe a way for craftsmanship to flourish under conditions of modern industry where capitalist relations of property and authority prevail.[57] However, both Veblen and Mills wanted to turn the individual problems of workmen into public issues by politicizing the authoritarianism in the workplace that made it impossible for craftsmanship to evolve. This was a very important point for Mills as it pertained to social scientists, for it was central to the exercise of the sociological imagination.

THE OVERDEVELOPED SOCIETY AND THE PERVERSION OF CRAFTSMANSHIP

Craftsmanship in the Millsian sense cannot flourish except in a "properly developing society." Mills advocated a society in which the spirit of craftsmanship would be a dominant reality. It would be a system in which people would be judged by their ability to develop along the lines of such a character model. The norms of craftsmanship would be the criteria utilized to measure not only individual character but social institutions as well. The ideal society would be one in which craftsmanship was the pervasive activity of the unalienated person and the primary condition for free development. Thus the most important question to ask was how to construct a social order that would give maximum encouragement to the development of craftsmanship and its relevant character traits?[58] It was evident to Mills that Veblen's "instinct of workmanship" had become contaminated under capitalism, so that community serviceability was now rated in pecuniary terms!

Mills distinguishes between the "properly developing society" and the "overdeveloped society" in terms that possess deep Veblenian roots. He believes that deliberately cultivated styles of life would be central in the properly developing society, and that decisions about standards of living would require citizens to debate choices between such life styles. Industrial equipment would be maintained as an instrument to increase the range of choice among these competing styles of life. He contrasts this pattern with the existing overdeveloped society where the standard of living controls life styles and where the people are dominated by the commercial framework. Here conspicuous production and consumption have become fetishes around which both work and leisure are organized. Here competition for status has taken the place of struggle for survival, as Veblen noted many years before.[59] The various forms of status emulation shape life styles in advanced industrial society. Ostentatious consumption, conspicuous production and waste, and conspicuous exemption from useful labor are all part of the apparatus of emulation. Fundamental human needs are often ignored in favor of status gratification through imitation. Mills' use of Veblen's ideas and language in his discussion of the overdeveloped society are pervasive.[60]

CRAFTSMANSHIP: INTELLECTUAL ORIGINS AND STRUCTURAL PARALLELS

Veblen used ideal types as polar opposites. Those he most commonly utilized were the peaceful and predatory. The traits of the peaceful or other-regarding type included the instincts of idle curiosity, parenthood, and workmanship. The opposite traits exhibited by the predatory type included the pecuniary instinct evident in moneymaking and the sporting instinct that was exhibited in such activities as hunting, militarism, and athletics and that involved the use of force and fraud. Mills and Veblen shared an overwhelming preference for the peaceful type and hoped that in the long run its normative humanism would prevail. In the meantime, Mills believed, the traits of the peaceful type should manifest themselves more among those involved in cultural and intellectual work.[61]

But to explain in more detail: Veblen's "parental instinct" is that altruistic tendency present in individuals who take more thought of others than themselves. It is the drive leading to a "parental solicitude for the common good." It starts with concern for one's offspring, but it can transcend this for a generalized concern with the well-being of large social groupings, including the nation or even mankind in the abstract. It corresponds with the ability of Mills' craftsman to understand the moral and political ramifications his work has for the rest of society.

Veblen's "instinct of workmanship" leads the individual to manipulate materials, create useful products, and be concerned with "devices and contrivances of efficiency and economy." Veblen believed that this instinct manifests itself in concern with practical expedients, creative work, and technological mastery of facts.[62] Much of the functional content of the instinct of workmanship is a capacity for taking pains. It is best displayed in the industrial efficiency of the worker and in the cumulative technological competence of the community.

The third instinct that played a significant role in Veblen's analysis and that influenced Mills is that of idle curiosity, that propensity "which drives men to inquire into the nature of things, to work out explanations of the world's events in mythological and, later, in scientific terms."[63] Again the structural parallels and value equivalents between this view and similar aspects of Mills' craftsmanship is apparent.

Mills' craftsmanship is thus essentially a composite of various traits found in the instincts that are characteristic of Veblen's peaceful type. In both there is an emphasis on the most efficient way to perform a task, although Veblen emphasizes this more than Mills. There is a stress on work as a developmental process in which learning continually occurs and from which satisfaction is derived. A parallel focus exists in Mills and Veblen on the altruistic aspects of work in which its moral and social implications are emphasized. However, Mills' eclecticism is again evident, for though Veblen was an important influence, we cannot ignore Marx's ideal of "unalienated labor," Mead's "aesthetic experience," and even Weber's idea of a "calling."[64] Mills' ideal of craftsmanship as a prescriptive norm thus has its ideological roots deep in the classical tradition of social thought.

Craftsmanship, Methodology, and the Social Role of Social Scientists

Both Mills and Veblen were displeased with the acquiescence of academic social scientists in the status quo. Veblen alluded to this conservatism on the part of university staff and administration in his

The Higher Learning in America. However, in his most direct analysis of the problem Veblen took his fellow economists to task for their uncritical support of capitalism. As he so satirically asserted:

> economic science should . . . be a science of business traffic . . . inbued
> with a spirit of devotion to things as they are shaping themselves under
> the paramount exigencies of absentee ownership. . . . [T]he body of
> economists in the degree in which they run true to form under the
> training of the schools and the market, should be partisans of this sys-
> tem, and of a reasonably intolerant temper. . . . [F]ollowing the lead
> given by the workday conduct of business traffic, the attention of the
> economists and their formulations of theory should converge on the
> ways and means of differential gain.[65]

Mills shared Veblen's indignation with academic social scientists who were uncritically engaging in the "Great Celebration" of American virtue without investigating the deficiencies of its social order. Mills charged the Establishment in the social sciences with methodological self-indulgence, unjustifiable support of Cold War policies, and acquiescence in social injustice. Inasmuch as academic social science had changed since Veblen's time, it would no longer suffice simply to repeat Veblen's attacks on orthodoxy. So Mills shifted ground in an attempt to undermine Establishment scholars and mainline social-science trends such as pluralism in political science, structural-functionalism in sociology, and consensus interpretations of American history.

Mills believed that much of what passed for "objectivity" in the social sciences was a successful attempt to garner research funds, obtain sabbaticals, and achieve promotion with little regard for the practice of intellectual craftsmanship. Mills divided academicians into two categories: those who were intellectual craftsmen, or aspired to be, and those whose activities were of a ceremonial nature. The former he dealt with as a subcategory of general craftsmanship; examples of the latter were the politically conservative academics whom Mills charged with indulgence in abstracted empiricism and grand theory. He writes in *The Sociological Imagination* of "The Method" and the "little mill of the Statistical Ritual" by which he means the infection of technique with ceremonialism. Social scientists become so committed to a particular methodology that they cannot study significant problems because of the methodological constrictions they place upon themselves.[66]

Although Mills and Veblen were alike in their assault on the methodological pretensions of mainstream social scientists, the main thrust of Veblen's attack was on the empty formalism of neoclassical economics, with its taxonomic rather than evolutionary approach. Mills, on the other hand, attacked the new formalism both of the abstracted empiricists for their trivialization of data and of the grand theorists whose vapory abstractions lacked empirical referents. In short, both men assaulted mainstream methodology for its formalism that meant failure to shed light on human problems and issues. As Mills put it in analyzing Veblen as a methodologist:

> . . . Veblen stands out as a live protest against these dominant tendencies of the higher ignorance. He always knew the difference between the trivial and the important, and he was wary of the academic traps of busywork and pretension. . . . Veblen was quite unable to be a specialist. . . . He was, in short, a social thinker in the grand tradition. . . .[67]

Veblen's and Mills' caustic criticism of formalistic methodology was due to their belief that it was a way of avoiding asking the "big questions": questions having to do with the legitimacy and use of the existing distribution of power and wealth. The avoidance, much to their chagrin, left the main power system untouched by mainline scholars as the bulwark of an unjust social order.

Status Emulation

Mills often used Veblen's theory of status emulation in his writings on various topics. Status emulation has long been regarded as an important contribution of Veblen to social theory and in his words it means that

> the leisure class stands at the head of the social structure in point of reputability; and its manner of life and its standards of worth, therefore, afford the norm of reputability for the community. . . . [T]he observance of these standards . . . becomes incumbent upon all classes lower in the scale. . . . The result is that the members of each stratum accept as their ideal of decency the scheme of life in vogue in the next higher stratum, and bend their energies to live up to that ideal.[68]

Veblen believes individual and collective character structure evolves in terms of the models available for imitation. Leaders are models of behavior and as such are sources of values. Mills, too, understands the emulative tendency to have political consequences. The use he makes of this insight is particularly evident in his discussion of the meaning for leadership of the "higher immorality" and the structure of "organized irresponsibility." For the deplorable state of public life he blames the moral decrepitude and political irresponsibility of top American leaders, since those who are politically active naturally emulate the most "successful" and visible statesmen. Veblen believed that status emulation rather than class analysis is often a better key to understanding the psychology of classes. For example, the struggle for existence has been changed into a "struggle to keep up appearances"—a struggle in which the appearance of success is becoming more important than the substance of success. Mills found Veblen's ideas of emulative consumption, ostentatious display, and conspicuous exemption from useful labor insightful for understanding the psychology of the new middle classes.

Veblen argued that the ordinary basis of self-respect was the respect shown to people by their neighbors. Only persons with deviant temperament could retain their self-respect when faced with the long-run disesteem of their cohorts. Mills elaborated on this theme in *White Collar* and in so doing reiterated Veblen's point that one does not impress others

> except by unremitting demonstration of ability to pay. That is practically the only means which the average of us have of impressing our respectability on the many to whom we are personally unknown, but whose transitory good opinion we would so gladly enjoy. So it comes about that the appearance of success is very much to be desired, and is even in many cases preferred to the substance. . . . [T]he means of sustenance and comfort [has become] so much easier to obtain as very materially to widen the margin of human exertion that can be devoted to purposes of emulation.[69]

But, for Mills, the most tragic aspect of the emulatory process described by Veblen is that individuals do not seek change in the emulatory system but want to be integrated into it. For in terms of happiness "to believe that they [the rich] are unhappy would probably be un-American. For if they are not happy, then the very terms of success in America, the very aspirations of all sound men, lead to ashes rather than to fruit."[70] Thus the emulatory problem is circular. The power elite set the standards and the rest of the social order uses these standards as criteria of their success. If they achieve this success, and become members of the elite, they in turn adopt the same values. Thus it is imperative for the radical political intellectual to reconstruct reality for others. Mills and Veblen hoped to break out of the elite-manipulated cycle of value circularity by undermining establishment definitions of social reality.

Mills' America differed from Veblen's in that status had become even more insecure. In Mills' view the enjoyment of prestige was often "disturbed and uneasy" because its basis, expression, and gratification were subject to strain that often took the form of a "virtual status panic." Thus it was no longer easy to borrow prestige from others as it had once been, although borrowing still occurred on a large scale. This was particularly true for white-collar employees who found it increasingly difficult to obtain prestige from their relations with both management and customers. Indeed, in the case of the sales clerk the prestige source now included the merchandise itself as well as the store.[71]

By the 1950s the American system of status emulation was more complex than in the 1890s when Veblen had first set forth his theory.[72] Mills, in using status emulation as part of his theory of the power elite, recognized the complexity when he argued that local society now looked to the cities of the Social Register, to corporations, and to the national centers of political and military power as emulatory models. Local society has thus become a satellite of a vastly more complex status system.[73] In particular the position held in the national corporation had become an important basis for the satisfaction of status claims. It was the organized power center of the owning classes. The propertied and managerial elites of the urban upper class, as well as local society, now looked to the corporation in claiming and in assigning prestige to one another.[74]

The national scope of the status system was made possible by the rise of the new media of mass communication that centralized the means of publicity. Mass communication made possible a celebrity system based on competition, but organized as a business with the stars selected and formed by the mass media for a profit. Thus there was discrepancy between the national hierarchy of status and the hierarchies of wealth and power. This situation was historically unprecedented since status has always been used to convert power into authority and thereby protect power from challenge. The change caused Mills to ask, "In due course will not those Americans who are celebrated come to coincide more clearly with those who are the most powerful among them?"[75] Here Mills' analysis of status and power attained its Veblenian climax:

> In America this star system is carried to the point where a man who can knock a small white ball into a series of holes in the ground with more efficiency and skill than anyone else thereby gains social access to the President of the United States. It is carried to the point where a chattering radio and television entertainer becomes the hunting chum of

leading industrial executives, cabinet members, and the higher military. It does not seem to matter what the man is the very best at; so long as he has won out in competition over all others, he is celebrated.[76]

Both Veblen and Mills recognized the unsuccessful attempts of outsiders to enter the status system. In Veblen's time this involved small farmers who wished to become absentee owners; for Mills, it meant labor leaders who wanted to be part of the power elite.[77] Neither believed that these outsiders would fully succeed in their quest, for they could engage in intensive status emulation without becoming part of the main power system. For these groups status emulation could only be a form of false consciousness.

Mills' work on the American middle class emphasizes the role that status emulation plays in its use of leisure time and in its consumption patterns. For Mills believed that the leisure of middle-class citizens was consumed in attempts to satisfy their status claims. The use of leisure had been made hollow by status emulation, especially in large urban areas where the breakdown of community made the realm of leisure and consumption even more crucial for status.[78] Those who are disturbed by the recreational vehicles strewn about the landscape of their suburban tracts may nod with gratification at the attack of Veblen and Mills on conspicuous consumption as the main American form of status emulation.

MILLS AND VEBLEN ON THE NATURE OF THE AMERICAN STATE

William T. Bluhm has argued that Mills' theory of the "exploitative state," as articulated in *The Power Elite*, is Marxian in origin and flavor.[79] In view of the similarities between Veblen and Marx in this respect, it is easy to understand why Bluhm would overreact. But Mills' eclectic interpretation of the nature of the state is probably derived more directly from Veblen's work, especially his *Absentee Ownership and Business Enterprise in Recent Times*, than from any other single source. Mills knew Veblen better and earlier than he knew Marx, and he recognized that Veblen's work, unlike Marx's, had the advantage of being based on firsthand knowledge of the American polity.

Veblen believed the modern state was an offshoot of the predatory dynastic governments of the late feudal and mercantilist eras. Like its predecessors, it engaged in four closely related forms of ceremonial activity. First, it supported a largely unnecessary military establishment that was often involved in unjustifiable war. Second, it was an instrument of waste and inefficiency serving the interests of those elements it employed at the expense of the underlying population. Third, it was also a tool of the vested interests with the courts, jails, policy, and legislatures serving primarily to protect the property rights of the upper classes. Fourth, it was an instrument of imperialism using force to protect the institution of absentee ownership abroad. Given the nature of these four claims, it is easy to see why Veblen viewed the United States government as an instrument of predation and coercion whose ceremonial activities were largely detrimental to the life process of mankind. Veblen was not a Marxist, but his interpretation differs in detail, not in substance, from the view that the "state is the executive committee of the bourgeoisie." The only apparent difference was that Veblen placed more stress on the waste and inefficiency of government than did Marx.

THE POWER ELITE: VEBLENIAN ORIGINS AND STRUCTURAL PARALLELS

What is most apparent in Veblen's analysis is the basically exploitative and manipulative nature of the modern state. For Veblen government in the United States is largely a tool of the vested interests and an instrument of predation. This became a central idea of great importance in Mills' theory of the power elite.[80] Mills' rejection of prevailing views of power and his long-term opposition to liberalism are obviously linked with Veblen's theory of the modern state. Although Veblen's theory is a "ruling class" theory as contrasted with Mills' "power elite" theory, they achieve a similarity of outlook. They share the view that members of the ruling group have similar social backgrounds, a common idelogy, an urge for power, the ability to effectively communicate with each other to achieve unity, and direct access to positions of institutional power. Although they differ in their attribution and location of institutional power, the difference can be explained by the fact that Veblen's last analysis is based on the early 1920s, whereas Mills' theory was articulated in the 1950s. Mills had the advantage of being able to view two significant developments: the enhanced position of the executive branch of the federal government brought about by the New Deal, and the militarization of American society due to the Cold War. To corporate power, which was the core of Veblen's ruling class thesis, Mills added the power both of the officer corps in the military apparatus and that of the president, his cabinet, and about 1500 of the top appointed officials in the executive branch of the federal government. Many of the basic differences between Veblen's "ruling class" and Mills' "power elite" can be reduced to the fact that the military and the executive branches of the federal government were far less important in Veblen's day.

Although *The Power Elite* cannot be traced to any single intellectual source, it was evident long before Mills published it that he recognized the inadequacies of the prevailing theories of power. The recognition was clear even before 1948 when Mills published *The New Men of Power* and noted the enhanced role of both the military and the federal government and their intimate relationship with large corporations.[81] The interchange of personnel among these three parts of the power elite resulted in greatly increased unity among them, and in Mills' view posed a theat to democratic control of the political order.

Mills classifies elite theories of power into four categories. The first category defined the elite by their possession of particular values, as those who had more valued possessions and experiences than anyone else. The second category consisted of those who were aware of belonging to the top social strata, who knew one another, and were thus part of an organized group. Another elite theory assumed unusual moral or psychological qualities in the elite that made it "superior" to the mass. Fourth was an elite theory based on institutional position.[82] Clearly, institutional position was the source of control used by Mills' power elite and Veblen's ruling class, although the first and second categories mentioned above are also relevant. In defining the elite partly in terms of institutional position, Mills was primarily concerned with (1) the nature and composition of the elite, (2) the social sources of its power, including its control over the state apparatus, (3) the different levels of power in the rest of society, and (4) the effect of elite rule.

Parallels exist in all four realms between Mills and Veblen. For example, compare Mills' view of the different levels of power with that of Veblen. To paraphrase Mills, there were three broad levels of power that were distinguishable although they were becoming increasingly unified and coordinated. At the top existed an elite whose power probably exceeded that of any small group in history with the possible exception of the Kremlin. The middle levels were a drifting set of stalemated forces which no longer linked the bottom with the top. The bottom was politically fragmented and increasingly powerless while beginning to emerge as a mass society. The decision-making power was now embedded in the top-level economic, military, and political institutions, which were developing a significantly greater ability to use and shape other social institutions.[83]

For Veblen corporate enterprise had increasingly become an organized power concentrate, competing with unorganized consumers. The upper levels of power were a cohesive but not monolithic monopoly, competing with deadlocked interest groups at the middle levels of power and with the politically fragmented masses at the bottom of American society. It is evident that in constructing his hierarchical theory of power with a power elite at the top, stalemated interest groups in the middle, and mass society at the bottom, Mills drew upon Veblen's analysis of the American system.

Like Mills' power elite, Veblen's ruling class is not a monolith whose will always prevails because it is an omnipotent conspiracy. Instead, he argues as Mills later did that:

> It foots up to a concert of action and policy enforced by the drift of circumstances, rather than by deliberation and reasoned plan looking to the long run. But by drift of circumstances—the drift of sound business principles and common solicitude—their several movements result, in effect, in such a convergence of forces and such a concert of policy and action as to merit the name.[84]

Veblen's *Absentee Ownership* focuses to a great extent on the organization and exercise of corporate power and is concerned with the relationships between what he calls the "Key Industries," "Manufactures," and the "One Big Union of Financial Interests." First, he identified the Key Industries as coal, steel, oil, lumber, railways, and waterpower. He designates Manufactures as "continuation industries" meaning those that are dependent for their existence on the Key Industries since they use or process what they produce. The management of the continuation has delegated power only, and their discretion is bounded by measures taken independently by the management of the key industries. Further, the One Big Union of Financial Interests is defined by Veblen as

> not precisely a trade union of bankers; although it is on the ground of investment banking and by use of transactions in credit and capitalization that the One Big Union's tutelage and regulation of business and industry goes into effect. . . . [T]he one big union of the interests appears scarcely to have had a settled local habitation and a name. Only in respect of the one big union's surveillance of note issues and rediscounts can it be said the Federal Reserve has given its membership a "central"—if one may take a metaphor from the usage of the telephone.[85]

Veblen's view of the interlocking set of relationships in the corporate structure is a tentative one based on an evolutionary analysis of its changing patterns. He made a discerning attempt to understand the ways and means by which the business community attempted to coordinate its activities and control its conflicts, while Mills focused on this *and* corporate enterprises's relationship with the military and political elites. In describing the One Big Union's tutelage and regulation of business and industry, Veblen wrote that

> ... the appointed custodians of these Interests . . . regulate these large matters, in point of tactics, scope and policy, not in point of detail maneuvers . . . except it be at a critical juncture, when the common good of the Interests is in the balance or when the fabric of credit and capitalizations is exposed to some imminent hazard.[86]

However, it is evident in Veblen's analysis that the American banking community is at the heart of the national power system, whereas in Mills' work the power of high finance is not neglected although attention is focused on large manufacturing corporations. Veblen believed that the use of the labor force and the industrial plant depended on the collusive fiscal strategy of those who controlled the financial structure of the American economy, although the powers and sanctions held by financiers were of a permissive sort.[87] He meant that they had a veto power on those activities that threatened to destabilize the whole system, including conflicts between different parts of the business community. Again Veblen relied on the dominant role of high finance to explain the existing pattern of conflict resolution when he wrote that it was a "question of how far the banking community will tolerate cross purposes between groups of industrial business concerns."[88] It is evident that when conflict reaches a sufficient level of intensity within industry, high finance will engage in conflict resolution of an unspecified nature. Conflicts occasionally arise between the different parts of Veblen's ruling class as they also do between military, political, and economic elites in Mills' power elite. But these conflicts are resolved by the dominant powers in both, *not* through a system of democratic accountability.

THE LOWER LEVELS OF POWER

Veblen's views on the different levels of power in American society also had their impact on Mills' thinking. For example, Mills' analysis of the old middle classes and its political role is based partly upon Veblen's analysis of the changing nature of competition in American capitalism. Veblen contended that under conditions of oligopoly, competition does not cease; however, instead of competition among producers it is competition between producers on the one side of the market and consumers on the other. As he put it, "these lines of business run on a settled plan of competition between the absentee owners and the underlying population on the principle of what the traffic will bear."[89] Veblen termed this phase of the development of capitalism "the stage of vested interest." Of course, Veblen was describing the absentee owners of an earlier period; but Mills thought the analysis now applied to the surviving remnants of the old middle classes as well, especially small businessmen and farmers.

According to Veblen one of the ways of vesting an interest is through "business sabotage." By business sabotage, Veblen meant informal agreement among businessmen not to compete in terms of price; this practice, of course, subverts competition. Mills felt that the small-business wing of the old middle class had devised its own form of sabotage. During the Depression small businessmen organized for the purpose of finding political solutions to their economic troubles. The "small business front," as Mills called their organization efforts, succeeded in sabotaging free competition through such political devices as the so-called "fair trade" laws. Thus Mills found Veblen's analysis of competition insightful for understanding the politics of regulated prices in the new society.[90]

From his analysis of interviews with small businessmen in middle-size cities, Mills concluded that despite their strong endorsement of competition what these small businessmen actually want is not free but "fair" competition. In other words, they wish to compete not among themselves but against consumers. Like Veblen's big absentee owners, these small owners want to become a locally vested interest. Earlier Veblen had detected attempts not only by business but also by farmers to achieve such a status. As he put it:

> The farmers who have to do with the great staples have, for some time past and repeatedly, endeavored to establish a collusive control of their market, with a view to narrowing and stabilizing the margin between the prices they get and the prices which the consumers pay; but so far with no substantial results.[91]

In Veblen's day the farmers merely aspired to become part of the vested interests and largely failed. In Mills' time, with the aid of government, part of the farm community actually achieved this status.

Mills saw in the findings of the Temporary National Economic Committee, a New Deal investigatory agency, a reaffirmation of much of the Veblenian creed with regard to corporate size, mode of operation, and levels of power. He also pointed to manifestations of cultural lag in the prevalent tendency to ignore the changes that had occurred in the structure of the American political economy. The T.N.E.C. documented "the manner in which competition has been hedged in by giant corporations, and by groups of small corporations. . . . [A]cting collectively, they have made clear the locus of the big competition and the masklike character of liberalism's rhetoric."[92] Like Veblen, Mills recognized the degree to which liberal ideology could not accommodate itself to the realities of corporate power. It was this recognition which stood as the common denominator in their indictment of the corporate sector of the American political economy. It also was to play a powerful role in Mills' analysis of John Dewey.

5

Mills' Critique of
Veblen and the
Conservative Institutionalists

Mills' critique of Veblen and the institutionalists is not completely original, for parts of it parallel main themes in other scholarly writings on Veblen. Was Veblen a technocratic elitist who wanted to turn over control of the American economy to engineers and technicians without responsible social control or accountability?[1] Was he a typical utopian without explicit means for achieving the ends he sought, divorcing means from ends and strategy from goals in a naive effort to achieve social reconstruction?[2] Was he a "scarcity economist" who urged unnecessary abstinence from consumption because of his failure to recognize the ability of an industrial economy to produce abundance for all?[3] Was Veblen a proponent of an extreme technological determinism,[4] and as a consequence of technological determinism did he believe the machine process would foster both functional and substantial rationality in the labor force?[5] These fundamental criticisms of Veblen resemble those made by Mills and aid in locating Mills' analysis in the body of Veblen scholarship. But parts of his critique of Veblen are novel contributions and it is these aspects of his analysis that I shall emphasize.

VEBLEN'S MISTAKEN FUSION OF
ARISTOCRATIC AND BOURGEOIS TRAITS

Mills claims that Veblen confused the aristocracy with the bourgeoisie by indiscriminately lumping them together as part of the same leisure class. But Mills overstated the case against Veblen, who recognized this distinction when he wrote that

The three conventionally recognized classes, upper, middle and lower are all and several pecuniary categories; the upper being typically that (aristocratic) class which is possessed of wealth without having worked or bargained for it; while the middle class have come by their holdings through some sort of commercial (business) traffic; and the lower class gets what it has by workmanship. It is a gradation of (a) predation, (b) business, (c) industry; the former being disserviceable and gainful, the second gainful, and the third serviceable.[6]

The fact that Veblen did not always adequately distinguish between classes as Mills alleged does not invalidate his theory of the leisure class, but it does make it more difficult to apply in those societies where the distinction is an important one. The reason for Veblen's sometimes casual treatment of this distinction lies in his belief that the economic functions of both classes are essentially ceremonial anyway; that is, rooted in waste and exploitation.

Mills was also critical of Veblen because:

The supposed shamefulness of labor, on which many of Veblen's conceptions of the upper classes rest, does not square very well with the Puritan work ethic so characteristic of much of American life, including many upper-class elements. . . . He did not want to call what the higher businessman does "work," much less productive work. The very term leisure class became for him synonymous with upper class, but there has been and there is a working upper class—in fact, a class of prodigiously active men.[7]

Mills adds that Veblen's disapproval of upper-class "work" and his refusal to give it that name "obscure" and "distort" our understanding of the upper classes as a social formation. Yet Mills claims that for Veblen to admit this would undermine his whole perspective, including its moral basis.[8] These comments by Mills are interesting because they suggest what surely is a strange argument for an American radical. In criticizing Veblen he implies that the work done by the working upper class is socially valuable and that Veblen weakens his own theory when he mistakenly fuses the idle and predatory traits of a true aristocracy with the Puritan work ethic that actually characterizes upper class life in America. To a degree this makes Mills a defender of the upper class and Veblen an unreasonable critic. But it also suggests that Veblen was a more consistent opponent of capitalist institutions.

In this same vein Mills also complained about the inaccuracy of Veblen's belief that destructive and pecuniary traits are found primarily in the upper classes. "One has only to examine the taste of the small shopkeeper to know that this is certainly not true."[9] Again, this interpretation of Veblen raises questions about Mills' own position, since Veblen's work is an indictment of the American upper classes, and yet Mills claims that small businessmen share the pecuniary and destructive traits of corporate capitalists. The quoted sentence may contradict Mills' view, which otherwise emphasized the upper strata as the main source for the formation and dissemination of pathological values. And yet it may also be indicative of small-business emulation of big business. If it is the latter, Mills is as Veblenian as Veblen.

Mills believes that Veblen's distinction between industrial and pecuniary employments is too simple. For Veblen most of the activity of the business community is of a ceremonial nature. Ceremonialism is based on invidious comparisons, hierarchical status rankings, and power inequalities, the exercise and maintenance of which amount mostly to waste in economic terms. But the business upper class may be prodigiously busy as Mills claims, yet in Veblen's eyes its activities are of no value in providing real service to the community. However, Mills may mean that, in the time that has elapsed since Veblen wrote, the ceremonial activities of business have diminished while the instrumental value of its work has increased. This construction makes Mills' position more intelligible, but again opens him to the charge that he is a less consistent critic of capitalism than Veblen.

While much of Mills' indictment of the corporate United States is penetrating, he failed to formulate an adequate value theory and apply it systematically. Admittedly, this would be a difficult task to accomplish. To illustrate: although Mills attacks corporations for the economic inequality they cause, the Marxian labor theory of value is not the value criterion he applies. It is evident that he believes corporate leaders lack Mannheimian substantial rationality but he does not consistently use this value criterion either. Also Mills employs Veblen's ceremonial-technological dichotomy, but does so in an unsystematic way. Mills' complaint that Veblen's sharp cleavage between business and industrial pursuits is too simplistic suggests that either the dichotomy is too crude and needs refinement, or that it should be discarded. Ultimately, Mills does neither with it. Mills' value theory is more eclectic than institutionalist, for its Veblenian roots are not fully assimilated into Mills' thought or consistently applied.

Veblen's Failure to Link Power with Status

Mills was fond of comparing John Adams' view of the status system in the United States with Veblen's perspective of it, usually to Veblen's disadvantage. Mills wrote that "Adams understands the status system of a nation in a way that Veblen does not, as politically relevant. . . . Just what does Veblen's theory of status have to say about the operations of the political economy?"[10] Mills answers his own question when he adds that "there is an elite demand for some sort of organization of enduring and stable prestige, which Veblen's analysis misses. It is a need quite consciously and quite deeply felt by the elite of wealth and especially the elite of power in the United States today."[11] Unfortunately, Mills' own investigations show a system in flux to such a degree that only the possession of money or power can guarantee the maintenance of status. But this was Veblen's own point!

A more penetrating comment is Mills' claim that Veblen tended to ignore the social function of the wealthy because, in analyzing the invidious basis of prestige of the American upper class, "Veblen laughed so hard and so consistently at the servants and the dogs and the women and the sports of the elite that he did not see that their military, economic and political activity is not at all funny."[12] Aside from the fact that Mills believed Veblen tried too hard to be funny, there is an important linkage between him and Mills in this respect. Mills was vitally interested in researching the interrelationships of the corporate rich, the military elite, and the political directorate. He focused on the impact of these institutions on mass society with regard to both social cohesion and conflict. Veblen also analyzed the factors of cohesion among groups in society while simultaneously examining the causes of conflict. For Veblen, who laughed at the upper class, and for Mills, who could not, it is not power alone that holds the American social order together—it is also status emulation and shared values.

Veblen's concept of predation in society is directly related to the level of economic development. As a consequence of economic growth, a power structure emerges that becomes predatory in nature. But, for Veblen, the important issue is not *whether* a ruling class exists, but the nature of its values, symbols, and lifestyles. As Ben Smith remarks:

> If one presumes that such a ruling structure has and will exist, he is not particularly shocked by its exposure nor highly driven to expose its particular power linkages. Rather, one may attack and ridicule the habits, the styles of life, and the moral beliefs in which men of high rank invest so much energy.[13]

The behavior of the leisure class established to Veblen's satisfaction its hostility to the public interest. Since the leisure class ultimately distinguishes between individuals by the criteria of force and fraud, repudiation of the ethical legitimacy of power is an important component of Veblen's social philosophy. Mills justifiably criticizes him for not being sufficiently explicit about this. It is evident, however, that their attitudes toward leisure class power are essentially the same though Veblen was even more inclined than Mills to explicitly link power with the class and status system.

MILLS, VEBLEN, AND TECHNOCRATIC ELITISM

A common allegation against Veblen is that he was a technocratic elitist. Critics focusing on *The Engineers and the Price System* claim that he advocated a political economy where engineers and technicians would control the system without accountability to the underlying population. Although this is a misconception of Veblen's prescriptions for the reconstruction of the American economic system, Mills himself vacillated between a moderate technocratic interpretation of Veblen and the view that Veblen was "at heart an anarchist and a syndicalist."[14] For example, Mills once wrote that

> Veblen set forth the industrial and economic situation out of which an association and group consciousness of technicians . . . might arise. . . . The modern technological system is indispensable to modern populations, and only the engineers can run it. In the technical planning and execution of work, "the technicians necessarily take the initiative and exercise the necessary surveillance and direction."[15]

Mills recognized the economic need for engineers and technicians and the strategic position they occupy in Veblen's analysis. But he argues that

> Veblen does not detail the means by which an association of engineers might come about. He does not examine political and class situations, and the differential chances of power holding and power grabbing do not come within his explicit purview. On this point he is ambiguous by irony, and behind this guise he states that, although they are indispensable to any overthrow, the technicians will not engage in such a line of action.[16]

In spite of his charge that Veblen was vague on the question of how the technocrats might seize power, Mills praised him for having no illusions about their revolutionary potential and attacked other writers like James Burnham who were predicting a take-over by the technocrats in the near future.[17] Mills did so because he could not accept the claim that technological imperatives make history since this claim rested on the invalid assumption that those who are functionally indispensable will have power. True to the logic of this argument, slaves should have been the ruling class on plantations in the antebellum South because of their vital economic role! Although he does not criticize Veblen for advocating technocracy in its more extreme forms, Mills does suggest that he mistakenly believed that if the functionally indispensable technicians and engineers chose (Veblen did not think they would), they could overturn the existing order.[18] Mills attributes a position to Veblen that he probably did not hold; namely that the functional necessity of certain occupational roles will soon transform itself into dominant social power. But Mills was also astute enough to recognize that the technocratic elitist strain in Veblen was offset by Veblen's anarchist and egalitarian tendencies.

VEBLEN—A SCARCITY ECONOMIST?

Mills also argues that Veblen was guilty of adhering to scarcity economics after they ceased to be applicable. "All this . . . was a sort of survival in Veblen's thought of classic economic conceptions of scarcity and betrays a lack of confidence in technological abundance which we cannot now accept in the simple terms in which Veblen left it."[19] Mills believed that Veblen's criticisms are outdated because the contrasts of extreme luxury versus great deprivation are no longer significant in our society. Mills' analysis assumes that Veblen entertains a theory of constant economic quantities, and that his main attack is against the deprivation of the poor by the leisure class. If the main thrust of Veblen's analysis were simply against deprivation, then Mills' critique would have merit. But if Veblen's indictment rests on deeper moral grounds, as it does, then this critique is misleading.[20] It is not necessary to accept Mills' caricature of Veblen as a proponent of static consumption patterns. Rather, the analyst may focus, as Mills himself did on other occasions, on a socially dysfunctional emulatory system made possible by economic growth and upper-class misappropriation of the resulting economic surplus. Veblen is not so much a proponent of scarcity economics as he is a critic of the way the vested interests use the growing abundance of goods and services.

TECHNOLOGICAL VALUES AND
THE PROBLEM OF RATIONALITY

Henry Kariel contends that the proper activity of all politics is to criticize false consciousness and to publicly review and reconstruct closed systems. These tasks require measuring the gap between what is and what can be, between reality and possibility, and between an alienated and an authentic existence. Kariel asks us to identify those aspects of the environment that are most oppressive. All arrangements that keep us frustrated, alienated, and nonpolitical must be located and brought to the center of attention. In short, he suggests we focus on all those institutions that needlessly limit our actions and undercut our promise.[21] All of this is an apt summation of the burden of the political intellectual earlier articulated by both Veblen and Mills.

Within the context of exploring the possibilities of human potential, Mills searched for a more adequate theory of value. His eclectic approach to this problem is evident in his combination of Mannheim's distinction between functional and substantial rationality, of Marx's dichotomy between false and true consciousness, and of Veblen's separation of ceremonial from technological or instrumental values. Mills never succeeded in fully integrating the core value systems or the analytic modes that underlie these concepts; however, he often used them as equivalents that can substitute for each other in measuring the performance of social institutions and processes. For example, he attributes to Veblen "the realization of this false consciousness all around him."[22] Actually, Veblen never used the term "false consciousness," but his idea of ceremonialism roughly parallels it. Mills put it this way:

> . . . For Veblen, technology, widely construed, stands opposite irational (ceremonial) institutions. And for both, in whatever other respects they may differ, the rational, the technical pole of history will come through; it will increase to dominate the social life of the West. . . . The irrational is identified with "pecuniary institutions."[23]

Mills learned from Veblen and Ayres that prices do not measure real values, but only quantify judgments made prior to price transactions. Whether those judgments are really good or bad should be determined not by the price system, but by their relation to the technological continuum. Ayres, in particular, distinguished between "price" values and "real" or "technological" values. In his view price values are frequently ceremonial values, and often reflect antiquated mores, the power of money, and class distinctions. In modern capitalism, use value is what has utility for an individual. But, as Ayres explained, this is not determined by some mystical "inner nature" of mankind thrusting itself outward in a demand for a particular good or service. On the contrary, what is useful or valuable for an individual is determined by the cultural environment in which he lives. Today, too often, this value-determining cultural environment comprises the backward-looking and change-resistant institutional complex based on traditional mores, beliefs, and attitudes rather than the technological or instrumental qualities that would enhance the life process.[24] Mills agreed with much of the method and logic of this system of evaluation, and yet he doubted the ultimate potential of the technological continuum as the basis for development of a fully adequate value theory.

He was also critical of Veblen's claim that technology would foster a new rationality in the working class and, by implication, in industrial managers. Nor did he think, as Veblen did, that this would also happen to scientists and make them capable of critically analyzing basic social institutions and values.[25] Extrapolating from this, Mills argued that Veblen mistakenly assumed that the development of "functional rationality" would be accompanied by "substantial rationality."[26] Veblen tended in his early works to believe that the industrial labor force would combine its insights into the nature of the industrial process with a broader understanding of complex social relationships. In short, an understanding of technical means would be fused with critical intelligence. As Veblen argued in *The Theory of Business Enterprise:*

> What the discipline of the machine industry inculcates therefore, in the habits of life and of thought of the workman, is regularity of sequence and mechanical precision; and the intellectual outcome is an habitual resort to terms of measurable cause and effect, together with a relative neglect and disparagement of such exercise of the intellectual faculties as does not run on these lines. . . . The machine throws out anthropomorphic habits of thought. It compels the adaptation of the workman to his work, rather than adaptation of the work to the workman. The machine technology rests on a knowledge of impersonal, material cause and effect, not on the dexterity, diligence, or personal force of the workman, still less on the habits and propensities of the workman's superiors.[27]

Mills did not believe that the increasing rationality of technology would make the individuals who operated the machines more rational, except perhaps in the functional sense. In fact, Mills argued that the judgment of engineers and technicians, combined with their capacity for substantive rationality in social and political affairs, was often no better than that of businessmen.[28] Mills judged Veblen's work from the perspective of the distinction between substantial and functional rationality. He found it strong in its claims that the machine process fostered the latter, but weak in its assertion that it encouraged the former. Mills warns against assuming that an understanding of means-ends congruence can be equated with ability to comprehend complex sets of social relationships. But a more careful analysis of Veblen's view of the psyche of industrial workers indicates that he portrayed it largely in negative terms; in terms of disbelief and distrust of convention and precedent. Veblen believed blue-collar workers were skeptical about the "natural rights" of property, freedom of contract, customary authority, and traditional religious beliefs. Perceiving this skepticism is not the same as claiming a positive causal relationship between interaction with the machine process and the development of substantive rationality. Veblen's claims would have to be more extreme than they were for Mills' attack to be fully justified.

MILLS AND VEBLEN ON LABOR

Mills and Veblen share many similarities in their views of organized labor. Both emphasize "business unionism" as the dominant type of labor union in the United States.[29] Mills typified such unions along Veblenian lines when he argued that business unions focus narrowly on bread-and-butter issues. As a result, they tend to identify the public interest with their own economic self-interest. They are more job-conscious than class-conscious in their seeking monopolistic control of a particular skill rather than pursuing schemes for the political and social reconstruction of society. Veblen and Mills both stress the strong disciplinary role of unions on the job and their willingness to engage in authoritarian tactics. They agree that business unions are adaptive creatures of the main business drift, seeking integration within the national power elite instead of undertaking independent political action. They are thus incapable of socialist consciousness. Such unions often join forces with employer corporations to fight against unorganized sections of the economy including small farmers, white-collar employees, consumers, and small business. Veblen and Mills agreed that organized labor often combined with capital to exploit other occupational groups and consumers and thus exercised generally detrimental effects on the community, such as inflation.[30]

By the late 1940s the political and economic environment of organized labor had changed. Conservative and pathological tendencies had become even more evident than they were in Veblen's time. Mills explains this phenomenon by arguing that:

> By offering labor a place among the coalition of pressure groups, the New Deal destroyed some of the reason-for-being of wider, independent political action on the part of labor. . . . Moreover the New Deal

left no instrument for liberal, much less radical activity for the use of labor; one of its effects, in fact, was to strengthen further 'the boss habits' among labor leaders.[31]

"Bossism" was viewed by Mills and Veblen as a pathological trait present within American unions. In fact, Veblen believed that the A.F.L. was officered by leaders skilled in bargaining with politicians and expert in intimidating employers and employees. The conservative and pathological tendencies that Mills observed intensifying within American labor leadership were due, in his estimation, to labor's partial integration in the national power system. Labor leaders had nearly attained membership in the national power system as part of the power elite and through bureaucratic machines they ran national pressure groups based on urban labor. They now conceived of the programs they wanted as capable of realization within the existing corporate framework and state apparatus. What they advocated was more power in the decision-making process and more firm integration within the corporation as well as a larger cut of the income stream produced by the political economy. As Mills put it "These unions are less levers for change of that general framework than they are instruments for more advantageous integration within it."[32]

As young men Mills and Veblen regarded trade unions as sources of potential structural change in American society. Veblen believed that the emancipating impact of the machine process would immunize the industrial worker against the ceremonial values and practices of the leisure class. Mills came to political maturity during the period of liberal New Deal reform in which the unions played an important role and promised to continue doing so. While Mills focused explicitly on trade unionists, Veblen made general assertions about the values and behavior of industrial workers, organized or not. As the two men grew older, however, they became more pessimistic about the role of unions as social-change agents. Mills called on the American left to repudiate the "labor metaphysic," while Veblen referred to the members of the A.F. of L. as "votaries of the full dinner pail." In Mills' words:

> What I do not quite understand about some New Left writers is why they cling so mightily to "the working class" of the advanced capitalist societies as the historic agency, or even as the most important agency in the face of the really impressive historical evidence that now stands against this expectation.
> Such a labor metaphysic, I think, is a legacy from Victorian Marxism that is now quite unrealistic.[33]

Mills came to believe that with few exceptions most labor leaders aspired to the national power elite, not to an egalitarian or participatory society devoid of such a ruling group. Labor supported the present system of property relations and the existing state apparatus, and had no independent vision of the good society. Thus it was an essentially adaptive creature of the main business drift. Veblen adopted a similar stance when he wrote that "The A. F. of L. is itself one of the vested interests, as ready as any other to do battle for its own margin of privilege and profit."[34] In short, the A.F.L. acted like organized labor did a generation later when Mills repudiated the labor metaphysic.

Why do Veblen and Mills take similar views in regard to labor? It is because both are convinced that organized labor is infected with the ceremonial values it shares with the middle and upper classes. These values, and the consumption patterns and life styles that result, make the working man, with few exceptions, largely impervious to radical egalitarian schemes advanced by political intellectuals on the left. It was a matter of common regret to Mills and Veblen that status emulation had corrupted the American labor movement. Mills' main differences over the role of labor were not with Veblen but instead with the more conservative institutionalists Hoxie, Perlman, and Commons. It is to them that we now turn.

MILLS AND HOXIE

Robert Hoxie had been a friend and colleague of Veblen at Chicago, and Veblen's views on labor greatly influenced him. However, as E. H. Downey put it:

> Veblen's persuasive and brilliant theory was at one time taught by him, not indeed, as final, but as sufficient for the purpose in hand. Gradually, however, he came to see that class lines in the concrete are less sharp than the contrasting disciplines of business enterprise and machine industry would apparently produce if acting alone, and that correlatively, political, religious, and educational influences are more important than he had at first supposed. He thus found himself more and more in sympathy with Professor Commons' conceptions of social control.[35]

Hoxie developed a typology based on five different kinds of unionism, the most prevalent of which he termed "business unionism." Business unionism was concerned not with the welfare of the working class as a whole, but with the economic betterment of its own membership. It provided a disciplined work force in return for higher wages and better working conditions. In trying to control the labor market, business unionists adopted the strategy that other businessmen used in controlling their own markets. Hoxie (and Mills) perceived unions as businesses exhibiting the same traits as other businesses because the structural pressures and ideological forces that shaped American businesses also molded unions. It is worth noting, however, that Mills, in using part of Hoxie's typology, recognized its inadequacies and tried to improve upon it:

> For a long time now it has been traditional to contrast business or market unionism with ideological or political unionism, as if these were types of unions or at least of ideologies. But it is more useful to think of these terms as simply indicators of two *contexts* in which unions operate. Unions may shift their attention to one or the other and may employ different tactics in one or the other, at the same as well as at different times. This shifting is one meaning of such assertions as that the market is political and the politics has relevance for the market and that labor must now operate in a political economy. Yet we have always to remember that "labor" also still operates in more local contexts and serves more local interests.[36]

Mills thus gained from Hoxie an important insight into the nature and development of American unionism. What better way than "business unionism" to describe the "bread-and-butter" orientation of so many American union leaders who are in the "business" of selling labor. Hoxie's term expresses what Mills came to believe was the primary trait of American unionism; its businesslike character.

MILLS AND THE COMMONS-PERLMAN THESIS

Mills took a course at the University of Wisconsin on the evolution of modern industry from Selig Perlman, the noted American labor economist, and held informal discussions with Perlman on various topics concerning American labor, social movements, and history.[37] Before coming to Wisconsin, Mills had studied under Edward E. Hale at Texas. Hale, too, had been a student of Perlman, and was undoubtedly influenced by Perlman's views on organized labor. So Mills had considerable opportunity to familiarize himself with the Commons-Perlman thesis on the nature of American labor unions.

Perlman had collaborated with John R. Commons in the writing of a famous multivolume history of the American labor movement, and had imbibed many of Commons' attitudes toward trade unions. More conservative than either Veblen or Mills, Commons and Perlman had an abiding interest in the problems of the American labor movement, and an intimate knowledge of the ideological orientation of its leaders. They believed that American workers were "job conscious" rather than "class conscious" and that American unions sought to control employment opportunities rather than fight for socialism. In short, the "scarcity consciousness" of the workers led them to impose collective control over the work opportunity to which their membership had access, rather than unite to achieve the social visions of radical intellectuals.

The influence of both Lenin and Perlman was apparent in the graduate seminar on labor that Mills taught at Columbia. The syllabus required students to compare Lenin's *What Is To Be Done?* with Perlman's *A Theory of the Labor Movement* in order to construct a theory to guide their investigation of specific unions. In a fifteen-page unpublished manuscript entitled "A Note on Professor Perlman's Theory on Unionism," Mills analyzed Perlman's theory, its ideological basis, and the reasons for its great influence.[38] Against this background, Mills' *The New Men of Power* can be seen as his own attempt to improve upon the theories of both Perlman and Lenin, as well as draw upon the insights of Veblen and Hoxie.

Like Lenin, Perlman accepted the idea that if left to themselves, workers do not develop class consciousness and will not engage in class struggle. Instead they will be content with what Lenin referred to as "economism," which is congruent with Perlman's belief that workers support trade unions only because they pursue limited economic objectives regarding working conditions and wages. Given the "natural" job consciousness of workers, the long-term success of unionism becomes dependent upon controlling local labor markets. Other objectives must remain secondary if unions are to succeed. Unlike Lenin, Perlman regarded this "spontaneous" development as desirable. His annoyance with "interference" by radical intellectuals was an important aspect of most of his writing on unions.

In his analysis of Perlman's theory, Mills suggested that it was still popular after a quarter of a century not because it was adequate, but because it was ideologically useful to union leaders and academic social scientists. Mills challenged its viability on several grounds. To paraphrase him, it failed to recognize the realities of power, it blurred the distinction between leaders and the rank and file, and it focused unduly on local labor markets. Finally, it was overly psychological in viewing the objectives of unions solely as manifestations of the attitudes of workers. Mills' critique of Perlman's theory was based on the premise that classes exist and struggle with one another in the United States.

However, Mills drew a sharp distinction between the objective existence of classes and their subjective awareness. Regardless of the motives and beliefs of the participants, classes and class conflicts *exist*. Perlman's theory, Mills wrote, "states a function of labor unionism only in a restricted context—the labor market—and then derides as intellectuals' ideologies all other attempts to examine functions of unions in larger contexts."[39] These statements of Perlman's were "often quite true but also quite irrelevant."[40] The real question was, should objective functions be ignored merely because those involved were unaware of them? Mills did not think so.

> Whether or not the leaders knows it, what he and what his union [are] doing . . . has consequences which although perhaps unintended by him and by his union's members add up to much more than the closure of a labor market for improving the conditions, the security, and pay of selected wage workers.[41]

Although Lenin and Perlman shared certain assumptions about the nature and role of labor unions under capitalism, they differed fundamentally in that Lenin was an advocate of revolutionary change while Perlman was an incrementalist. Lenin endorsed militant class consciousness while Perlman supported a narrow job consciousness. Lenin stressed the socialist aspirations of the proletariat while Perlman focused on economic gain. The one advocated the leadership of radical intellectuals while the other favored leadership indigenous to labor. Lenin stressed the seizure of state control; Perlman emphasized collective bargaining. Socialist militancy was a key phrase in Lenin's vocabulary while consciousness of scarce employment opportunities was its counterpart in Perlman. Lenin emphasized workers' relationship to the state as an organized political force. Until late in his career, Perlman placed little faith in the ability of government to aid organized labor.

It is evident that the labor ideology shared by Veblen and Mills would be somewhere left of center along a continuum starting with Lenin on the extreme left and ending with Perlman on the right. Mills and Veblen could agree with much of the descriptive elements in the Perlman theory, yet they could not endorse its normative implications. However, in spite of his disagreements with Perlman, Mills did recognize the great importance of his work on the American labor movement. When he edited *Images of Man* Mills commented that "The necessary limits of a book have, of course, limited my choice of selections. Were it possible, I should have reprinted from . . . N. Lenin and Selig Perlman (on labor.)"[42] On balance Mills' disagreements with Perlman are stronger than their agreements, especially in the prescriptive realm. This is particularly evident in his discussion of class consciousness versus job consciousness:

> Job consciousness is a polemic term . . . standing against class consciousness. But these two don't make up the whole field of possibility. Between job consciousness and class consciousness there are many things not carefully noticed in . . . Perlman's philosophy. . . . It's necessary in such matters to separate the leaders from the led. One might say that workers are job-conscious, plant-conscious, corporation-conscious or industry-conscious, and at time even class-conscious. . . . But whether or not workers are conscious in any of these ways, it is still a fact that unions do fight "class conflicts." There can of course be objective class conflict without class consciousness.[43]

Mills thus argues that America is a class society without class consciousness.

Objectively, class divisions exist and they are important. But, subjectively, these divisions are often ignored by various social strata. The class system has not produced a corresponding recognition of its existence, and Perlman's theory is itself an ideological expression of the obfuscation of objective class interests. Its widespread acceptance, to Mills, was a manifestation of "false consciousness" among the academic intellectuals who so uncritically endorsed it. Mills contended that the Perlman thesis was wrong because it held the union to

> . . . be a kind of closure group by means of which manualists control and ration out job opportunities. All this stands in polar contrast to the "businessman" who has a consciousness of abundance for "unlimited opportunities." This is indeed a strange characteristic of businessmen, rural or urban, big or little, in 1952. In fact farm entrepreneurs have done a more effective job of closure tactics than labor unions, and certainly little business men yearn with all their consciousness for the same kind of guarantees, which big business men often have been able, in fact, to secure, as for example during recent wars.[44]

In challenging Perlman on this point Mills asks satirically, "Where today is 'free competition' more of a sin against one's fellows than among certain business groups?"[45]

At this point in his career, Mills recognized how little influence radical intellectuals like himself had in trade-union ranks, and how prone Perlman was to take satisfaction from their impotence, while denigrating any form of socialist influence on labor. In fact, in Mills' analysis of the Perlman thesis, he comments that "The influence of alien political intellectuals increases with the objective weakness of trade union control of the job situation. Only the weak can afford the luxury of wider views."[46] This ironic comment is, of course, an attack on Perlman's view that the stronger and more mature the unions are, the less inclined they will be to heed the advice of leftist intellectuals.

Another serious fault in Perlman's argument was his view of union attitudes toward the state.[47] During the period when the Perlman-Commons thesis was formulated, American unions made little effort to gain state support for the welfare and regulatory mechanisms that the New Deal later brought into being. They asked little more than to be left alone by government. Government usually responded by so doing, pursuing an interventionist role only when violence seemed imminent or when strikes appeared likely to succeed, thus necessitating court injunctions to break them. However, the New Deal changed the voluntarist ideology of the craft unions into a demand for large-scale government intervention. As Mills put it:

> The political roles of unions are certainly no longer so distrustfully voluntaristic as the Perlman theory assumes. The union view of the state's role in economy has undergone great change. I would like to underline J. B. S. Hardman's recent suggestion that "the notion that workers are distrustful of the state be closely re-examined." Neither workers or unions are so foolish as to assume that it was not . . . government action and the resultant social atmosphere of the later Thirties and early Forties that made possible their rise to truly national stature.[48]

About the time Mills encountered Perlman at Wisconsin, Perlman had revised his opinion about the proper relationship of labor unions to the federal government. Instead of prescribing laissez-faire as the proper attitude for labor, he recognized that the New Deal had permanently revolutionized the relationship. Earlier, government had been a "broken link" for labor to rely on, but it had since become a strong supporter of labor under the auspices of the Roosevelt administration. Now unions would have to go far afield in actively engaging in politics and legislation. This was an abrupt about-face from the perspective Perlman adopted in 1928 in his *A Theory of the Labor Movement*. His change in attitude toward government escaped Mills' notice for he persisted in attributing a voluntaristic, antistatist position to Perlman even after he had begun to abandon it.[49]

Mills disagreed with much of the conservative institutionalist analysis, especially its more prescriptive aspects, as well as with the status quo orientation of the unions that this analysis endorsed. It is likely that the beginning of his disillusionment with labor's potential to initiate and sustain structural change stems from his contact with Perlman and his students. In later years he had close ties with labor intellectuals such as J. B. S. Hardman, and he did a great deal of empirical work on labor leaders, much of which was incorporated in *The New Men of Power* (1948). So his disillusionment with the potential of organized labor as a social-change agent was a gradual process which did not reach fruition until the mid-1950s, when he started to attack the "labor metaphysic." However, the seeds of his disillusionment were sown years earlier when he listened to Perlman expound his analysis of labor, with its prescriptive focus on material gain and control over job opportunities, its lack of any broad conception of the public interest, and its antiradical prejudice. Mills undoubtedly realized that beneath the political and ideological bias of the Commons-Perlman thesis lay a partly realistic assessment, if unjustifiable endorsement, of some painful truths about the American labor movement. However, unlike the conservative institutionalists, he did not abandon the search for agents of social change. Instead he shifted his attention from the working class to the intelligentsia.

Mills was thus of two minds regarding the ideas of the central figures in institutional economics. The conservative institutionalists such as Robert Hoxie, John Commons, and Selig Perlman who were really political liberals he respected even when he did not agree with the normative aspects of their work. His judgment of them was tempered by his appreciation of their analytic, descriptive, and conceptual strengths. On the other hand Mills greatly admired the work of Thorstein Veblen, who was easily the most radical of the group; he was particularly enamoured with Veblen's normative orientation. When he was critical of Veblen, it was usually because he found theoretical aspects of his work flawed, not because he thought Veblen's heart was in the wrong place.

6

George H. Mead
and Mills' Social Psychology

It is impossible to understand C. Wright Mills without recognizing his
indebtedness to the American pragmatists. As he put it in the fall of
1938:

> My intellectual godfathers were pragmatists; when I first awoke I dis-
> covered myself among them. Hence it has come about that the majority
> of beliefs I think most tenable at present has been built by critically
> craw-fishing from this originally pervasive intellectual pattern.[1]

Mills' intellectual ties with pragmatists and pragmatism were formed
early, were of an intimate nature, and had lasting, but gradually di-
minishing, impact. They stem primarily from his experience at Texas,
where he studied under three pragmatists—Clarence Ayres, David
Miller, and George V. Gentry. The three had completed their doctor-
ates in philosophy at Chicago, Ayres in 1917 and Miller and Gentry in
the early 1930s.[2] All had been students of George Herbert Mead, the
now eminent American philosopher and social theorist, who earlier
had been a colleague of Dewey and Veblen. Clarence Ayres, from
whom Mills took courses on economic theory and history and with
whom he had much informal contact, had become an exponent of Dewey's thought and had systematically applied it to his own study of
economic institutions and thought. Mills' knowledge of pragmatism
and institutional economics undoubtedly owed much to his work with
Ayres. Mills took seminars in American pragmatism and social-science

methodology from George Gentry, a skilled interpreter of the philosophy of Charles Sanders Peirce and a devotee of physiological psychology.[3] David Miller, from whom Mills took courses in the philosophy of science, helped edit and compile Mead's papers and became a leading Mead scholar. It is evident that Mills' understanding of Mead is not primarily the result of his use of "symbolic interactionist" literature as such.[4] (Indeed, this body of literature hardly existed when Mills first began to study Mead in the 1930s.) Instead, it more likely results from his own textual exegesis of Mead's work and from the influence of Professors Ayres, Gentry, and Miller while Mills was at the University of Texas. Mead's writings that most influenced Mills were *Mind, Self and Society, The Philosophy of the Act*, the section on Karl Marx in *Nineteenth Century Movements of Thought*, and several articles published in professional journals.

In view of the great impact of Mead on both Mills and his professors at Texas, a short biographical sketch of Mead is in order. Mead was born in South Hadley, Massachusetts, in 1863 and died in Chicago in 1931. His father, Hiram Mead, came of a long line of clergymen and was himself minister of the local Congregationalist Church. Through his mother, Elizabeth Storrs Billings, Mead was descended from some of the most distinguished names in American civic and cultural life who could trace their ancestry to Englishmen who had settled in New England in the seventeenth century. When Mead was seven his father became professor of homiletics at the newly founded theological seminary at Oberlin, Ohio, a position his mother was to hold after his father's early death. As an undergraduate at Oberlin Mead read widely in the classics, philosophy, literature, and history while emancipating himself from subservience to the Congregationalist creed. Mead worked for a few years after graduation as a surveyor and a teacher and then enrolled at Harvard for the academic year 1887–1888. As a graduate student in philosophy he studied under the idealist Josiah Royce while living in the home of William James and tutoring the James' children. After completing his M.A. in philosophy at Harvard he went abroad to study at the Universities of Leipzig and Berlin. In Germany he worked under Wilhelm Wundt, the originator of gestalt psychology, and several other noteworthy German scholars, including the philosopher Wilhelm Dilthey. Mead intended to write his doctoral dissertation under the direction of Dilthey at Berlin, but he ultimately abandoned this plan because of difficulties he encountered in fulfilling the residency requirement there.

His first academic post was at the University of Michigan, where he was a colleague of John Dewey. Both were soon to become exponents of pragmatism and join James and Peirce as part of the great pragmatic quartet. A few years later, when Dewey moved to the University of Chicago as chairman of the philosophy department, he took his friend Mead with him. At Chicago both Mead and Dewey were colleagues of Thorstein Veblen from 1894 to 1904 when Dewey departed for Columbia. Veblen's exodus to Stanford followed shortly. Little is known about Dewey and Mead's relationship with Veblen although they were certainly in personal and intellectual contact with him.[5]

MILLS AND MEAD

In 1943, in his doctoral dissertation, Mills lamented the fact that he had not been able to evaluate Mead from the perspective of the sociology of knowledge as he had analyzed Peirce, James, and Dewey. As Mills put it:

> An account of George H. Mead must be included. It is true that many features of Mead's thought are treated by the consideration given to the work of John Dewey. However, in view of the course of the pragmatic movement and of Dewey's differential evaluation of Mead and James, the inclusion of James and the omission of Mead is an unrepresentative act that is intellectually unwarranted.[6]

It is evident and noteworthy that long before Mead achieved his present lofty status as a preeminent American social theorist, he had achieved this status in Mills' eyes to the extent that Mills thought him, roughly speaking, as much worthy of study as Peirce, James, and Dewey. The importance of Mead to Mills was also evident in another context when, after mentioning the founders of modern sociology— Comte, Spencer, Marx, Weber and Freud—Mills wrote that:

> If it seems to be a shortcoming of these eminent Europeans to become, in certain phases of their work absolutist, it is a distinct contribution of American pragmatists, notably George H. Mead, to purge sociological thinking of such elements and to open up our minds for the pragmatic explorations of reality.[7]

Mills also wrote that "behaviorism's most fruitful outcome was George Mead's work, especially his daring effort to anchor personal consciousness itself in the social process."[8] Plainly there can be no rational denial of Mead's impact on Mills. At this point in our analysis the question is not whether Mead influenced Mills but how. We must now turn our attention to Mills' employment of Mead's social psychological constructs.

THE GENERALIZED OTHER

Mills' use of a Meadian vocabulary, especially in *Character and Social Structure*, is significant since it leads him toward utilization of Mead's concepts and theory. Mills uses Mead's concepts of the "generalized other," "significant other," "significant symbol," and the "I"/"me" distinction; he employs them in Meadian ways after fusing them with structural sociology. In his own work Mead's concepts tend to become disembodied from social institutions, but Mills reintegrates them with the class structure and power matrices of society. Mills thus adds structural and historical anchorage to otherwise contextless ideas.

Mills uses Mead's concept of the "generalized other" more than any other Meadian idea. His often rich and inventive utilization of it in his own historically rooted macrosociology is evident in *Character and Social Structure*. For example, with regard to leadership, Mills asserts that

> Externally, the instituted leader . . . applies sanctions against those who fail to meet instituted expectations [. . . these sanctions range] from the lifted eyebrow of the club leader to the death penalty imposed by the state. Internally, the members incorporate the institutional head's expectations as a more or less crucial component of their particular or generalized other, and then punish themselves when they are out of line.[9]

Here Mills uses Mead's generalized and particular other to explain how leaders and their followers are affected by the generalized other and how this is used to legitimate formal and informal sanctions. At times the generalized other simply buttresses the existing system of authority, while on other occasions it can become the fulcrum of social revolution.

Mills believed most institutions regulate the generalized others of their members. One function of leadership is to bring larger codes into the subgroup that is led. The "leader" is thus a mediator between the members of his group and the larger social structure. As the head of his family or of his enterprise, for example, he is held responsible for what goes on in his family. The father is thus accountable to the public-school teacher for the behavior of his children.[10] On the other hand, a radical cult or movement leader might urge children to defy those in authority.

When neurotics are under the domination of an unusually demanding generalized other whose demands cannot be fulfilled, they may develop guilt feelings and thus punish themselves. In extreme cases such tendencies to self-hate may cause a distraught individual to attempt suicide or to seek punishment by committing a crime. Mills thus uses the "generalized other" to explain socially induced neuroses and deviancy.[11]

Institutional conflict undermines the coherence and even the identity of the self. To paraphrase Mills, the rival demands of conflicting roles, when the individual becomes aware of them, elicit "conscience," which is an important part of the generalized other. Compartmentalization of roles and of role obligations will function adequately to suppress conscience so long as the generalized other is not concerned, that is, so long as no universal moral principles are involved. But when ethical universals are invoked the Christian who claims to be an honest businessman may not cheat his partner without ignoring or betraying his own conscience.[12]

Mills utilized Mead's "particular other" and "generalized other" by relating them to the division of labor and to occupational roles. Institutions select persons by formal and informal roles of recruitment and dismissal, and then resocialize them by particular types of training that may require the individual to develop a new or different generalized other. Certain traits may be socially rewarded and strengthened, or socially tabooed and diminished in importance, by institutional pressures.[13] In the Meadian sense, this resocialization means sensitizing the employee to norms that become part of the individual's generalized and/or significant others.

Mills is eager to give Mead's concepts a stronger structural focus by viewing them as processes within particular social institutions. The conditions that affect the chances for a generalized other to develop are themselves undermined by broader conditions of social structure. Career patterns will not change much when, for example, there is little upward social mobility. Hence, no conflicting expectations arising from changing careers will be experienced. In such stable societies harmonious relations are more likely to be dominant. On the other hand contrary circumstances may produce conflict or disharmony.[14]

Interestingly, Mills gives the "generalized other" a specifically political meaning it often lacks in Mead's own work. The generalized other typical of particular social aggregates may change. To paraphrase

Mills: if, for example, the norms of a society erode, new significant and authoritative others will come forward to formulate new values and loyalties, since a crisis now exists in every person's conscience because their authoritative others have changed. The person is reappraised, and he reappraises himself as well as the selves of others. Such shifts have occurred several times in the course of Western history, for example in cases of political and religious turmoil. Also, crises of this sort are pervasive in industrial societies in connection with totalitarian parties.

Reconstruction of the composition of the generalized others can originate in many parts of society. In political and economic revolutions, the authoritative other of civil leaders may initiate the process of reappraisals. Parents and teachers may assimilate these reappraisals and present them to those of an impressionable age. Or, shifts in interpersonal circumstances may bring about such reconsiderations, which will then be conveyed to politicians and civil statesmen, thus forcing profound structural changes.[15] Mills believed this could lead to an expansion of the generalized other which might stimulate revolutionary goals in crisis circumstances by changing the symbolic context of charismatic revolutionary groups.[16]

The Social Nature of Individualism

It would be difficult for the author of an important American book on social psychology to avoid explaining the origins of individualism. Mills did not shirk this task. He pointed out that "conscience" can emerge only when a degree of individuation exists that in turn requires a detachment from roles, and a distance from the expectations of others when particular roles are adopted. Such detachment and individuation may arise when conflicting expectations exist in the course of a career due to changes within our circles of significant others. Individuation of the self results from the variety and scope of voluntary actions that it is possible to undertake. It involves the reality of individual decision and responsibility for personal choices.[17] The chances for an individual to emerge and to control himself by a generalized other are decreased as the variety of voluntary choices and decisions which confront persons diminish. Thus Mills shared Mead's belief that individualism itself is socially induced, and more likely to flourish in complex industrial societies than in primitive tribal communities.

Through repeated participation in social transactions people come to share the viewpoint of other participants, who constitute the generalized other which is a filter that selectively transcends that of particular individuals. Although Mead saw human beings as inextricably involved in groups, he also stressed the importance of individuality. Each person, although a product of society, retains his distinctiveness, for he incorporates the generalized other from a unique standpoint. To Mills, this was probably an attractive feature of Mead's thought for it preserved individualism while simultaneously showing that it was socially produced. In this respect, Mills' thought is more like Mead's (and Dewey's) than it is like Veblen's, for the latter tended to submerge individuals into the community, thus ignoring their unique features.

SIGNIFICANT OTHERS AND THE GENERALIZED OTHER

Mills offers the following definition of "significant others":

> Significant others . . . are those to whom the person pays attention and whose appraisals are reflected in his self-appraisals; authoritative others are significant others whose appraisals sanction actions and desires. The generalized other is composed of an integration of the appraisals and values of the significant, and especially the authoritative, others of the person.
>
> The generalized other of any given person does not necessarily represent the "entire community" or "the society," but only those who have been or who are significant to him. And some of those who have been significant others may not operate in the generalized other, but may have been excluded from awareness—a fact that is in line with the principle of selecting as significant those others who confirm the desired image of self.[18]

To paraphrase Mills, only the evaluation of those who are significant to the person explains the construction and preservation of his or her self-image. In many social orders the mother is the most significant other to the child, since she is socialized to satisfy its physical needs. Consequently, the picture the child has of himself is often the picture his mother has of him. But as children mature, many different significant others may impact on them. If an observer can understand who has been and who is presently significant to the person's image of self, then the observer knows a great deal about that person.[19]

Mills links the idea of the significant other with the generalized other by arguing that the content of a person's generalized other largely depends upon the normative attitudes of "the society" only as these attitudes have been selected by those who are authoritatively significant to the person. Accordingly, persons who pursue different occupations will feel quite different attitudes in regard to given actions. And, on the other hand, persons who have held similar jobs will have the same generalized ones.[20]

Through conversation, different roles are fitted to patterns of expectations, but when a person does not respond to the expectations of significant others, the person will usually try to rationalize his or her behavior. In such dialogue statements of motive begin to function. Indeed, an important part of Mills' early work deals with those types of vocabularies of motive that mask the actor's real intent. But the main device by which institutions form persons involves the circle of significant others that the institution establishes. This device is important because it causes institutional members to change their generalized other. By internalizing the expectations of institutional heads, as particular others, the persons who perform the institutional role come to control themselves—to act out their roles in accordance with the constraints thus built into their characters. As they develop as institutional members, these constraints are often generalized, and are thus linked psychologically with particular institutions.[21]

Where the unity of a social structure is disintegrating, the grip of institutions upon people relaxes, with the consequence that no general and stable systems of premiums and taboos can operate. The responses and traits of people are accordingly less predictable, for then a greater range of action is possible and experimental types of character may arise. Some of these types may eventually create a new system of premiums and taboos that will, in turn, structure the development of new traits in other persons.[22]

SIGNIFICANT SYMBOLS

When a sound that a person makes evokes similar responses in those who hear and in those who make it, then the sound has a common meaning. It is what Mead calls a "significant symbol." When a particular symbol has a common meaning to a group, the persons in the group make up a community of discourse. In general, symbols will have the same meaning to this community insofar as they are used by persons acting in coordination. Mills pointed out that if two persons understand a symbol differently, the joint task they are performing may become disjointed. This uncoordinated conduct, arising from the symbol's failure to unify the actions of the participants, will aid in correcting the wrong interpretation, that is, the one not usual and common. In this way, the common meaning of a symbol, that is, the response it usually calls out in various persons, is maintained.[23]

The relationship between symbols and roles is an important one in

Mills, for those symbols that legitimize and rationalize the institutional arrangement of the order are its master symbols.[24] Such master symbols are used in a hegemonic manner to assure continued dominance by elites. "Countersymbols" thus become the tool of critical intellectuals when they attempt to undermine the use of master symbols by the dominant political forces. Mills himself was a potent creator of countersymbols and an implacable user of them in his efforts to undermine the powers-that-be.

ROLES AND ROLE-TAKING

Mills' approach to role theory is largely Meadian. To illustrate this let us examine a quotation from Mills that fuses role theory with the generalized other.

> In a society in which the roles certain persons may play are consistent, and in which few choices exist, the problem of the consistency of the self is socially solved. For then no one person may take it upon himself to achieve an individual integration of self. But in a society where there are inconsistent expectations exacted of the person, and hence alternatives offered, each person will have to achieve such consistency and unity of self as he can. In this process, man is individuated, and this individuation involves the building of a generalized other from the conflicting expectations of significant others.[25]

Role theory of the Mead type is used by Mills to depict leadership in which leaders are role-determined or role-determining. It is the institutional context the leaders choose that in turn sets the role they play and provides images of them that justify their authority and motivate their leading and others' following.[26] Mills believed that there was a crucial distinction between role-determined and role-determining leadership and that the role-determined leadership is more determined when the institutional sphere is stable, less determined when the sphere is breaking up or at least changing rapidly.[27] Thus periods of political and social transition were most likely to enhance and facilitate creative leadership.

MILLS' USE OF THE "I" AND "ME"

Voluntary conduct is a sequence of adjustments in which a person responds to himself as well as to the rest of his perceptual field. To study this process Mead used his concepts of the "I" and the "me"; these terms refer not to agents but to phases of activity. The "me" is the object one forms of oneself from a conventional standpoint, and the "I" is the reaction of the unique individual to the historical situation as he perceives it. Characteristic tendencies to react differ from person to person; in fact, the succession of "I's" constitutes the basis of individuality. In speaking of behavior as being built upon the interaction of the "I" and the "me," Mead was stressing both the novel and the stable aspects of human conduct. Thus, an individual's line of conduct is constructed as he adjusts to a succession of perceptual objects, images, and anticipated reactions of other people. Mills' use of the Meadian "I"/ "me" distinction is best illustrated in the analysis he gives of the reaction of the old Bolshevik leaders to the crimes they were charged with by Stalin.

> Their circle of significant others, in brief, was confined to party members, and the party formed, as it were, the only social locus of their generalized others. So, it may be that their confidence in themselves, in their ability to think and decide, was tied to their faith in the party, the I and the Me having no clear-cut border line in their conscience. Therefore: no thought, no feeling, no consciousness outside the party. In liberal terminology their commitment was not provisional or partial; it was permanent and absolute. And since they had no social anchorage for individual behavior outside the party, their last individual act was to sacrifice themselves for the party.[28]

The remarkable psychological aspect of this has to do with the "confessions" of the old Bolshevik vanguard. They "confessed" to actions which it is generally conceded they did not commit. Because they had been party members most of their adult lives their existence would have little meaning outside the party.

MILLS, MEAD, AND THE SOCIOLOGY OF KNOWLEDGE

Mills' early work in the sociology of knowledge relied heavily on Mead and was closely linked with Mills' later studies in social psychology. Mills found Mead's concept of the "generalized other" a useful device by which to explain how social processes enter as determinants into reflection. The generalized other was the internalized audience with which the thinker converses. Selected social experiences brought into the mind make up the generalized other with whom the thinker talks. The habits and character of the audience, as constituent parts in this interaction, shape the thinker's internal dialogue and help solidify the beliefs that develop from the exchange. Thus thought was not an interplay between two separate entities; rather it was a dynamic, fluctuating process. As Mills put it "The elements involved interpenetrated and modified the existence and status of one another. Imported into mind, this symbolic interplay constitutes the structure of mentality."[29]

When we talk to ourselves as we think, a generalized other containing certain rules of logic channels the directions of that thought, for logical rules provide parameters for most ideas. Taking his cues from Mead, Mills thought that, in general, conformity to logic was an necessary condition for the acceptance and diffusion of ideas. However, in attempting to effectuate our interests and thought, we use a socially derived logical apparatus. In the mind the generalized other works as a socially derived mechanism through which logical evaluation operates. For Mills the generalized other is part of the "reflective process"; it is even the locus of the apparatus of logic.[30]

For Mead and Mills, language is part of a system of social control. Symbols, as part of language, gain their status as meaningful events because they produce a similar response in both the utterer and the hearer. To paraphrase Mills: communication must establish common modes of response in order to be communicative; the meaning of language is thus the common social behavior evoked by it. Symbols are the "directing pivots" of social behaviors and are an indispensable prerequisite of mind. Word meanings originate in and are sustained by the interactions of human collectivities, and thought is the manipulation of such meanings.

> Mind is the interplay of the organism with social situations mediated by symbols. The patterns of social behavior with their "cultural drifts," values, and political orientations extend a control over thought by means of language. It is only by utilizing the symbols common to his group that a thinker can think and communicate. Language, socially built and maintained, embodies implicit exhortations and social evaluations. By acquiring the categories of a language, the value-implicates of those "ways," our behavior and perception, our logic and thought, come within the control of a system of language. Along with language, we acquire a set of social norms and values. A vocabulary is not merely a string of words; immanent within it are societal textures—institutional and political coordinates. Back of a vocabulary lie sets of collective action.[31]

The symbolic forms, including language, thus structure the way we think and the way we perceive our social existence.

Mills and Mead: An Appraisal

In recent years Mead's work has begun to receive the attention it deserves from radicals and Marxists. They characteristically argue that Mead has no adequate ideas of class, power, alienation, and exploitation. They also criticize Mead's work because they think it is astructural, apolitical, and ahistorical. It is interesting to note that even though these are the kinds of criticisms one would expect to find in Mills' analysis of Mead, in fact they play only a minor role.[32]

Robert Paul Jones has correctly asserted that one reason why Mills did not select concepts from pragmatism's model of society is that there was no pragmatic sociology as such. In Mead's work, for example, there was little between the community and the larger social process, for Mead's "society" was often a formless and timeless process. In the early Dewey's work, "society" and "culture" were sometimes unanalyzed residual categories into which he lumped everything involving social interaction. Though Dewey's "society" was historically located, it remained a distant and vague framework. Since the pragmatists saw society only as a process, they lacked the conceptual tools to analyze its more durable features. Jones believes that in place of pragmatism's amorphous society, Mills used concepts from classical social science to understand a structured society and he did so without abandoning the pragmatic idea of process. Rather than focusing exclusively on process as the pragmatists had, Mills focused instead on structures in process.[33] This focus, undoubtedly, is what many social scientists find so stimulating in his work.

Mills believed that Mead's use of the term "generalized other" mistakenly incorporated the whole society. Consequently, Mills thought his own use of the term differed from Mead's in one crucial respect in that it stood for selected societal segments. Although David Miller has correctly argued that Mills misunderstood Mead's generalized other, Mills did try to give it more historical and structural specificity than it had in Mead.[34] Mead's generalized other is a valuable concept in explaining the social nature of mind, but Mills recognized its vagueness and ambiguity. As Mills once put it:

> But one's generalized other, one's "field of mind," does not, despite Mead's assertion to the contrary, stand for or incorporate "the whole society." One's generalized other is built through one's social behavior and experience; vicariously and directly it is built by selectively cumulative processes. . . . His statements to that effect are functions of an inadequate theory of society and of a certain democratic persuasion.

These are not, however, logically necessitated by the general outlines of his social theory of mind.[35]

Mead's radical critics including Mills have often failed to notice that human society, in Mead's formulation, contains many generalized others. The individual can be a member of different groups simultaneously and can conduct himself with reference to different generalized others at different times; or he may broaden his view of the generalized other to include a "larger" community than the one in which he has hitherto been involved. He could thus become a member of the human race as such rather than simply be a member of a particular nation. For the self is not necessarily confined within the limits of any one generalized other.[36]

CONCLUSION

Mills probably viewed Mead as a "consensus theorist" who at times had difficulty coming to terms with the reality of social conflict and the disharmonious development of political life. This criticism is serious for it suggests that Mead's thought is partly an ideology that covers up (or "mystifies") the sometimes ugly realities of American society. It is very similar to the judgments Mills mistakenly made of the later Dewey but in the case of Mead it is a more accurate assessment.

Many critics have commented that Mead's thought lacks political focus. Although Mills does not stress this deficiency in Mead, he avoids it in his own work when he uses Mead's ideas. For example, Mills wrote that

> We may "locate" a thinker among political and social coordinates by ascertaining what words his functioning vocabulary contains and what nuances of meaning and value they embody. In studying vocabularies, we detect implicit evaluations and the collective patterns behind them—"cues" for social behavior. A thinker's social and political "rationale" is exhibited in his choice and use of words. Vocabularies socially canalize thought.[37]

It is not hard to demonstrate that Mead's theoretical position is inadequately anchored in the "harder" aspects of human existence. Although he was a brilliant and original theorist he suffers from a deficient understanding of social institutions and environment, like Dewey before 1918. Also, like the early Dewey, he displays an unwarranted degree of optimism, which is expressed in his sometimes naive faith in science and social ameliorism, dogmatic preference for incremental change, and fixation of middle-class values. Like the classical American pluralists, he believes that rational men of good will can somehow compromise their differences through a process of bargaining and accommodation. However, unlike Dewey after 1918, he does not sharply veer toward an analysis that is more historical, political and structural in its orientation. Instead, right up to his death in 1931, he remains an unreconstructed liberal, even after his friend Dewey turned to the left and incorporated social radicalism and class conflict more fully into his philosophy. It is important to note that Mills in his interpretation of Mead places far less stress on this ideological position than he did in his account of Dewey. Mills made a strong indictment of Dewey for his refusal to adopt a structural analysis that was sufficiently political in tone, but he let Mead off the hook even though his work had the same failings. Perhaps the difference resulted from Mills being more interested in using Mead's social psychology in *Character and Social Structure* than in attacking his liberalism. Consequently, his work on Mead contains little genuine criticism of Mead's ideological underpinnings but much successful exploitation of his ideas.

7

Dewey and the Pragmatic Influence on Mills

A Biographical Sketch

George H. Mead's close friend and sometime colleague John Dewey had a great influence both positive and negative on C. Wright Mills; consequently, a brief sketch of Dewey's life is in order. He was born in Burlington, Vermont, in 1859 and died in New York City in 1952. He was of English descent and came from an old New England Congregationalist family whose lineage could be traced back for centuries. His father owned a small store in Burlington where John and his older brother Davis Rich Dewey, later an eminent economist in his own right, were reared. Since the University of Vermont was located in his home town, it was natural that Dewey and his brother would matriculate there. After graduating, Dewey taught school for a year in Pennsylvania but his love for philosophy and the encouragement he received from other professional philosophers led him to decide on a career as an academic philosopher.

Like Mead, Dewey had a particular interest in German idealism and, like Veblen, he wrote his doctoral dissertation on Immanuel Kant. As graduate students at Johns Hopkins during the early 1880s, he and Veblen both studied under Charles Sanders Peirce, although Veblen soon transferred to Yale to finish his doctorate. Their academic careers overlapped again at the University of Chicago from 1897 to 1904, and at the New School for Social Research after World War I. They also served as editors of *The Dial* for a short time during Veblen's stay in New York City in the early 1920s. However, their professional acquaintanceship and their common institutional affiliations should not lead one to the conclusion that they were part of the same intellectual movement during the Progressive Era. Indeed, it is only after 1918 when Dewey veered sharply to the left that his social philosophy came to vaguely resemble Veblen's. Even then important political differences still separated the two men.[1]

Dewey's academic career began in the mid-1880s at the University of Michigan, where he taught until the University of Chicago opened in 1892. George H. Mead was his colleague at both institutions. At Chicago Dewey's work with the experimental school and his writings on the philosophy of education achieved nationwide notoriety. He also found time to work with Jane Addams at Hull House, a settlement house that engaged in social-uplift activities in a poor neighborhood of Chicago. His career at Chicago was highlighted by many publications that received widespread attention in the world of philosophy and made him one of the preeminent American philosophers. However, Dewey became disillusioned with the administration at Chicago, and in 1904 took a position at Columbia University in New York City, where he remained for the rest of his life.

At Columbia, Dewey continued to produce a steady stream of books and articles that embellished his already lofty reputation. His published work covered current political and social issues, political and social philosophy, ethics, logic, epistemology, aesthetics, metaphysics, the history of philosophy, and the philosophy of education. Few if any other American philosophers have written on such a staggering array of topics with such a degree of competence.

At this same time Dewey also became intensely active in political organizations and social-reform movements and often assumed a position of leadership in them. It is doubtful that any other American of his time lent his name and his energies to so many liberal causes. To illustrate, Dewey organized or led the following organizations at some point in his long career: the Progressive Education Association, the League for Industrial Democracy, the American Federation of Teachers, the People's Lobby, the American Civil Liberties Union, the American Association of University Professors, and the League for Independent Political Action. Many other organizations could be added to this list.

After a lengthy and illustrious career, Dewey retired at Columbia in 1930 although he retained emeritus status until 1939. Retirement meant little to Dewey for he continued to work at a pace that would have exhausted a much younger man. Indeed, some of his best work was published after he was seventy. He also continued his activism in social and political organizations and became more militant and radical than he had ever been before. Perhaps his best known role during the late 1930s was as chairman of the International Tribunal that investigated the charges made against Leon Trotsky by Stalin and the Soviet government. The tribunal cleared Trotsky of the allegations that he had engaged in treasonous activities by attempting to aid the Fascist powers in subverting the Soviet regime. Although Trotsky and Dewey continued to have important political differences Trotsky expressed his admiration and respect for him.

Since Mills' work on Dewey's career and thought essentially ends with the onset of World War II, it is unnecessary to extend this biographical sketch of Dewey beyond 1940. While Dewey's reputation among professional philosophers is not as high as it once was, he probably has had more influence on American philosophy than any other American. As Mills could attest, he also had a great impact on American education and on the development of the social sciences in this country. The nature of Dewey's influence is readily evident in Mills' own work.

PRAGMATIC INFLUENCES ON MILLS

This chapter and the next one focus on the impact of Dewey on Mills. Because Mills was primarily a political sociologist and social critic it is appropriate that Dewey, whose work was more political in nature than that of the other leading pragmatists, be used to illustrate the pragmatic influence. Although occasional references will be made to other pragmatists, Chapters 7 and 8 are not really concerned with them, except insofar as their major philosophic positions coincide with those of Dewey.[2] In any case, in *both* the positive and the negative sense, Dewey's influence on Mills was more pervasive than that of William James or Charles Sanders Peirce. Even when he disagreed with Dewey, which was often, Mills gave very explicit reasons.

A common interpretation of Mills' intellectual development among those who understand his grounding in American philosophy is that he gradually abandoned pragmatism. For example, Irving L. Horowitz suggests that although Mills "internalized" pragmatism as a way of life, he abandoned it "as a theoretically adequate system of thought."[3] However, it is more likely that Mills, who was intellectually self-conscious at an early age, simply borrowed what he found useful in the pragmatic tradition and discarded the rest. It would be correct to assume that although he was greatly influenced by the pragmatists, he was not a pragmatist in the literal sense. His attitude toward pragmatism was not too different from that towards any other school of thought except that he was more familiar with it. He was too critical and independent a thinker to be regarded as an intellectual "disciple" or as a member of a "school" of thought.

What Mills most objected to in pragmatism was not the epistemology, logic, or ethics of its founders, but the later Cold War stance and political opportunism of "pragmatic liberals." As Horowitz put it, "Mills retained a basic regard for liberal values if not for the liberals who sought to carry forth such values; and a basic regard for pragmatic philosophies, if not for the pragmatists who acquiesced in the 'conservative mood' of the 'political directorate.'"[4] The pragmatic movement had lost whatever coherence it once claimed as its proponents went in diverse ways, but for Mills many pragmatists were proponents of the political status quo. Indeed the professionalization of philosophy caused pragmatists to concern themselves more with the technical aspects of their discipline than with the promotion of reform efforts. The public concerns of a John Dewey or a William James had given way to a narrow focus on the intricacies of epistemology, logic, and language analysis.[5] Pragmatists sometimes became indistinguishable from logical positivists in their mutual disengagement from politics and from pressing social issues. Henry Aiken put it well when he wrote:

> In his later writings, Mills seems to think that the pragmatic tradition cannot transcend the historical limitations which have circumscribed and in some respects emasculated the thoughts of the great pragmatists. Accordingly, he tended to move out of the orbit of pragmatism. . . . it was the failure of the pragmatists to develop an adequate theory of, or response to, the developing revolutions of the twentieth century which drove Mills at least half-way into the arms of the Marxists.[6]

In this context Mills expressed his own disappointment at the use to which Dewey's vaunted "method of intelligence" had been put by social scientists. He contended that the method of intelligence, instead of being incorporated into liberalism as the pragmatists had recommended, had worked itself out into a "bureaucratic practicality." Its capacity for critical analysis and for the promotion of structural change had become enmeshed in bureaucratic restraints. In short, it has been so absorbed into institutional research that it lost its potential to disturb and emancipate.[7]

Epistemology: Divergence and Convergence

Although Mills often wrote on methodology in later years, he rarely dealt with epistemology after he left Texas in 1939. Consequently, his epistemological position was not formally articulated again although he occasionally made intriguing but indecisive comments about it. There is much ambiguity in what he says about the fact/value dichotomy in his unpublished papers, especially those written when he was in his early twenties. This is evidence that he was caught in an intellectual cross fire between the logical positivists who denied cognitive status to values and the pragmatic philosophers he worked under who awarded cognitive status to values. The result of the intellectual tension this engendered in Mills was uncertainty and vacillation.[8]

Alfred J. Ayer had intensified debate over the cognitive status of values with the publication of his *Language, Truth and Logic* in 1936. He argued for a rigid segregation of judgments of fact from judgments of value since he believed that the latter were noncognitive. In short, value judgements were essentially emotive in nature and were an expression of nothing more than the sentimental feelings of those who gave vent to them. Although contrary to Dewey's, Ayer's view soon became popular in certain quarters in both Britain and the United States. The conflict between the two presented a dilemma for Mills, for even though he did not fully agree with either on the cognitive status of values, he was unable at the time to formulate a consistent position of his own. Dewey had argued that the practical import of the positivist position

> . . . may be inferred from the fact that according to it the differences as to value cannot be adjudicated or negotiated. . . . serious cases of ultimate difference can be settled, if at all, only by "bashing in of heads." . . . [A]t the present time serious differences in valuing are in fact treated as capable of settlement only by recourse to force.[9]

Whereas many years later Mills put it this way:

> We cannot deduce—Hume's celebrated dictum runs—how we ought to act from what we believe is. Neither can we decide how anyone else ought to act from how we believe we ought to act. In the end, if the end comes, we just have to beat those who disagree with us over the head; let us hope the end comes seldom. In the meantime, being as reasonable as we are able to be, we ought all to argue.[10]

Although Mills agrees in this instance with the positivist position that ought cannot be derived from is, he still contends that debates on moral issues are valuable. We ought to have adequate reasons for behaving in certain ways even though we cannot determine whether moral assertions are true or false. Discussion is relevant, or arguing would be senseless. In his characteristic way, Mills then reduces an abstract philosophic debate, to which he saw no satisfactory solution, to a question of sociopolitical power. He asserted:

> when there are values so firmly and so consistently held by genuinely conflicting interests, that the conflict cannot be resolved by logical analysis and factual investigation, then the role of reason in that human affair seems at an end. We can clarify the meaning and the consequences of values, we can make them consistent with one another and ascertain their actual priorities, we can surround them with fact—but . . . if the end is reached, moral problems become problems of power, and in the last resort . . . the final form of power is coercion.[11]

What is at issue between Mills and Dewey is not the meaning of the fact-value distinction since Mills never fully solidified his position and Dewey's view was rather vague. Instead, what is at stake is the sociopolitical question of how to deal with value differences when they become irreconcilable. Mills tended to assume that they would be resolved by force without necessarily intending to endorse such means, while Dewey emphasized avoidance of such a "solution" if possible.

Although Mills soon moved away from a technical philosophic concern with the epistemological status of facts and values, he did indicate in his unpublished papers that he was not fully satisfied with the positivist's position or with that of Dewey. He complained that Dewey badly confused moral exhortation with hypotheses that were empirically verifiable.[12] Yet only a few months before he said that:

> The logical positivists are fond of saying that the function of value predicates are "merely emotive" not assertive. I agree that in many cases there probably is a "feeling" within the speaker as a condition for his utterance of a judgement containing a value term. But to say that the *function* of a value term is emotive is not, it seems to me, to say very much. . . . To understand the function of value judgements we must come away from a purely logical analysis such as that of the positivists and work empirically within a social context.[13]

Mills' efforts to deal with epistemology from a pragmatic perspective are also evident in his conception of the meaning and significance of truth. The first of the traditional views of truth is the coherence theory characteristic of Continental rationalism, which makes truth a function of the internal logical consistency of an argument. Truth consists in coherence, for the more beliefs hang together in a system the truer they are. Another view is the correspondence theory, identified with British empiricism, which focuses on congruence between ideas on one hand and facts on the other. Truth thus consists in correspondence between theory and fact. A third view is associated with American pragmatism and holds that the most significant test of truth lies in its workability, that is, the fruit ideas bear and the results to which they lead. Thus for the pragmatist, a statement is true if it expresses a fact or describes a situation upon which we can act and secure the anticipated results. Last is a composite theory of truth that combines insights from the other three so that truth becomes identified with the internal logic of an argument, its accordance with facts, and whether it "works" or not. From outside the discipline of philosophy may be added a sociology-of-knowledge perspective in which truth is viewed relative to socioeconomic determinants and power relationships. This approach can focus, as Mills himself did, on the approval or rejection by various elites of particular verification models as the appropriate means by which to ascertain truth.

The heavy influence of pragmatism on Mills is thus revealed in the fact that his outlook draws more from it than from the coherence and correspondence theories. It is evident, however, that his view of truth is sufficiently eclectic so as to be legitimately called composite since it draws insights from all four viewpoints. However, in spite of Mills' eclecticism, John Carbonara was probably correct when he wrote that:

> In Mills' critical empiricism the pragmatic argument type is the central inferential principle. In this type of argument, one argues from the *value* of the consequences to the truth or falsity of the principles that precipitated the initial action that led to these consequences.[14]

It is clear that Mills' early epistemological inquiries were stimulated by his encounters with pragmatism, logical positivism, and the sociology of knowledge. Even though his perspective was not identical with Dewey's, Ayer's, or Mannheim's, it is evident that he used both of the latter in his critique of Dewey's epistemology, and in his efforts to develop a more adequate social-science methodology.

PRAGMATIC SOURCES OF MILLS' METHODOLOGY

In his early writings Mills viewed methodology in terms of the pragmatic interpretation of science. But in his later writings, he usually justified his methodological prescriptions by linking them not with pragmatism but with the classical tradition of social theory of which pragmatism was but a part. This tendency deceived many of his interpreters about the intellectual origins of his methodology. As Darnell Rucker has shown, the Chicago pragmatists, especially Dewey and Mead, developed a methodology that gave social scientists a frame of reference, a perspective, and a sense of continuity.[15] It was a methodology whose main characteristic was flexibility, for it did not offer forms or languages to which social problems had to be adapted. Instead, method had to be developed so that its form and language grew out of the problem itself and manifested its particular traits. Mills used the term "intellectual craftsmanship" to approve the social scientist who was his own methodologist. In his view the scholar is the originator of concepts and the creator of methodology. New concepts and methodologies must arise from efforts to overcome obstacles to successful research. Methodological and technical innovations resulting from the influence of Dewey on Mills probably include the ideal of scholarship as a unique life style that fuses personal and intellectual life and the development of methods to communicate more effectively with an educated public. The latter includes techniques for becoming both a participant and an observer of social structure. All show evidence of the instrumentalist linkage between theory and practice and of its incorporation into the scholar's work life.[16]

There is a tendency in Mills to fuse the realms of methodology and epistemology. His identification of the two is an example of the persistent residues of Dewey's influence decades after he ceased to write about him.[17] The impact of Dewey in this regard is evident in Mills' earliest writings on methodology, for in language and ideas reminiscent of Dewey, Mills warned against scientific concepts which were defined ontologically and *a priori* rather than by their performance. Mills believed that social science could not adequately develop without a basic concern with answerable problems. In approaching this aspect of experience, the researcher should inquire, "What difference in whose behavior does this factor make?"[18] This is a question of great methodological significance best understood by social scientists like Mills who were influenced by Deweyan instrumentalism.

The Relationship between the Natural and the Social Sciences

Another important methodological source of influence on Mills was Dewey's belief in methodological symmetry between the social and natural sciences. This influence is not immediately evident in Mills' work, for Mills often argues that the wholesale transplantation of methodology from the natural sciences to the social sciences is an error that leads social-science inquiry astray. His rationale is that the methodological constraints imposed by such a transplantation make study of the big problems and important issues difficult or impossible. But there is a critical difference that Mills did not fully grasp. It is between Dewey's view of the verification process that opens the possibility of transcending immediate experience and a more constricted view of verification that does not. For Dewey the process of knowing necessitates a distinction between direct and indirect knowledge. The latter kind of knowledge gets beyond what is immediate by transitions and connections in experience. However, a constricted operationalism assumes an immediate correspondence between thought and object, and sees the foreground as the only source of valid information. This was the type of methodological constriction Mills criticized in the social sciences and his opposition to it was in line with Dewey's thinking on the subject.

Mills interprets Dewey's analysis of social-scientific inquiry to mean that it should follow the paradigm of the natural sciences. He attributes to Dewey the belief that there is only one scientific paradigm. Whether or not this is an adequate interpretation of Dewey is doubtful. However, it is important to understand the modifications Mills insists upon whether the basic thesis is Dewey's or not. Mills contends that Dewey's writings were characterized by a failure to understand the problems associated with the natural-science paradigm of inquiry, especially the conception of "experiment" when applied to social data.[19] In Mills' view, most social situations have characteristics which experiments in a laboratory cannot produce. Dewey's alleged inability to recognize this suggests a further need to evaluate social researches in their intellectual and existential environment, and to formulate the rules that are implicit in them. When this is done, it will be possible to transcend the *a priori* assumptions made by Dewey regarding the similarity between social science and physical science inquiry.[20]

In this same vein Mills believed that George Lundberg's work in sociology was methodologically deficient. Lundberg was a well-known proponent of logical positivism in the social sciences who believed in the ideal of a value-free sociology. Mills thought that Lundberg, in insisting upon emulation of the physical sciences, had forgotten the way actual social inquiries were performed. He disregarded how the methods of physical science were really derived from interaction with data in favor of a grand methodological fiat that created a "science" of social inquiry. For Mills, the methodology employed in future social inquiry must be derived from the process of inquiry itself, not from the philosophers of physical science.[21] Mills' position at this time anticipated criticisms he was later to direct at Lundberg's intellectual descendants when they came to dominate the behavioral movements in the social sciences. Mills continued to attack the claim that the methodology of physical science is applicable to social science.

> You cannot get at social data directly, as you can . . . the data of physical science. In the latter the attempt is made to determine the patterns of relationships between orders of events themselves, not their relationships to man's social behavior and intentions. You try to determine "objective meanings," i.e., the meanings of events in terms of the interaction with one another and with physical instruments. But with social data, every *item* handled must be viewed not in "itself" but as it lies in the experience and behavior of *some* social agent. Only so viewed is it human, social data.[22]

Mills' methodological criticisms of both Dewey and Lundberg are launched from a position that is more genuinely pragmatic than either. His point is simply that the methodologist is not warranted in making any ontological or *a priori* assumptions about the applicability of natural-science methodology to social-science inquiry. Instead, a case-by-case analysis of problematic situations is necessary to ascertain where such importations are valid and where they are not. Mills has found a chink in Dewey's intellectual armor in an unexpected place.

Mills adopted the essentially Deweyan view that the process of inquiry may transform the situation or problem under study.[23] But Mills believed that an unfortunate situation had developed in the social sciences, where the method used determined the area of study. Only that which lent itself to statistical manipulation was studied and the result was "the methodological inhibition." In firm pragmatic fashion Mills charged the discipline of sociology with lacking any solid connection with substantive problems or pressing social issues. Both Dewey and Mills felt that the main purpose in amassing a body of knowledge was to serve human needs; knowledge ought to be useful. By adopting this position they extended the analysis of what is to the analysis of what ought to be. Knowledge would provide the power to bring about a desired future state of affairs, and it would be achieved through this methodological prescription. Although Mills did not entirely share Dewey's epistemological stance, they both attempted to link what is with what ought to be. Although fact and value ultimately merge in Dewey, he probably never intended to proclaim facts as what "ought" to be. Rather he and Mills sought out the socially relevant facts: in

Dewey's case those that contributed to the process of "growth"; for Mills those contributing to the "emancipation of reason." They are what both believed "ought" to be in spite of their epistemological differences.

Dewey and Mills disagreed with the view that inquiry is genuinely scientific only as it systematically abstains from all concern with matters of social practice. Thus the proper moral mission and methodological orientation of social-science inquiry are important issue areas for both. By way of illustration, Dewey believed that scholarly work was inherently social and that this fact implied a deep moral obligation. Thus philosophers have a moral responsibility as instruments of human progress. However, Mills felt that the moral objectives Dewey gave to philosophy were intrinsic to the social sciences. Consequently, the ethical and methodological aspects of Mills' position require research designs and strategies that not only promote understanding of the subject matter under study but also leads to fundamental social reconstruction. Thus, in spite of their epistemological differences, they do not separate values and morality from social investigation. In Dewey's words:

> Anything that obscures the fundamentally moral nature of the social problem is harmful, no matter whether it proceeds from the side of physical or of psychological theory. Any doctrine that eliminates or even obscures the function of choice of values and enlistment of desires and emotions in behalf of those chosen weakens personal responsibility for judgement and for action.[24]

It is this particular stance of both Dewey and Mills that provides an introduction to the analysis of their conception of praxis.

THE THEORY OF PRAXIS

Mills objected to the view that the human was a passive recipient of external sense data that were thrust upon it, and to the belief that the mind contained innate ideas fixed at birth by inheritance. He thus avoided the difficulties of both classical empiricism and rationalism. Consequently, epistemology takes on political significance because Mills links it with an instrumentalist view in which ideas are defined as plans of action. Theory and practice, ideas and action, ethics and politics thus bear an integral relationship to each other. Man is neither a mechanistic cipher passively accepting his fate, nor is his mental apparatus fixed in any rigid way in his constitution. He is thus capable of using what he learns in order to reconstruct society and his own place in it. Mills and Dewey incorporate in their theory of praxis not only a particular way of relating theory to political activity but also a rationale for individual commitment to a specific kind of political involvement. Consequently, both emphasize self-realization simultaneously with enrichment of the lives of others. This is achieved through organization of the social conditions leading toward ultimate human emancipation. As Mihailo Marković defines it, praxis is a "free human activity with definite aesthetic qualities . . . in which people 'objectify' all their 'potential powers,' affirm themselves as personalities, and satisfy the needs of others."[25]

At the beginning of his career Mills sought in pragmatism the unity between theory and practice. The vehicle he thought could bring the two together was the labor movement in coalition with political intellectuals. Although much of his early writing was premised on this basic assumption, he gradually lost faith in the working class as an instrument of structural change. By the mid-1950s he was denouncing the labor metaphysic and looking for other sources of change. While he did not completely write off the entire working class his attention was diverted instead to students, ethnic minorities, intellectuals, and foreign revolutionaries as agents of social change.[26]

The way in which Mills defined "the sociological imagination" is another clue to the pervasive influence of pragmatism on Mills' style of thought. The pragmatist defines ideas as plans of action; they are defined by what they do, not what they are. Mills became increasingly critical of the new intellectual classes because they confused knowledge as a goal with knowledge as a technique and instrument.[27] It was evident that his conception of praxis required the political intellectual to recognize ideas as instruments of socio-political change, not as ends in themselves aloof from pressing social issues. Mills was pragmatic enough to recognize that ideas that have no consequences in the political arena may have no consequences at all. Although he always emphasized the necessity of political action he was an intellectual who "acted" through his writing. However, he did not believe in action for its own sake, but rather in the importance of purposive action even to the extent of criticizing Dewey for failing to take "party stands."[28]

Mills' conceptualization of praxis was partially elucidated in an unpublished manuscript dated September 19, 1953. In it Mills dealt with two images of self-realization which he labeled "The Hemingway Man" and "The Wobbley." He wrote that:

> The Hemingway Man is spectator and an experiencer; he is also a world traveller, usually alone or with changing companions, he is the ob-

server, who has become romantic about his experience and cultivates only one value, skill in expressing his experience. For the rest he lives well and enjoys the best, the most exciting, the most comfortable, except when he courts danger or safe nearness to it. . . . The Wobbley is an actor and a political man.[29]

However, Mills stated that while he had never been either of these types, he had acted out, often without knowing it, both of them. He also wrote that

the image which unites the Hemingway Man and the Wobbley . . . and both of them with my "real" occupational role as a professor of social science . . . is the image of the political writer. This is the idea of the man who stands up to nonsense and injustice and says no. Say[s] no, not out of mere defiance or for the sake of the impudent no, but out of love of truth and joy in exercising intellectual skills. My task is to shape and work with this role in such a way as to make it more satisfying of what it does not now satisfy in the other two images which still float in upon me, often unawares.[30]

There is an evident tension in his theory of praxis between individual gratification and social obligation; that is, between individual self-interest and fulfillment on the one hand and altruism on the other. The "Hemingway-Wobbley" dichotomy is evidence of his recognition of the need for reconciling the two.

For both Mills and Dewey, to adhere seriously to a social philosophy means to commit oneself to bringing it about. In so doing the intellectual faces an ethical dilemma in relating theory to practice. To solve this dilemma it is essential to have applicable values from which to choose, for values are not truly "available" when offered merely in the form of ideals. Availability requires that the value be practical. And to ensure practicality a value must be attached to a theory with an adequate empirical base. Theory is valuable for its aid in achieving the clarification and ranking of values and for helping the actor get from others the cooperation he needs to put the value into effect. Thus, theory for both Mills and Dewey is necessarily oriented toward action. However, to view theory as such is not to achieve "praxis," which is the integration of theory with action. No matter how viable a theory, it cannot be brought into action without a *commitment* to do so.[31] It was this commitment to act that Mills felt "pragmatic liberalism" lacked in the post era, after World War II.

For Dewey and Mills the active character of thought is taken for granted. Action, so to speak, is at the heart of ideas. Thus the tradi-

tional separation of theory and practice must be eliminated because
knowing is itself a type of action. Mills believed that Dewey's lifelong
attempt to break down the classic separation between theory and practice was embodied in his effort to modify the distinction between judgments of value and judgments of fact. In a penetrating commentary,
Mills summarized Dewey's fusion of is with ought and his linkage of
both with human action.

> "The 'ought' is itself an 'is'—the 'is' of action." Around that sentence a
> great deal of the thought of John Dewey pivots. For the understanding
> of his total thought it is one of the most important sentences he has ever
> written: (a) The category of the act, linked with theory, is an answer to
> the separation of the *is* and the *ought*. And this separation operates
> elsewhere as science and morals, as science and art or value, etc. It is
> 'action' with which he gets them together. (b) In so using the category
> of *action*, it becomes the repository of morals. It replaces ought.[32]

For Dewey any doctrine of fixed ends is likely to divert attention
from the examination of consequences. But in Mills' analysis of Dewey
it is evident that Mills is more committed to a creed of fixed ends, or at
least to a more explicit articulation of them. This becomes an important issue separating the two, for Mills makes the claim that exercise
of Dewey's method of intelligence will lead to "implemented aimlessness," that is, to futile engagement in directionless processes. Democratic goals may not be separable from democratic means, as Dewey
argued, but such means may lead to futility and stalemate. Mills claims
that since Dewey failed to adequately define his ends any means he
urged would be inadequate to achieve his aims.

To illustrate, for many radical critics the Roosevelt administration
was the incarnation of pragmatism in action even though Dewey, himself, was a staunch critic of the New Deal. Many on the left tended to
equate Deweyan instrumentalism with the New Deal in arguing that
both had led to aimless experimentation, an indifference to guiding
principles and definitive goals, and hence an uncritical drift toward the
revival of laissez-faire society. Earlier, however, Dewey had given
what seemed to him a convincing answer to accusations of this sort
from both left and right. He wrote that

> The person who holds the doctrine of 'individualism' or 'collectivism' has
> his program determined for him in advance. It is not with him a matter
> of finding out the particular thing which needs to be done and the best
> way under the circumstances of doing it. It is an affair of applying a

hard and fast doctrine which follows logically from his preconception of the nature of ultimate causes.[33]

It was probably Dewey's occasional vacillation and vagueness that caused Mills to claim incorrectly that

> Dewey has not taken party stands. He has stood for many 'programs' and attitudes and very specific issues like the trials of Negro sharecroppers. Sidney Hook, who surely should know, has written: 'none of the conventional labels of left-wing politics can be affixed to him. This is what we should expect about anyone faithful to the spirit of the experimental philosophy.' We can see Dewey fumbling for words that are politically neutral: 'There is no word which adequately expresses what is taking place. 'Socialism' has too specific political and economic associations to be appropriate. 'Collectivism' is more neutral, but it too, is a party-word rather than a descriptive term.'[34]

Manifest in this criticism is Mills' implicit complaint that for Dewey there is no *a priori* model that if followed would insure a "good" state or society. Mills' does not go so far as to insist that Dewey lay out an elaborate blueprint. But he thinks that Dewey's failure to define his ends is a prime shortcoming in his work. Mills was as much interested in the specific nature of a reconstructed social order as he was in developing methodologies for studying the existing one. Thus he was disappointed with Dewey's emphasis on the development of a satisfactory method for studying society as contrasted with Dewey's relative indifference to the structural forms the good society should incorporate.

Praxis, Politics, and Social Reconstruction

Mills' view of needed changes in the American system resembles those recommended by Dewey. Mills argued that the political structure of a modern democratic state required the existence of at least six conditions. First, to paraphrase him, he claimed that the public should be a forum for a politics of real issues. Second, nationally responsible parties should debate openly and clearly the important issues. Third, a senior civil service (composed of skilled men who were genuinely independent of any private corporate interest) was needed to link knowledge and sensibility together. Fourth, an intelligentsia would be needed to engage in a dialogue on the big issues and problems facing Western civilization. Its work must be influential among parties, movements and publics. Fifth, a "media of genuine communication" must be accessible to this intelligentsia. With its aid they could translate the private troubles of individuals into public issues, and public issues and events into their meanings for private life. These conditions were essential if leaders were to be held responsible and if there was to be an end to the isolation of the intellect from public life. Finally, democracy required that there be associations free from external control linking families, smaller communities, and publics on the one hand with the state, the military establishment, and the corporation on the other.[35]

From where did Mills derive his theory of social praxis and political reconstruction? By repudiating the labor metaphysic, Mills indicates his belief that the proletariat by itself, even with the leadership of radical intellectuals, cannot serve as the class base of structural change. This belief of Mills' differs from the classical Marxian conception of social praxis, which emphasizes the fusion of theory and action in the revolutionary behavior of the working class.[36] Also, Mills possessed a significantly stronger commitment to the institutional forms of liberal democracy than that held by Marx and many others claiming to belong to the Marxian tradition. He regrets that American political and legal institutions are not being used to promote structural change and an expanded civic consciousness, instead of maintaining that these institutions are primarily tools of the upper class and should be discarded along with the rest of the capitalist system. Thus, in reference to the class base through which social praxis is to be realized, and with regard to institutional forms and processes, Mills' view is closer to that of Dewey than to that of Marx.[37]

What Mills and Dewey also share is a similar view of political reconstruction based on (1) a belief that structural change will have to be carried out in the United States by a multiclass political coalition, not a proletarian party; (2) a conviction that political intellectuals must promote a political realignment in the United States so that the parties become structured along ideological and programmatic lines; the party system would thus develop a cleavage based upon philosophic differences and clear-cut issue orientations; (3) a belief that major structural change will be accomplished only when a genuine civil service is developed that is capable of resisting the encroachment of predatory interest groups and spoilsmen, and that recruits quality personnel on the basis of genuine merit and competence; (4) a view that debating publics must be developed who will connect a plurality of voluntary associations with the top of the power structure. What will then be characteristic of the system will be a two-way flow of information and communication instead of the present system where communication is based on a one-way flow—*from the top down*. There is a significant parallelism between these four prescriptions for political rejuvenation in *The Power Elite* and similar themes in Dewey's *The Public and Its Problems*. The parallels illustrate once more the probability of the Deweyan origin of many of Mills' most basic ideas.

HUMAN NATURE, MORAL AUTONOMY, AND SOCIAL CONSTRAINT

Society, for Mills, demands the contrast of good and evil in order to make available effective chances for its citizens to choose between the consequences of alternative decisions. In this sense he shared the pragmatist's interests in the cultivation of personal capacity for choice. Unfortunately, the subtle pervasiveness of bureaucratic power hid the truth about bureaucratic aims and their moral implications. It contributed to the public mood of moral uneasiness and political expediency because choice was made to appear as inconsequential or unnecessary. Mills was impressed by the volitional aspects of Deweyan individualism, which he regarded as appropriate in nonbureaucratic societies. Such individualism was characteristic of conduct and decision-making in problem situations that are on the edge of traditional social structures. However, Mills thought this kind of individualism belonged essentially to the American past and was being swept aside by bureaucratization. Both the individual's perspective and his movement were now limited by social institutions. This situation necessitated a stronger focus on power and accessibility to physical force and domination, factors which in Mills' view Dewey tended to ignore.[38]

To argue that bureaucratization displaces opportunities for individuals to take responsibility is to suggest that the loss of this moral option is unfortunate. The pragmatic idea of responsibility as a moral standard assumes that one quality of human beings is their potentiality for ethical autonomy. Mills held to the Deweyan ethic that individuals not only *are* but *ought* to be in charge of their own destiny within the limits permitted by environment. Thus individual character development takes place to the extent that persons can and do decide on alternative courses of action. So the psychology of pragmatism is grounded upon an assumption of freedom of choice through the exercise of which individual character is formed even though in Mills' analysis it is constrained by the growth of bureaucratic impediments.[39]

In accord with the pragmatic perspective, Mills does not have a deterministic view of the American past or future. He does not believe that the "mindlessness" and "irresponsibility" he describes are the only possibilities for the United States. The hope of his critique is that it will bring about change. His charge to political intellectuals in *The Causes of World War III* was that they act in a politically responsible manner, and his aspirations were that they would do so. The idea of purposive conduct is contained within the liberal view of individual freedom and tied to the idea of social reconstruction. Although Dewey was one of the key articulators of this concept, Mills thought Dewey's position was inadequate because he did not place sufficient weight on the language categories through which the individual expresses his motives and anticipates consequences. It was possible that other institutionalized motives operated that were not utilitarian. To paraphrase Mills, his criticism of Dewey is that he cannot account for actions contrary to self-interest—the alternative acts available are themselves selections from possible alternatives, and these "acceptable" selections are tied to the ideals of the social order in question. In some situations the alternatives are expressed through such words as "useful" or "practical"; however, other situations may call forth such nonutilitarian categories as "self-sacrifice," "nobility," or "charity." Dewey's analysis requires a definition of utility that is synonymous with self-interest; but Mills points out that social alternatives are not always couched in terms of self-interest.

The language categories that signify alternatives are themselves structured by the social order, which permits only a selection of possible alternatives. Consequently, the individual does not have unlimited "choice" among alternatives, but must confine his choices to those that the existing social order makes possible. The Deweyan position suggests that enlightened self-interest can make possible "unstructured choices," but Mills contends that not all possible realistic choices are "seen," only those that have been "named" by the social order. Again, however, Mills has exaggerated what are at most minor tendencies in Dewey's work, for Dewey was hardly oblivious to the manner in which the social environment constrains individual choice.

Mills and Dewey both believed that the trouble with the old social psychology was its mistaken attempt to explain conduct in terms of constant qualities of human nature. Clearly, "immutable traits" could not account for variations in behavior. Mills thought that the tendency of American social psychologists to focus on social experiences and the impact of social roles was a step in the right direction. But Mills felt that Dewey had not succeeded altogether because he did not have an adequate conception of social structure. This was a deficiency Dewey shared with many other American writers who, at best, had a "milieu" rather than a "structural" sociology.

On the whole, the Dewey-Mills conception of human nature suggests that few limits can be placed upon the capacities of human beings. Consequently, "human nature" cannot be regarded as determining social organization. On the contrary, social organization is to be seen as determining human nature. Take, for example, the question of motivation. Motives are often thought to be essentially "private" or "individual," but in the Dewey-Mills analysis there is not a single human motive that is not a motivation of the culture itself. Why any one culture places a premium on certain motives as against others can only be answered by a study of the nature of that culture. As Gerth and Mills showed in *Character and Social Structure*, motives for which there is no social reward are likely to disappear, become disguised, or never emerge in the first place.[40] Consequently, they concluded that human nature cannot be described in fixed categories because it is not immutable.

Mead, Dewey, and Mills have pointed to the fact that the "self" is expressed in social patterns, social institutions, and social habit. What has not been so apparent, however, is their claim that our very "selves" are created in the process. We do not so much "express" social habits as we are formed by them, or to put it more explicitly, that we *are* our habits. As a result, not merely our habits but ourselves are largely social in origin.[41] Although Mills clearly shared with Dewey and Mead a perception of man as a product of environment conditioning, he believed Dewey's particular way of saying this had important political implications. Mills claimed that

> In putting the problem on a social plane he (Dewey) gets away from the conservative who would seal the status quo in the nature of man. In recognizing the force of habit and custom he avoids the "shortcut revolutionary" who would urge a change of conditions very quickly, for writes Dewey, "man is a creature of habit, not of reason nor yet of instinct."
>
> The conception of habit, which is one of the three key terms of Dewey's psychology, is ideally calculated to mediate the instinctivist with a conservative political implication, and extreme environmentalism with its revolutionary import. "Habit" could have been deduced by Dewey to fulfill this mediation.[42]

Mills thinks Dewey's view of human nature is logically and empirically linked with his political liberalism because he designed it to underpin a liberal politics. In Mills' view, it was part of Dewey's attempt to under-mine both radicalism and conservatism; yet Mills ignored Dewey's view that habituation is subject to change, even radical change. This attitude is consistent with Mills' refusal to acknowledge the existence of any radical political implications in Dewey's work.

TWO SIMILAR THEORIES OF PUBLICS

Important similarities exist between Dewey and Mills' conception of "publics." Dewey's use of the term "public" rests on his distinction between the direct and indirect consequences of social transactions. Upon the basis of this distinction, Dewey further distinguishes be-tween the private and public, the latter identifying those who are affected by the indirect consequences of private acts. Thus in Dewey's work on publics there is a general theory of political order that as-sumes the necessity of regulatory political organization. In his words:

> Consequences are of two kinds, those which affect the persons directly engaged in a transaction, and those which affect others beyond those immediately concerned. In this distinction we find the germ of the dis-tinction between the private and the public. When indirect conse-quences are recognized and there is effort to regulate them, something having the traits of a state comes into existence. When the conse-quences of an action are confined mainly to the persons directly engaged in it, the transaction is a private one.[43]

Dewey assumes that publics consist of people who are organized, or soon will be, and who seek to extend or modify their existing organiza-tion in the interest of themselves and the community.

Mills, however, was careful to distinguish "publics" from "mass" society. The latter was beginning to emerge in the United States and it contained negative features, such as centralized and irresponsible manipulation of public opinion, that produced passivity and apathy on the part of the common man. Consequently, for Mills a public could exist only when four conditions were met. These conditions were that (1) there be an opportunity for as many to give opinions as there are to hear opinions; (2) there be a setting such that the receiver of an opinion has an opportunity both to reply and to publicize the response; (3) there be opportunities for effective action to implement these opin-ions; and (4) the group be free from external penetration and control by the central government.[44] In *The Power Elite* Mills argues that the concentration of political and economic power is leading to a decline of publics, not to the resurgence of them anticipated by Dewey. Mills was less optimistic about the possible emergence and maturation of publics than Dewey was when the latter wrote *The Public and Its Problems* in the mid-twenties.

A problem of mutual concern to both Mills and Dewey was the identification of publics as they began to emerge out of an amorphous unformed stage into an organized entity. Related to this was the growing awareness of the emerging public as to its own identity and common interests. In Dewey's view it was important for the public to achieve such recognition of itself as would give it weight in the choice of its representatives and in the assignment of their responsibilities and rights.[45] However, an unformed public was capable of organization only when indirect consequences were understood and when it was possible to create agencies that would anticipate their occurrences and order their effects. Until such governmental entities were established as would canalize the streams of social action and thereby regulate them, the publics would remain amorphous and unarticulated.[46] It was not that there were no publics; it was that publics could not for any length of time identify and hold themselves together because they were too fragmented and diffused.[47]

Another fundamental problem of mutual concern to Mills and Dewey was that of ensuring elite responsibility to the electorate. Given the immature and unformed nature of many publics and the likelihood of manipulation, how could elite accountability be achieved? In short, what were the proper relationships of experts to democratic publics?[48] Dewey believed that technical experts were essential to the proper functioning of modern governments at every level.[49] He lays more stress [on this facet of politics] than Mills. However, as he once said:

> It is not necessary that the many should have the knowledge and skill to carry on the needed investigations; what is required is that they have the ability to judge of the bearing of the knowledge supplied by others upon common concerns.[50]

The lack of *consciousness* of the indirect consequences of behavior in the United States is not necessarily a denial of the *existence* of such indirect consequences.[51] Thus both Dewey and Mills were able to develop a viable conception of the interests of publics though little political awareness of these interests existed in the public at large. However, in his analysis of publics, Dewey focused on indirect consequences as the public's business while Mills concentrated more on the lack of conscious awareness among publics of their common interests. This difference is further evidence of Dewey's view that publics were emerging on a large scale and of Mills' belief either that the publics have not formed or that if they have they are disintegrating into mass society. Mills feared the withering away of publics into a mass society. Indeed, he thought that the United States had advanced quite far in the direction of massification, which meant centralization of power and dependent relationships. Ultimately, it produced the alienated, anomic creature Mills described as a "cheerful robot." Dewey optimistically looked to the creation of new publics that would hasten the crystallization of opinion by groups of citizens arguing for recognition of new needs for governmental action. However, Mills' pessimism is evident in his view that a mass society is evolving that has traits the opposite of those prized by him and Dewey. Although his work has nostalgic overtones, Mills preferred the renovation of existing publics and the creation of new ones rather than the restoration of older publics that had long since withered. However, Mills had moved beyond Deweyan publics in his recognition of American evolution toward a mass society. Although he found both the theories of publics and those of mass society dated, they were still useful in showing the general social trends. The United States was no longer a collection of primary publics in the Deweyan sense, nor was it yet a mass society of the sort described by Karl Mannheim, although it was moving in that direction. Mills' use of both normative and descriptive aspects of each theory is indicative of his fundamental eclecticism, which fuses insights from American pragmatism with aspects of European social theory.

8

Mills' Attack on Dewey and American Liberalism

C. Wright Mills was obviously not John Dewey's first critic.[1] The social and political thought of Dewey has been under sustained attack since World War I when Randolph Bourne criticized his views on American involvement; a partial survey of writers critically concerned with Dewey's thought in ways related to Mills' critique of it includes many who failed to grasp Dewey's role in the American radical tradition. This involves Marxists, particularly, and other radicals who believe instrumentalism is an ideological rationalization of the capitalist order. They contend that Dewey had an inadequate conception of class structure, little appreciation of the role of the working class, an unworkable commitment to incremental rather than radical change, and an unwillingness to confront squarely the problem of corporate power in capitalist society.[2] It also involves religious critics, such as the Protestant theologian Reinhold Niebuhr, who think structural reform can be achieved only by overcoming group egoism and self-interest. Niebuhr believes that Dewey ignores these considerations because of his unwillingness to face the difficulties of attaining change in a hostile environment.[3] Nor can disillusioned pragmatists be ignored, like Bourne who emphasized the propensity of instrumentalism to degenerate into a philosophy of political expediency in which ends are subordinated to means and vision to technique.[4]

The tendency to disregard Dewey's radicalism also exists among recent critics, some of whom argue that Dewey avoids serious reflection about values, especially political values, because he is preoccupied with the process of choice at the expense of criteria of choice.[5] Still others make the related claim that Dewey never asked the question about ultimate values or purposes, an assertion of obvious political significance if social or political reconstruction is sought.[6] For example, Morton White contends that Dewey's liberalism supplies us with no specific political position that can be acted on, only a plea for intelligence.[7] In a similar vein, A. J. Somjee argues that Dewey's approach to the problems of political manipulation is unrealistic and naive,[8] made so by inability to grasp the basic difference between the manipulative operations of civil or mechanical engineers on the one hand and political "engineers" on the other. Finally, still another adversary argues that Dewey's thesis on the proper relationship between the natural and social sciences is utopian because, although natural science has enjoyed success in its own realm, it will not be successful in dealing with problems of a completely different kind.[9] This list of criticisms of Dewey could be extended almost to infinity, but the majority of them are articulated by scholars who are oblivious to Dewey's later radicalism; that is, to his abandonment of Progressivism after World War I and his subsequent acceptance of democratic socialism.

From Bourne's attack on Dewey during World War I to the present there is a reiteration of the same criticisms. Since Mills' writings contain these criticisms they can serve as a vehicle for ascertaining the substantive value of his work on Dewey. Although he mounted his challenge from the political left, Mills distinguished himself from other radical critics of pragmatism by the exceptional breadth of his analysis. No other social scientist has explored so many different facets of Dewey's thought with such penetration. Nevertheless, in analyzing liberalism, Mills unjustly accuses Dewey of epitomizing it. Mills fails to do justice to Dewey because he inaccurately categorized Dewey as just another liberal thinker, although a very important one. But Mills fails to recognize that his real argument is not with Dewey so much as it is with the American liberalism of Mills' own time. Indeed, this deficiency in Mills' analysis is related to his failure to distinguish between Dewey's early liberalism and his later role in the American radical tradition.

MILLS' ANALYSIS OF LIBERALISM

Mills' critique of American liberalism focused on these five points:

1. the liberal claim that the state achieves a balance of power between conflicting interest groups and classes;

2. the liberal theory of public opinion assumes that government is the obedient instrument of a sovereign public guided by those views that prevail in the market place of ideas:

3. the view that locates all human problems between man and nature, instead of between men and men;

4. the assumption that competition is a fair way of fusing merit with compensation; and

5. the view that a harmony of interests exists between the business community, especially its corporate segment, and the rest of society.

Mills attributed these five basic assumptions both to Dewey and to American liberalism and found them wanting. He failed to see how Dewey tried to emancipate liberalism from these shortcomings.

Most of Mills' analysis of liberalism is found in embryo form in his masters's and doctoral dissertations on the American pragmatists and is expanded in his later work. But it is not always clear what Mills means by the term "liberalism." He often shifts from the nineteenth-century usage of the term when it meant laissez-faire to the twentieth-century usage when it signifies welfare and regulatory state collectivism. However, in Mills' perspective, the two kinds of liberalism have much in common inasmuch as they share the assumptions of balance and harmony. These are his justification for attacking premises he believed intrinsic to both types of liberalism. But many of Mills' criticisms of Dewey miss the cutting thrust of Dewey's later radicalism and strike instead against his earlier liberal philosophy. Dewey well recognized the deficiencies of this older liberalism: First, he understood it to be dogmatically committed to a private enterprise devoid of social control and based upon the sanctity of private property. This kind of liberalism did not always inhibit change, but rather it limited the course of change to a single channel, that of laissez-faire capitalism.[10] Second, the earlier liberals lacked historic sense and interest. This lack blinded them to the fact that their own special interpretations of liberty, individuality, and intelligence were themselves historically conditioned and time-bound. In consequence they regarded their own versions of these ideas as immutable truths and forgot their sociohistoric relativity.[11] Dewey argued that originally liberalism meant emancipation from such oppressive forces as slavery, serfdom, dynastic rule, and inherited legal customs that hampered the rise of new forces of production. More recently it had come to signify liberation from material insecurity and from the restraints that prevent the masses from using the cultural resources that are available. As Dewey argued:

> The direct impact of liberty always has to do with some class or group that is suffering in a special way from some form of constraint exercised by the distribution of powers that exists in contemporary society. Should a classless society ever come into being the formal *concept* of liberty would lose its significance, because the *fact* for which it stands would have become an integral part of the established relations of human beings to one another.[12]

The primary source of Mills' critique of liberalism was probably Veblen, who had attacked the hedonistic view of human nature incorporated in Economic Man who knows his economic interests and acts accordingly.[13] He also satirized the invisible hand of competition that claims to balance the economy for the benefit of all. Influenced by Veblen and Ayres, Mills concluded that no natural harmony of interests exists. In the spring of 1938 he wrote that

> . . . only a believer in that ideological myth of a commercialized culture, classical economics, could possibly maintain that science "serves the entire community" and responds to the "needs" arising from the "community's" efforts of adaptation. . . . This precisely is the assumption of classical economics . . . that there is an "unseen hand" guiding each individual business man's activity [into a sum of] activities resulting in the good of all . . . that there is a "preestablished" social harmony of interests. Institutional economics and the facts of history have completely shattered any intellectual respectability such a view might ever have had.[14]

However, inasmuch as the liberal theory of politics assumed a natural harmony of interests, it served "as the ideology of dominant groups, by making their interests appear identical with the interests of the community as a whole."[15] Because of its assumption of a natural harmony of interests, Dewey's biological theory "serves to minimize the cleavage and power divisions *within* society, or put differently, it serves as a pervasive mode of posing the problem which locates all problems between *man and nature* instead of between men and men."[16] When social problems are conceptualized not as problems of power and conflicting values but instead as problems of intelligence, then the answer to them is more and better education. Consequently, Mills thought that Deweyan instrumentalism, as a form of liberalism, served as an ideological veil for the existing pattern of power distribution. Dewey's liberal faith in science, Mills asserted, was also misplaced because it too was based on unacceptable assumptions of harmony. Science and technology were not, as Dewey believed, instruments by which the whole society adjusted to new conditions. On the contrary, they served the interests of big business at the expense of the rest of society.

While the democratic state was not limited merely to adjusting group conflict, Dewey believed such adjustment must be achieved. Through adjustment together with the socialization of the forces of production the enduring values of liberalism could be preserved and expanded. The method of intelligence would serve to achieve this. But what would provide support for this method on such a scale as to make it politically viable as an ideology? Dewey's answer was the provocative claim that "There is nothing in the inherent nature of habit that prevents intelligent method from becoming itself habitual; and there is nothing in the nature of emotion to prevent the development of intense emotional allegiance to the method."[17] It is evident that while Dewey may have been *prescriptively* correct in his claim that a culture ought to act so in order to survive, he was *descriptively* incorrect in that cultures and species have shown no marked inclination to institutionalize the method of intelligence.

Mills rejected the liberal theories of balance of power that pluralists had developed.[18] The idea of balance of power assumed an equality of power, but as Mills argues, "One man's honorable balance is often another's unfair balance."[19] Mills' rejection of the theory of political balance was both a reaction to the deficiencies of pluralism in the 1950s and part of his broader attack on liberalism. Mills' main criticism of American liberalism and of Dewey was that both lacked ideological, institutional, and programmatic autonomy from the corporate structure. They were adaptive creatures of the main drift rather than formative in their orientation toward corporations. Consequently, they were unable to formulate a convincing analysis of the corporate power system and a related set of policies for harnessing it to the public purpose. Although Mills was correct in making this allegation against liberals, he thought it especially applicable to Dewey. In so doing he overlooked Dewey's statement that

> It is foolish to regard the political state as the only agency now endowed with coercive power. Its exercise of this power is pale in contrast with that exercised by concentrated and organized property interests. . . . The regime is in such large measure merely the agent of a dominant economic class in its struggle to keep and extend the gains it has amassed at the expense of genuine social order, unity, and development.[20]

Dewey did not focus as sharply or as dramatically on corporate power as Mills and other radical critics wished, but he cannot accurately be accused of ignoring the subject in the 1930s. In spite of occasional vagueness and inconsistency, he did not slight recognition of corporate power or the problem of harnessing it to the social interest. As he said in 1934, "the cause of liberalism will be lost for a considerable period if it is not prepared to go further and socialize the forces of production, now at hand, so that the liberty of individuals will be supported by the very structure of economic organization."[21]

Mills argued that liberalism wrongly assumes that competition is an equitable way of rewarding merit. However, Mills claimed that the incorporation in American novels of this Horatio Alger theme was becoming less common. More often, success was attributed to luck or manipulation, rather than hard work, virtue, or intelligence. Thus a basic premise of liberalism was recognized as outdated insofar as it assumed competition would reward merit with just compensation. This was part of Mills' repudiation of the way in which market economies distribute income.

Originally the liberal theory of political balance included a theory of public opinion. According to the liberal theory of public opinion the public is the seat of legitimate power, opinion emerges from the competition of ideas, and government is the obedient instrument that reacts to it.[22] Here again Mills discerned the ideology of eighteenth-century liberalism. As the free market consists of competing entrepreneurs, so the public is composed of competing opinion peers. As price results from transactions in the market, so public opinion emerges from discussions in the public.[23] As does the theory of economic balance, the liberal theory of public opinion assumes a natural harmony of interests. Mills rejected the latter for the same reasons that Veblen rejected classical economics. Veblen's description of what was happening to the market was similar to what Mills believed was also happening to public opinion. As the economy became more concentrated, competition increasingly took the form of a battle between big business and consumers. Likewise, with the rise of new media of communication, competition of opinion was increasingly between "the manipulators with their mass media on the one hand, and the people receiving their propaganda on the other."[24] Mills believed that the concept of a "free marketplace of ideas" was untenable from its very inception. It was used to mask and legitimize the competition among opinion elites for support from the general public opinion.

Although the influence of Veblen upon Mills' critique of Dewey and American liberalism is ambiguous, Mills was in reading contact with Veblen at the time that his views on liberalism were formulated. Mills found in Veblen's attacks on neoclassical economics ammunition that he used to belabor liberals like Dewey, especially in his denials that there is a natural harmony of interests between capital and labor. Mills could not accept the view that the main struggle is between man and nature, *not* between men and men, nor did he believe that there is a power balance between groups and classes in society with the state functioning as a neutral balance wheel. He also found liberal views of the formation and role of public opinion grossly inadequate and denounced competition as an equitable way of mating merit and compensation. All of these critical views of liberal doctrine closely parallel those held by Veblen. Because Mills believed liberalism was the prevalent ideology and served to "orient" Americans to their existence, he made a career of attacking liberalism for he believed it was not only too influential but was also politically moribund and morally indefensible. Much of Mills' writing aimed not only at exposing the deficiencies of liberalism but at forcing liberals to rethink their position. His exposé charged that liberalism was suffering from cultural lag for it originated in the United States under conditions which no longer prevailed.

MILLS ON DEWEY'S INCREMENTALISM

Dewey's incrementalism as policy prescription and political philosophy was suspect because it failed to consider total social structures.[25] Focusing on Dewey's concept of adaptation, Mills writes that the "biological model strengthens the drive toward the specificity of problems and this specificity implements . . . a politics of reform of the situation. Adaptation is one step at a time; it faces one situation at a time."[26] What he apparently means by "incrementalism" are programs that deal with parts of a problem instead of the whole. Such programs deal with secondary issues rather than fundamentals. Consequently the aspects of the problem that are dealt with are those for which a "product" solution is possible. The solutions chosen are such as will constitute the least amount of disturbance to the social fabric. Incrementalist reform efforts were associated with the New Deal, the Fair Deal, and the New Frontier programs. Mills faults this kind of piecemeal construction, for

> Mills is committed in a partially Deweyan sense to a continual social reconstruction, simply because our knowledge of the social order keeps changing and increasing. He differs from Dewey and other liberals in that he does not advocate a "piecemeal" reconstruction. This in his view is doomed to failure, because partial reconstructions never really take into account the entire social order. What is required is a broad reconstruction along many, if not all, fronts simultaneously.[27]

An analysis of Dewey's proposals for socioeconomic reconstruction during the depression provides a picture different from that articulated above. Dewey supported government ownership of basic industries and natural resources. This structure would involve a mixed system in which supervision and regulation of industry would be jointly administered by the government, which would represent the public interest in general and the consumer interest in particular. It would also require a role for management and one for workers through their democratically controlled trade unions. To achieve socialization Dewey advocated heavy taxation on upper income groups; this revenue could then be used to compensate owners of industries that were nationalized, and also to redistribute wealth through subsidizing social-welfare programs.[28] These are hardly the policy prescriptions of a liberal ameliorist. Dewey summarized the ideal relationships between radical and incremental social change when he wrote:

> Liberalism must now become radical, meaning by "radical" perception of the necessity of thoroughgoing changes in the set-up of the institutions and corresponding activity to bring the changes to pass. For the gulf between what the actual situation makes possible and the actual state itself is so great that it cannot be bridged by piecemeal policies undertaken ad hoc. The process of producing the changes will be, in any case, a gradual one. But "reforms" that deal now with this abuse and now with that without having a social goal based upon a inclusive plan, differ entirely from effort at re-forming, in its literal sense, the institutional scheme of things.[29]

Although it is difficult to square Dewey's views with Mills' interpretation, Dewey's radicalism was inconsistent since he vacillated between advocacy of welfare-state capitalism and genuine socialism. Nevertheless, several years before the New Deal began, he wrote prescriptively that:

> We are in for some kind of socialism, call it by whatever name we please, and no matter what it will be called when it is realized. Economic determinism is now a fact, not a theory. But there is a difference and a choice between a blind, chaotic and unplanned determinism, issuing from business conducted for pecuniary profit, and the determination of a socially planned and ordered development. It is the difference and the choice between socialism that is public and one that is capitalistic.[30]

Should it be thought Dewey's commitment to massive structural change is exaggerated, a glance at a summary of his position during the New Deal suggests otherwise. Admittedly, this is the period when Dewey moved furthest to the left, but it was the period of Dewey's work with which Mills was most familiar and about which he was most likely to generalize. Edward Bordeau has written that

> Dewey could not accept Roosevelt's compromise with capitalism for he saw clearly that the New Deal permitted power and rule to remain essentially in the same hands as those that brought the country to its present state—dominated as those hands are by the profit motive. . . . While the New Deal was not, to Dewey's mind, radical enough in terms of his socialism, it was nonetheless greatly under the influence of his instrumentalism and pragmatism even if this pragmatism was more ad hoc and headless than his own. Dewey genuinely applauded what he, Roosevelt, had accomplished, but the New Deal was merely an attempt to save capitalism and "only a new system which destroys the profit system can banish poverty and bring the American people the economic liberation which modern science and technology is prepared to bestow upon them."[31]

Mills underestimated Dewey's commitment to radical reform, albeit Dewey's advocacy of radical change throughout his career was inconsistent. Dewey's sometime commitment to radicalism was more evident in the interwar period than earlier. Consequently, Mills' indictment of the liberal, as opposed to the radical aspects of his work, is more accurate when aimed at Dewey before 1918 rather than during the depression.

POLITICAL ACTIVISM AND SOCIAL INVOLVEMENT: A COMPARISON

Although Dewey shared the liberal reformist political views of his colleagues, his early publications did not reveal a strong focus on political issues nor an overriding concern with pressing social problems.[32] But though Dewey did not often discuss pressing social problems, his lectures in such courses as "Contemporary Theories Regarding Ethical Relations of the Individual and Society" and the "Sociology of Ethics" did. Certainly the public talks he gave and the discussions he led at Hull House were so concerned with social matters as to demonstrate beyond doubt that he considered himself a liberal. Thus, had Mills focused on the Michigan and Chicago phases of Dewey's career and cited his published work from that era more extensively, his criticisms would carry more weight. For despite Dewey's liberal social activism, his writing had more of the deficiencies Mills attributed to it. Unfortunately, Mills all too often generalized about Dewey's work not from this early period when his criticism was applicable but from the 1920s and 1930s when it was not.

Dewey's voting record indicates that he was an independent. Most of his votes were cast for socialist or progressive third-party candidates, although occasionally he supported a Democrat for the presidency. To illustrate, he voted for Democrat Grover Cleveland in 1884. In 1906 he voted for Charles Evans Hughes, a progressive Republican, for governor of New York. In 1912 he supported socialist Eugene V. Debs for president. In 1916 he voted for Democrat Woodrow Wilson for president. In 1924 he backed Robert M. LaFollette, the Progressive reformer, for the presidency, and actively supported the LaFollette-Wheeler ticket in the campaign of that year. On one occasion he appeared as the principal speaker at a LaFollette rally of college students in New York City.[33] In the presidential campaign of 1928, which pitted Herbert Hoover against Al Smith and in which Norman Thomas ran as the Socialist Party candidate, Dewey's sympathies were with Thomas and the Socialist Party. He wrote that "If I had any special confidence in what can be accomplished by any party, with reference to our specifically political needs, I should vote for Norman Thomas, because I think those needs are connected with a much more fundamental facing of the issues of economic reconstruction than we shall obtain from the Democratic party under any conceivable circumstances."[34] But, practical politics dictated that he support Smith. Among his reasons was the "humane and sympathetic spirit" with which Smith approached social problems as contrasted with Hoover's hard "efficiency," an efficiency that "works out to strengthen the position of just those economic interests that most need weakening instead of strengthening."[35] Dewey did not foresee the time a few years later when Smith would become a Liberty Leaguer and an archconservative critic of the New Deal.

After several years of proposing radical measures through his League for Independent Political Action, Dewey finally endorsed Norman Thomas in 1932. The explanation for Dewey's electoral support for the Socialist Party was the fact that the planks he proposed through the L.I.P.A. were almost identical to those favored by the Socialists. Only the Socialists' dogmatic insistence on the evitability of class warfare prevented Dewey from assuming a more active role in the Socialist cause.[36] In view of Mills' strictures against Dewey, it should be kept in mind that it was during this period that Dewey wrote:

Our entire history and experience proves that the financial and industrial leaders of the nation will not make these changes voluntarily—they will not, except under compulsion, surrender their most profitable share of a system which has concentrated four-fifths of the nation's wealth in the hands of one twenty-fifth of the people.

The federal government alone has the power to force the wealthy owners of the nation to surrender their control over the lives and destinies of the overwhelming majority of the American people and the first step is to compel them to pay taxes commensurate in sacrifice with that of people with very small incomes.[37]

Dewey also supported Norman Thomas in 1936 and 1940. The only other indication of his later voting record reveals that he voted for Franklin D. Roosevelt in 1944. On October 20, 1944, the *New York Times* ran an article in which Dewey indicated that he distrusted the "isolationism" of the Republican Party and intended to vote for President Roosevelt as the man most likely to "lead us forward."[38] Clearly Dewey had long realized the importance of third-party pressure in offering the public real alternatives through formulation and propagandization of progressive programs. His willingness to support the Democratic Party emerged primarily when third-party agitation seemed fruitless, as was the case during World War II.

It is important to note that both Mills and Dewey voted for Norman Thomas, the Socialist Party Candidate, for president in 1940 because this may indicate that they were not as far apart as Mills thought.[39] In spite of Mills' attacks on Dewey's conception of the linkage between theory and practice, he came to the same conclusion about whom to give his political support. Mills fancied himself further left in the ideological spectrum than either Dewey or Norman Thomas. Nevertheless, when forced to choose, he chose Thomas, whose views he preferred to those of Stalinists, Trotskyites, and other radical splinter groups. Perhaps the main difference between Mills and Dewey in the arena of electoral politics was that Dewey was willing to support non-socialist "progressive" or "liberal" parties and candidates, while Mills usually abstained from supporting them on the grounds that they were not sufficiently "radical."

Dewey was a supporter of American entrance into World War I and he attempted to show that the method of intelligence did not preclude the use of force in international politics. He thus tried to demonstrate the fundamental compatibility between pragmatism and war. After the Versailles Peace Conference he rapidly became disillusioned with the Allied cause and with American participation in the war and gravitated toward what was essentially a pacifist position.[40] Ultimately the doctrine of pacifism became a basic part of his pragmatic approach to social affairs. After war started again in 1939, there was no pragmatic justification for the use of military force in Dewey's work. For, in spite of his strong dislike of totalitarianism and fascism, Dewey's support of the war was halfhearted. His politics during this period was directed toward waging battles on behalf of civil liberties and civil rights as well as toward a program to avert future war.[41] Although any direct Dewey influence on Mills cannot be demonstrated, it is interesting to note that Mills' view of American participation in the war was similar. As Dewey was, so Mills was critical of intellectuals who unequivocally endorsed the war effort and its rationale and stratagems. He probably believed that the only two viable alternatives to such endorsement were the pacifist one and one of critical, conditional support.

DEWEY'S AUDIENCE

In *Sociology and Pragmatism* Mills evaluates the nature of the "publics" for whom Dewey wrote. These upwardly mobile groups include students, educators, professional philosophers, and those actively concerned with social and political problems. Mills locates Dewey's political anchorage and his reading publics in those business and professional groups from a rural or small-town background to whom the "formality, intellectuality, and tentativeness" of Dewey's thought correspond and appeal. He indicates that Dewey's audience found his commitments to incremental reform, avoidance of violence, and "mugwumpism" convincing. Mills asks rhetorically, "Could the political character of Dewey's concept of action be imputed to the fact that none of the groups to which he is oriented have aspirations to rule?"[42] It is evident to Mills that Dewey's theory of action and his social philosophy are well tailored to the views of his audience. However his criticism explains the deficiencies of liberal analysis rather than accuses Dewey of opportunism:

> Liberalism recognized new irrational spheres; for instance class struggles and power fights. But it is intellectualistic in so far as it attempts solely through thought, discussion and organization to master as if they were already rationalized, the power and other irrational relationships that dominate here. . . . From all these factors mentioned comes an explanation for why there is no power problem in pragmatism. For it is precisely individuals who coming from varied strata have arrived at modus operandi among themselves that conceive of all problems being solved by intelligence and discussion.[43]

In spite of these strictures Mills soon abandoned any belief in the revolutionary socialist potential of the American working class, deeming it an archaic residue of the "labor metaphysic." He directed his political analysis to many of the same groups that earlier he criticized Dewey for having in his reading audience. For it was evident that, if structural changes were to be achieved, intellectuals must play a prominent role. Thus, despite his original skepticism about the political orientation of Dewey's publics, Mills arrived at similar conclusions about the socio-occupational affiliations of the likely catalysts of political change. Although he spoke to those groups in more radical language than Dewey used, the composition of their audiences was similar. Mills was wrong about the makeup of Dewey's audiences, for Dewey addressed his ideas to all sorts of people, including revolutionaries like Leon Trotsky.

Mills said that Dewey's model for individual action assumed either a rural setting or a small community. Yet the majority of the population lived in large urban areas. In Dewey's scheme the basis for social action and orientation was in the context of close relationships. He believed individuals identify with the people with whom they merge their private lives. From this convergence of private and community life comes the overall social orientation. Mills claimed that communities of this type were rapidly disappearing. Close relationships with neighbors had become less likely to exist. Increased urbanization and role specialization interfered with the primary relationships that Dewey assumed were dominant. As Mills put it, Dewey saw "the good society organized communally . . . in a way that is unmistakably rural."[44] Just as there is nostalgia in Dewey for America's rural communal past and the set of social relationships it fostered, so also is there in Mills. The Power Elite, in particular, is replete with nostalgic references to those archaic traits Mills believed were characteristic of Jacksonian America.[45]

"Biologization" versus the Cultural Apparatus

Mills believed that Dewey's explanation of human behavior was too biological because his sequence of adjustment was a simplistic, mechanical one of organism-environment-adaptation. Mills contended that urbanized existence was virtually independent of biological factors, for explanation of social action is cultural, not biological. But, in Dewey, physical characteristics were set against mental characteristics while inadequate attention was given to cultural factors. Mills argued that Dewey's psychology thus failed to take adequate account of the fact that in the evolution of cultural conduct from organic behavior there is genuine novelty and irreducible qualitative differentiation. Thus, behavioral patterns are culturally fostered and cannot be reduced to biology and physiology.[46] The political significance of this is evident in Mills' claim that the power elite is able to manipulate the cultural apparatus to its own advantage to establish ideological dominance. Thus, Dewey was guilty both of using a mechanistic adjustment model to explain human behavior and of inadequate recognition of the cultural and symbolic aspects of the political environment.

According to Mills, Dewey's value theory made him prone to overlook power inequalities, ideological differences, and conflicts of interest. Linked to this criticism was his claim that Dewey's biological model of action was an evasion of the value problem. As Mills stated, "The biological model of action, 'adaptation,' by its formality enables one to avoid value-decisions. . . . By its usage value-decisions as value-decisions are assimilated into the biological and hidden by formality."[47] Mills reads Dewey as believing that value phenomena are embedded in a biological, adaptationist matrix that is a central cause of Dewey's failure to confront the necessity of value choice.

So often did Mills make the charge that Dewey was guilty of biologizing human behavior and values that it is patently not a snap judgment on his part. As Mills argued:

> It is anthropologically patent that the relation of volitional and social-attitudinal complexes to the conditions necessary for biological survival are extremely tenuous. Yet, in the new *Logic* a wholly biological statement of "need" as lack of integration and equilibrium of organic energies and environmental conditions within the activity of an organism is carried over without redefinition.[48]

Mills charged Dewey with believing that since the human species has evolved from lower animals, all human actions, even those on the highest cultural level, have developed from biological adaptation of organisms to their natural environment. Thus, human actions remain similar in form and function to those organic processes in which they originated. They differ from them only in such secondary characteristics as complexity, indirectness, and range of adaptability. Mills concluded that because of his biological reductionism Dewey's conception of human nature was hardly distinct from animal nature. Thought was a capacity that was more refined than "instinct" but barely different in kind. Thus Mills read Dewey as limiting his concept of action to adaptation, a concept whose ideological use within the framework of centralized power suggested very restricted types of political action that could not transcend the status quo.[49]

Despite Mills' allegations that Dewey is guilty of biologizing human behavior, an analysis of Dewey's later writing shows such charges to be wide of their mark. It is a too common tendency of critics to think of instrumentalism as a way of patterning only low-level organic disruptions. On the contrary, for Dewey, problems are not limited to practical difficulties in any narrow sense, but include the full range of intellectual, moral, political, and artistic perplexities.[50] Mills' claim that Dewey didn't give sufficient recognition to cultural factors in explaining human behavior, but rather used a biological-adaptationist model is easy to rebut. For example, Dewey says in *Reconstruction in Philosophy* that

> . . . man lives in a world where each occurrence is charged with echoes and reminiscences of what has gone before, where each event is a reminder of other things. Hence he lives not, like the beast of the field, in a world of merely physical things but in a world of signs and symbols. . . . And all this which marks the difference between bestiality and humanity, between culture and merely physical nature, is because man remembers, preserving and recording his experiences.[51]

Nearly twenty years later Dewey reiterated the point when he wrote that

> To a very large extent the ways in which human beings respond even to physical conditions are influenced by their cultural environment. . . . To indicate the full scope of cultural determination of the conduct of living one would have to follow the behavior of an individual throughout at least a day . . . the result would show how thoroughly saturated behavior is with conditions and factors that are of cultural origin and import. Of distinctively human behavior it may be said that the strictly physical environment is so incorporated in a cultural environment that our interactions with the former, the problems that arise with reference to it, and our ways of dealing with these problems, are profoundly affected by incorporation of the physical environment in the cultural.[52]

Dewey believed that all human behavior could be explained by either the biological or the social factor or both. Transformation from organic behavior to intellectual behavior was a product of life in a cultural environment, and the most important single facet of this environment was language, although Dewey never lost sight of other relevant cultural processes.[53]

However, Mills was convinced that Dewey was so given to biological-adaptationist interpretations of social phenomena that it even affected his view of the history of philosophy. As Mills argued, "pragmatists would have us believe that *all* ideas are plans of overt action addressed to 'problems' in an act of 'adjustment.' This is not an adequate nor exhaustive model of intellectual history."[54] Yet, of all Mills' criticisms of Dewey, his charge of "biologization" is the least convincing because it cannot be validated through textual exegesis of Dewey's work.

Mills and Dewey on the Method of Intelligence

In view of Mills' attack on Dewey for "methodizing" problems that were not methodological, a brief restatement of what Dewey meant by the "method of intelligence" is in order. He did not define it in an abstract, technical way, but as a kind of knowledge that results when methods are employed that deal competently with whatever problems arise. In this sense the doctor, artist, mechanic, or electrician can all claim to be "scientific." The method of intelligence rests upon the idea that

> known objects exist as the consequences of directed operations. . . . We may . . . give the name intelligence to these directed operations. Using this term, we may say that the worth of any object that lays claim to being an object of knowledge is dependent upon the intelligence employed in reaching it. In saying this we must bear in mind that intelligence means operations actually performed in the modification of conditions, including all the guidance that is given by means of ideas, both direct and symbolic.[55]

For Dewey, what was needed to make social inquiry more fruitful was a method that proceeded on the basis of the interrelations of observable acts and their results.[56] The investigator had to choose between blind acceptance of the *a priori* on the one hand and a discriminating criticism employing intelligent method and a conscious criterion on the other.[57] For Dewey "judgement" was an integral part of the method of intelligence and was used to select and arrange means and to choose ends. A man was intelligent if he could correctly estimate the possibilities of a situation and act in accordance with it.[58] Dewey believed that inquiry must, if it was to be genuinely scientific, (1) be related to real social frictions, aspirations, or problems; (2) have its subject matter determined by the conditions that are means of bringing about a unified situation, and (3) grow out of an hypothesis which is both a plan and a policy for resolving a conflicting social situation.[59] In sum, Dewey once defined "inquiry," a fundamental part of the method of intelligence, as "the controlled or directed transformation of an indeterminate situation into one that is so determinate in its constituent distinctions and relations as to convert the elements of the original situation into a unified whole."[60]

For Dewey it was important that democracy institutionalize the procedure of trial and error. He focused strongly on social and political experimentation, for he believed that it was experimentation that gave natural science its strength. By experimentation a society could find solutions for its problems, but Dewey argued that only a democratic form of government would permit such experimentation.[61] Mills' charge of "implemented aimlessness" against Dewey's alleged lack of a specific goal orientation is incorrect because directed trial-and-error experimentalism avoids the element of blindness involved in undirected trial-and-error procedure. It does not leave the process of trial and error to accident, for the procedure of trial and error is directed toward desired ends. What is required is a correct understanding of the problematic situation and the alternatives to it that are wanted.[62] Mills thus overlooked the important distinction Dewey made between *directed* and *undirected* trial-and-error methods and the oversight weakens his attack on Dewey's alleged "methodolatry." Much of Mills' criticism of Dewey assumes that it is impractical to think conflicts over public policy can be settled by appeals to scientific intelligence. This criticism seems misplaced when Dewey's own caveats on the subject are heard. He once wrote that "Vested interests . . . are powerfully on the side of . . . hindering the growth and application of the method of natural intelligence. Just because these interests are so powerful, it is the more necessary to fight for recognition of the method of intelligence in action."[63]

Dewey thought moral progress was most likely to be achieved through social reform, and that the chief obstacles to it were vested interests and ideas. He believed that one effective means of overcoming these barriers was through development of the social sciences together with a wide dissemination of the results of scientific inquiry. As he put it, "The duty of the present is the socializing of intelligence—the realizing of its bearing upon social practice."[64] Mills believed Dewey guilty of thinking that most important social problems could be solved if the findings of social scientists were widely enough diffused.[65] However, Dewey was not so naive as Mills imagined him to be, for social science inquiry, technical skill, and altruistic moral impulses must be fused together in order to combat upper-class power.[66]

Ultimately even these combined would not suffice in a class-oriented power struggle if they were not harnessed to the appropriate political vehicle. In rebuttal of such criticisms as Mills', Dewey had written that

> What is applied and employed as the alternative to knowledge in regulation of society is ignorance, prejudice, class-interest and accident. Science is converted into knowledge in its honorable and emphatic sense only in application. Otherwise it is truncated, blind, distorted . . . [and used] for pecuniary ends to the profit of a few. At present, the application of physical science is rather *to* human concerns that *in* them. That is, it is external, made in the interests of its consequences for a possessing and acquisitive class.[67]

Although Mills and Dewey could sometimes agree on the cause of social conflict, they often could not agree on the proper means for resolving such conflict. Mills probably believed that a class-oriented, confrontationist politics was the best way to resolve such differences while Dewey, who was not oblivious to class-rooted politics, warned that his method of intelligence viewed with suspicion "the erection of actual human beings into fixed entities called classes, having no overlapping interests and so internally unified and externally separated that they are made the protagonists of history."[68] It is evident that Dewey preferred compromise and bargaining, in short an "accommodationist" politics, to the "confrontationist" politics preferred by Mills at this point in his career.[69]

Mills' charge of "methodolatry" meant Dewey should do more than endorse the method of intelligence to resolve social problems. He felt that Dewey should also indicate what the solutions were or ought to be. Thus Mills succumbed to the common tendency to search Dewey's writings for an answer to moral difficulties and intellectual doubts instead of using Dewey's prescribed method to resolve them himself. In so doing, Mills fell prey to what Dewey warned against in his attacks on conservative orthodoxy. Dewey's point is not that values are antecedently given as traditional theories of value have maintained, but that they are developed as outgrowths of operational thinking. Value judgments, like judgments of matters of fact in science, derive their validity not from their correspondence to something antecedent, but from their success in bringing about anticipated consequences after the designated operations have been performed. However, Mills' critique of this position suggests that while it may be productive of forward movement, it will lack direction and coherence and ultimately fail. Dewey maintained that his theory of valuation was a special case of his general method of inquiry, that valuation judgments and a unified logical method are needed for the solution of all problematic situations. But, as Mills and other critics have pointed out, he did little to show how specific features of his general method of inquiry are used in solving problems of valuation.[70]

Mills believed Dewey guilty of

> . . . the assimilation of problems of political power and of moral goods to a statement of thinking, of method to a model of action and thought imputed to "science." . . . But the model is generalized by Dewey into education and into the discussion of politics. . . . "scientific method" becomes "the method of intelligence" and this method is equated with "liberal democracy."[71]

Thus, where Dewey perceives problems as emanating from failure to use the "method of intelligence," Mills views them as resulting from power, wealth, and status inequalities originating in institutions, and from value conflicts rooted in the class structure. Such problems cannot be solved by resorting to methodological manipulation or by the shibboleths of experimentalism. Instead, Dewey should have squarely confronted the structural problem of power in modern capitalism. But he would not do so because "the professionalizing or methodizing of value questions already assumes for its happy operation a kind of community that nowhere exists."[72] Unfortunately, Mills pays insufficient attention to Dewey's recognition that many situations arise in hostile environments where the method of intelligence can be expected to accomplish little. As Dewey once wrote:

> If intelligent method is lacking, prejudice, the pressure of immediate circumstances, self-interest and class interest, traditional custom or institutions of accidental historic origin are not lacking, and they tend to take the place of intelligence.[73]

However, Mills is correct in asserting that Dewey is unnecessarily brief about the kinds of environments in which the method of intelligence will not succeed because of structural obstacles. Dewey's position would be stronger had he given a more detailed analysis of the institutional barriers that prevent utilization of his method. It would be even more convincing had he shown how the method could be used to overcome these barriers. But then neither Dewey nor any other modern political theorist has been able to articulate such an effective political technology.

Mills argues that Dewey was wrong in believing that the method of science is self-corrective. Dewey paid inadequate attention to the sociology-of-knowledge perspective, which shows how acceptance of a particular methodology depends upon the distribution of social power. For what is "scientific" is often an ideological rationale for what is useful to elites who perceive science as a device for enhancing their own sociopolitical position. Consequently, models that are dominant in the scientific community, including the procedures of laboratory science upon which Dewey relied too heavily, may reflect little more than the existing power structure. This is especially true when these procedures, adapted from the "hard sciences," become the methodological core of inquiry in the social sciences. Dewey's work on social and political issues performs a "masking" or ideological function that weakens its potential as an agent of social change, for as Mills says, "It should be clear that . . . the angle of sight of these conceptions are not conducive, indeed prohibit the discernment or the reconstruction of power-issues and structural antagonisms."[74]

In summation, Mills thought that the methodizing of social problems signified a belief that these are soluble through the method of intelligence.[75] He believed that through such methodization Dewey escaped having to formulate concrete sociopolitical ends.[76] By shifting the locus of the value problem, Dewey was able to avoid the trials that beset those who are committed to structural change. Mills believed that the heart of moral and political questions was the compulsory character of judgment, and Dewey avoided this through "intellectuality" of a kind that blurred the "demands of the moral life."[77] Mills also complained that Dewey's methodizing of value questions assumed in advance for its successful operation a kind of harmonious community that did not exist and thus failed to adequately situate his concerns in a realistic setting.[78] Nonetheless, it is difficult to avoid the conclusion that Mills inflated the case that can be made in each respect.

GROWTH AS SOCIAL END
OR AS AVOIDANCE OF BASIC ISSUES?

Dewey was a strong critic of absolute or fixed ends. He took the view that values were relative to situations and that the criteria to be used for judging values must vary from one circumstance to another. However, he linked situationally derived value criteria to human growth and development, so he cannot rightly be charged with advocating moral opportunism in the radically relativistic sense. Although Mills was not an absolutist who believed that there were fixed ends to be striven for, and absolute values worth sacrificing anything to achieve, he differed over the extent to which values are situationally derived and oriented. Precisely why he felt this way remains obscure, but he charged Dewey with advocating "implemented aimlessness," which meant supporting directionless change. He suggested that instrumentalism was morally adrift because of uncertainty over the character of its substantive goals. However, Mills consistently overstated the case that can be made against Dewey in this regard. But his exaggerations are not due solely to an impetuous youthful radicalism, inasmuch as they became an enduring part of his stock-in-trade in criticizing liberalism. Perhaps what disturbed Mills more than anything else about Dewey was his refusal to commit himself to any particular set of ends or social goals except human growth, and his failure to be explicit about the nature of growth itself. Dewey was often guilty of refusing to discriminate between values by contending that their worth is approximately the same. A good example of this was Dewey's claim that "every case where moral action is required becomes of equal moral importance and urgency with every other. . . . Anything that in a given situation is an end and good at all is of equal worth, rank and dignity with every other good of any other situation, and deserves the same intelligent attention."[79] It was just such indiscriminate endorsement of all goods that lent strength to Mills' critique. However, Dewey did offer other more discriminating criteria in his efforts to estimate the effects of growth on individuals. He believed that people should be judged not by whether or not they fall short of some fixed end, but by the direction in which they are moving. The bad man is the individual who is beginning to deteriorate, while the good man is improving, no matter how morally unworthy he has been.[80]

Since the ends Dewey sought to promote were those of growth, he often refused to specify in advance the precise nature of the social environment he ultimately sought to achieve.[81] For who could say *a priori* which particular set of institutional arrangements would be most likely to facilitate maximum growth in all situations? It was only through the use of experimental method that such knowledge could be ascertained and then only tentatively.[82]

> To say that the welfare of others, like our own, consists in a widening and deepening of the perceptions that give activity its meaning, in an educative growth, is to set forth a proposition of political import. . . . Our moral measure for estimating any existing arrangement or any proposed reform is its effect upon impulse and habits. Does it liberate or suppress, ossify or render flexible, divide or unify interest? Is perception quickened or dulled? Is memory made apt and extensive or narrow

and diffusely irrelevant? Is imagination diverted to fantasy and com-
pensatory dreams, or does it add fertility to life? Is thought creative or
pushed to one side into pedantic specialisms?[83]

This explicit delineation of growth weakens Mills' charges of directionless action or "implemented aimlessness," for Dewey had a strong
faith in the almost limitless development of human potentialities. People are most likely to grow in an environment that gives them maximum scope for expression and action. Consequently, he laid great
emphasis on the creation of an environment conducive of continuous
growth.[84] In endorsing growth as a prime value Dewey makes the
principle of continuity the main criterion for judging a growth experience. He asked where a particular experience leads and what its potentiality is for physical, intellectual, and moral growth. Is there
increase of ability to direct subsequent experience into richer channels? For the meaning of growth to be concrete it must meet a number
of criteria. First, it must be an aim in the individual's experience and
education. Second, the aim must be flexible in the sense of being both
able to guide activity and modify it. Third, the aim must function to
liberate or free action in a planned sequence.[85] Dewey often used the
term "education" in a normative sense. For Dewey, not every
modification of behavior is educative; it may, in fact, be miseducative.

The growth of morality in the individual should follow the three
ideals of harmony, variety, and expansion. As Dewey put it "to convert strife into harmony, monotony into a variegated scene, and limita-
tion into expansion."[86] Moral growth also requires development of the
powers of initiative and reflection essential for choice and foresight, an
interest in modification of character, and a trend of conduct leading to
more varied and self-conscious choices and larger areas of unimpeded
action.[87] Dewey focused not on final, ideal ends, but on interruptions
and recoveries. Although it was important to judge progress by pur-
ported "ultimate" ends, "growth" was a standard for evaluating qualitative change in process whose final outcome was not known.
Nevertheless, in spite of his familiarity with these many examples of
Deweyan growth criteria, Mills doubted that Dewey had established
adequate standards for determining when growth occurs.[88] Perhaps
Mills should have been more specific about the nature of "adequate"
standards in this context?

However, although Dewey's criteria for measuring growth are
meaningful, the measurement does not lend itself to quantification or
precision. It is understandable that Dewey's critics would find them
vague. Mills remained confirmed in his belief that Dewey "repudiates

the notion of education as "unfolding," or as "preparation." Either view would lead to questions of goal setting. But education as growth is calculated to avoid just such questions."[89] Mills charged Dewey with lacking criteria for differentiating between good growth and bad growth to such a degree that he could not explicitly face the value problem. This was evident in his unwillingness to throw growth issues upon the "moral, political plane where decisions between adults must be made." However, although Dewey was sometimes vague about the difference between good and bad growth, he did not portray growth as neutral or amoral development. For it was life directed along the lines of the enrichment of present and future development. As Dewey put it:

> . . . a man . . . who starts out on a career of burglary may grow in that direction, and by practice may grow into a highly expert burglar. Hence it is argued that "growth" is not enough; we must also specify the direction in which growth takes place, the end towards which it tends. . . . That a man may grow in efficiency as a burglar, as a gangster, or as a corrupt politician cannot be doubted. But from the standpoint of growth as education and education as growth the question is whether growth in this direction promotes or retards growth in general. Does this form of growth create conditions for further growth, or does it set up conditions that shut off the person who has grown in this particular direction from the occasions, stimuli, and opportunities for continuing growth in new directions?[90]

Dewey said that growth means increasing rationality in the sense of development of ability to formulate ends as well as select and arrange means for their realization.[91] Growth thus becomes a matter of discovering our possibilities and of devising methods to achieve them. Growth must give the individual "a personal interest in social relationships and control, and the habits of mind which secure social changes without introducing disorder."[92] Dewey also argued that growth is an "added power of subsequent direction or control" which makes one better able to "prepare in advance so as to secure beneficial consequences and avert undesirable ones."[93] The political significance of Dewey's position becomes evident in his claim that educational institutions must be structured so as to avoid the perpetuation of economic and cultural class differences when growth occurs. Thus, because growth has no end beyond itself, society must develop those institutions which will foster growth to a maximum degree.[94] In Dewey's writings on education there is a strong focus on growth as a desirable social end. He indicates that the child should be molded into a citizen who has the attributes of sociality, self-discipline, cooperative inquiry, and responsibility for self. The student must have an affection for others, an appreciation of scientific inquiry, and an interest in the welfare of society.[95] The real test of an educational system and of the use of leisure-time activities is whether or not they contribute to intellectual and emotional growth, to a liberal and humane outlook on affairs, and to a deeper sympathy for those who suffer.[96] Dewey's painstaking efforts to articulate an educational theory based on a proper understanding of human growth and development are evident. Contrary to Mills' belief, these are not the views of a social critic who wishes to avoid a discussion of political values and social ends.

A survey of Dewey's writings will provide substantial information on the nature of his theory of growth as well as criteria for judging it. However, in no single one of his published works does he present *all* his fundamental ideas on the subject. Since Dewey wrote approximately 42 books and between 700 and 800 articles, it is not surprising that the author of a doctoral dissertation, only part of which was on Dewey, would have been unable to master the corpus of his work. The conclusion cannot be avoided that Mills did not fully assimilate or understand Dewey's writings on growth. Like many other radical critics, he did not appreciate the degree to which Dewey articulated concrete social ends. Mills was so eager to convince his audience that Dewey was just another indecisive liberal that he neglected to mention that which weakened, or even contradicted his main criticisms.

MILLS' CRITIQUE OF DEWEY'S POLITICAL SOCIOLOGY

Much of Mills' analysis focuses on the implications of Dewey's work for political sociology, but since he did not write systematically on the subject Mills had to piece together these views from many sources. Mills' primary concern was with Dewey's alleged assumption of an already existing democratic decision system and social order. Mills ignored Dewey's view that the best organized social forces, not the most virtuous men, control public policy in general, and that these forces are dominated by economic elites. However, Mills' analysis rests on his belief that Dewey was oblivious to concentrations of corporate power. While it is true that Dewey does not focus as dramatically or as sharply on the corporate structure as he might have, it was hardly an aspect of American society that he ignored. Even before his most radical phase during the depression he wrote that:

The forms of associated action characteristic of the present economic order are so massive and extensive that they determine the most significant constituents of the public and the residence of power. Inevitably they reach out to grasp the agencies of government; they are controlling factors in legislation and administration. Not chiefly because of deliberate and planned self-interest, large as may be its role, but because they are the most potent and best organized of social forces. In a word, the new forms of combined action due to the modern economic regime control present politics, much as dynastic interests controlled those of two centuries ago. They affect thinking and desire more than did the interests which formerly moved the state.[97]

From 1920 to 1940 Dewey devoted considerable attention to the class structure of capitalism in the United States and to the ways in which it was integrated with the power matrix of the system. He was not an apologist for the inequalities of power and wealth that were characteristic of the American social order at the time. Nor was he an admirer of the moral character and social values of the upper class. As he once put it:

There is something horrible, something that makes one fear for civilization, in denunciations of class-differences and class struggles which proceed from a class in power, one that is seizing every means, even to a monopoly of moral ideals, to carry on its struggle for class power. This class adds hypocrisy to conflict and brings all idealism into disrepute. It does everything which ingenuity and prestige can do to give color to the assertions of those who say that all moral considerations are irrelevant, and that the issue is one of brute trial of forces between this side and that.[98]

However, it is evident that Dewey feared the outbreak of class warfare as a possible consequence of polarization caused by a predatory and irresponsible upper class. He believed no common moral ground and no uniform standard of appeal existed between propertied classes and wage earners.[99] Dewey hoped the method of intelligence would prevail as the means for avoiding open class warfare, but he was far from certain that such would be the case.

There is a difference of emphasis between Dewey and Mills in that Mills focuses more on exploitation while Dewey, although not ignoring it, emphasized the anachronistic aspects of control by the vested interests. For him it is a matter of cultural lag in which the upper classes fail to adjust to the potentialities of science and technology.[100] However, his use of the cultural-lag theory gives an ambivalence to

Dewey's thought that provides Mills with the opening wedge for which he was searching. No sooner does Dewey finish denouncing capitalists by saying that "industrial entrepreneurs have reaped out of all proportion to what they sowed," than he comments that "the new industrial forces tended to break down many of the rigid class barriers that had been in force, and give to millions a new outlook and inspire a new hope—especially in this country with no feudal background and no fixed class system."[101] It was Dewey's occasional vacillation between praise and indictment of capitalism and his inconsistent use of different theories for analyzing it that provided Mills with ammunition for portraying him as another vacillating liberal.

Mills argues that Dewey's experimental conception of action is not an analysis of power relevant to the politics of mass-based parties. Dewey's concept of action, when applied to social orders, was built upon an unequal distribution of power and thus aided the elite. The relationship between thought and action in Dewey is unobstructed. There are no "power" implications in the formation and pursuit of goals within Dewey's framework. Once the solution to a problematic situation is discovered, it is put into effect. However, Mills was wrong to accuse Dewey of ignoring the power facet of social existence, for as Dewey once stated:

> It is not pleasant to face the extent to which, as a matter of fact, coercive and violent force is relied upon in the present social system as a means of social control. It is much more agreeable to evade the fact. But unless the fact is acknowledged as a fact in its full depth and breadth, the meaning of dependence upon intelligence as the alternative method of social direction will not be grasped.[102]

Mills objects to Dewey's inadequate conceptualization of the nature and role of power, and to his naive endorsement of the method of intelligence as an alternative to the use of force.[103]

According to Mills, one of Dewey's ways of avoiding the problems of power was to focus upon education as a means of ameliorating social problems. This device served to mask the inequalities of power and conflict of interest, which were more characteristic of American society than the existence of community and harmony. A central theme in Mills' work is that Dewey is all "too ready to root conflict in a 'logical nature' which man is up against; he is too reluctant to admit the facts of conflict within the cultures of men."[104] Mills enlarged this assertion into the claim that because of its assumptions of harmony of interests, Dewey's model of action "serves to minimize the cleavage of power divisions *within* society, or put differently, it serves as a pervasive mode of posing the problem which locates all problems between *man and nature* instead of between men and men."[105] Passages in Dewey's work lend themselves to this interpretation, although not to the degree Mills claimed. For example, in 1939 Dewey wrote that

> . . . the technologies, which are the practical correlates of scientific theories, have now reached a point in which they can be used to create an era of abundance instead of the deficit economies that existed before natural science developed. . . . [W]ith an era of abundance and security the causes of conflict would be reduced. It may be mentioned as a hypothetical illustration [that if] the economic regime were so changed that the resources of science were employed to maintain security for all, the present view about the limitation of science might fade away.[106]

Mills believed Dewey dealt with the problems of power and force technologically by transforming these concepts from political into technical ideas. Power was energy, violence was waste, and organized force was synonomous with efficiency. Thus Dewey avoided a concrete recognition and analysis of the problem of political power and "depoliticized the vocabulary of social struggle." Mills exaggerates, for as Dewey asserted:

> Human power over the physical energies of nature has immensely increased. In moral ideal, power of man over physical nature should be employed to reduce, to eliminate progressively, the power of man over man. By what means shall we prevent its uses to effect new, more subtle, more powerful agencies of subjection of men to other men? . . . The thing still uncertain is what we are going to do with it. That it is power signifies of itself it is electrical, thermic, chemical. What will be done with it is a moral issue.[107]

Mills would be more convincing had he pointed, instead, to Dewey's failure to adequately distinguish between power as a material force affecting inert matter and power as a social phenomenon affecting mankind. Although Dewey's model often focused on conflict between man and nature, he did not ignore simultaneous struggles occurring between men and men. Mills disregarded this fact in arguing that Dewey's position had several pernicious effects. One effect was that the social sciences, under his influence, were permeated with the belief that fundamental social problems result from inability to manipulate and control nature. Mills was convinced that these problems could not be resolved because disparities of power, wealth, and status give the upper hand to the dominant class. The other effect was the widely held belief that the solution to social problems was more and better education, a prescription about which Mills remained skeptical throughout his career.

There are fundamental differences in the way that Dewey and Mills perceived the role of science and technology. In *Liberalism and Social Action* Dewey wrote "the rise of scientific method and of technology based upon it is the genuinely active force in producing the vast complex of changes the world is now undergoing, not the class struggle whose spirit and method are opposed to science."[108] Mills viewed Dewey's interpretation of the role of science and technology as incorrect because it was based on untenable assumptions of a natural harmony of interest. Technology was not an instrument by which the whole society adjusted to new conditions. On the contrary, its prime function was to serve the interests of big business.

> Technological power is then socially neutral and those who would celebrate it must face the question: Power for what? Dewey has celebrated "man's" growth of power through science and technology; he has not clearly answered the question involved in that celebration. To do so would have committed him to face squarely the political and legal problem of the present distribution of power as it exists within this social order. And this Dewey has never done. . . . Just how this technology is to be taken from those pecuniary individuals who now monopolize it, we are not told.[109]

Again Mills has overstated the case. As has been shown, Dewey's ideas about how to deal with corporate power and its misuse of technology, at least during the 1930s, were not unlike those of other radicals including Mills. It is ironic that his structural criticisms of Dewey were similar to those later made of Mills himself by his Marxist critics.[110]

Conclusion

Mills once wrote of Clarence Ayres that one of Ayres' points about Dewey was "too reminiscent, too localized; it represents a phase of thought . . . and could not hold of the entire career and periods through which Dewey has moved."[111] Although Mills did not intend it as such, this was an apt summary of Mills' own work on Dewey. He should have paid closer attention to his criticism of Ayres as it applied to Dewey and to the advice he once received from James H. Tufts, Dewey's old friend and collaborator, who told Mills that

One general remark, growing out of my long friendship and discussions with Dewey is this. Many criticisms of his supposed views have been based on passages in his writings taken as though they represented his whole thought on the topic. That has not infrequently resulted in distorted or one-sided conceptions. It is not his habit to guard very meticulously all his statements. When he wishes to make a point he often does not take pains to note all possible qualifications or exceptions. He drives at the central idea. And then, perhaps at another time and in another connection brings out other aspects.[112]

Although Mills' work on Dewey represents a significant intellectual achievement for a scholar in his mid-twenties, it contains several deficiencies not yet given adequate treatment that mar it. First is his tendency to ignore the evolution of Dewey's thought by disregarding the stages of his intellectual development. Mills wrote as though Dewey composed the entire corpus of his writings in a short period of time, and as though any single publication was necessarily characteristic of all the rest. Mills' compression of Dewey's writings into a short time frame caused serious distortions to appear when he generalized about the bulk of it. Second, Mills often criticized Dewey from a sociological perspective without recognizing that philosophers do not ordinarily adopt a structural view of the sort that is commonplace among political sociologists. When Mills accuses Dewey of lacking an adequate understanding of social structure he is correct, but why should he have expected otherwise from a professional philosopher? In summation, my criticisms are that Mills ignored the evolution of Dewey's thought over time, that he worked too hurriedly and read too selectively, and that he unjustifiably expected Dewey to have a sociological perspective. Nevertheless, despite the shortcomings of Mills' analysis it is one of the most original commentaries ever written by an American radical. But it shows this merit primarily if it is viewed as a penetrating assault on the unexamined assumptions and deficiencies of liberalism rather than as an adequate analysis of Dewey.

Still we must ask, how convincing is Mills' criticism of Dewey? The answer to this question is value-laden and lies as much in the realm of political philosophy as in that of scholarly method. The art of textual exegesis and the insights of political biography are relevant, but no more so than the scholar's ideological reaction to Mills' and Dewey's political values. Mills understood his analysis of Dewey to be a dialogue between radical and liberal, with all the implications this has for political confrontation between opposing camps. However, Mills underestimated Dewey's commitment after World War I to organizations oriented toward structural change, including several with a strong political focus.[113] In fact, he and Dewey were closer in political and intellectual orientation than Mills admits, for their common interests and values are more striking than their differences. Both share a desire for an egalitarian and participatory society that has much in common with the ideals of guild socialism. As political activists they spent much of their careers outside the framework of the two-party system as leftist independents, although Mills was much less a joiner than Dewey.

The "liberalism" of Dewey was at times quite radical in its programs and implications and, therefore, different in substance and spirit from the dominant ideology of interest-group or pragmatic liberalism. But it is also evident that Dewey's political thought had some of the deficiencies that are intrinsic to American liberalism. In this regard Mills' criticism of Dewey serves as a valuable antidote and corrective. However, though Mills was often wide of the mark in attacking Dewey's liberalism, his evaluation is not irrelevant to the larger analysis of American liberalism. His interpretation is not an adequate view of Dewey as a political thinker, but it is a compelling criticism of present-day liberal doctrine and practice. The flaws Mills attributed to Dewey are much more prevalent among the contemporary proponents and practitioners of interest-group liberalism. Specifically, they include a strong tendency to reduce problems of issues to problems of method and to take as problems of method those social ills that are rooted in the class structure and power matrix of American capitalism. Evident, too, is a refusal to consider the possibility that "lack of awareness of objective self-interest," as Mills put it, is fostered by a cultural apparatus dominated by powerful elements that benefit from disseminating the folklore of political and intellectual pluralism. Contemporary liberalism often sanctions an evasion of the problems of corporate power and upper-class wealth in a way that Dewey never did during the 1930s. As an academic stance of which Mills was critical, it endorses morally dubious efforts to separate humanistic values from social-science inquiry in ways contrary to instrumentalist doctrine. As a political posture it often ignores the failures of the welfare and regulatory mechanism and promises more of the same on an incremental basis. In short, the same tendencies Mills caricatured in Dewey are, instead, part of liberal thought and practice.

9

Native Doctrine and Indigenous Insurgency in Mills, Veblen, and Dewey

While excellent biographies of Thorstein Veblen and John Dewey are available,[1] no really clear picture of C. Wright Mills as a person has yet emerged. At times he appeared both noble and petty, naive but sarcastic, idealistic yet sometimes self-pitying. Although Mills rightly and courageously criticized American political intellectuals for surrendering to the temptations of the marketplace or to an inflated urge for professional respectability, he, himself, was not immune to egocentricity. Mills could be self-righteous and dogmatic when involved in academic or political infighting and these personal qualities inflamed existing ideological debates. Even without this exacerbation, however, the fundamental doctrinal differences he had with liberals would have remained. It would be an error to assume that all that separated Mills from his liberal critics was his sometimes abrasive personality.

Nothing was more important to Mills than his own views of right and wrong; he was forever trying to remake the world according to his own lofty ideals; Dewey and Veblen were also committed to radical reconstruction, but they acted in a less bellicose manner. Yet like these predecessors, Mills remained a supreme individualist, holding fast to his own private conceptions of morality, for his philosophy was one of individual struggle rather than social acquiescence or withdrawal. Mills may not have believed in the illusion that one can conquer time or escape from history, but his strenuous assault on the status quo gave that impression.[2]

Mills' respect for Veblen both as a man and a scholar was epitomized in his admiration for the solitary individual who revels in his opposition to major institutions and to the conventional wisdom. To Mills, Veblen was an intellectual "wobbly," one of those "masterless men" who refused to acknowledge the moral legitimacy of existing authority. Contemporary radical sociologists may think of Mills as the originator of a radical "new sociology" but before him was Veblen, whose career and work suggest important parallels with Mills. Both men were trained in philosophy at the same time that they were educated in the social sciences. Mills' criticism of "grand theory" and "abstracted empiricism" echoed Veblen's attack on the formalism of neoclassical economics, and both of the critiques paralleled Dewey's assault on formalism in philosophy. Both developed a form of evolutionary institutional analysis as the key to understanding social processes. Their language and writing styles were similar owing in part to the fact that Mills adopted such Veblenisms as "conspicuous consumption" and the "main drift" of society. Both became sardonic and eminent social critics who wrote about similar topics for audiences larger than the academic community. Finally, a certain heroic mythology has developed around the personalities and intellectual contributions of both men, who by their examples have influenced social scientists on the left.[3]

Although Mills had a grudging admiration for Dewey's idealism and his intense involvement in political organizations, it would be hard to imagine two men of more different temperament and personality. Mills' swashbuckling and bellicose behavior contrasted sharply with Dewey's taciturn and shy demeanor. But aside from these personal differences much of Mills' criticism of Dewey's work seems misplaced because Mills' real target was the American liberalism of the 1940s and 50s, not Dewey's radical liberalism of the period after World War I. All too often Mills aimed his penetrating shafts at a target he thought was Dewey, but instead hit some liberal Cold Warrior. In spite of what he thought were major politico-ideological differences with Dewey, their works showed marked intellectual parallels, for Mills had assimilated more of the instrumentalist philosophy than he imagined. Mills and Dewey were more sympathetic toward volitional individualism than Veblen, who in his more pessimistic moments felt individuals could exercise little control over the future. Mills' and Dewey's liberalism was evident in their insistence on the role of human intelligence in transforming institutions, their regard for individual freedom and self-expression, and their emphasis on the need for action in problematic situations. Mills and Dewey diverge from Veblen in their overt commitment to these aspects of liberal thought. Mills' convictions that will power and commitment do matter, and his willingness to test all programs and theories in the laboratory of social experience made him a loyal, if ambivalent, disciple of John Dewey long after he ceased to study Dewey's work or consider himself a pragmatist.

BETWEEN AND BETWIXT THE
NEW LEFT AND LIBERALISM

The New Left's inability to develop a new radical theory that would both incorporate and go beyond liberalism left it sadly deficient, for a sustained theoretical overview was needed and it was not forthcoming. That none developed partly explains the New Left's abysmal collapse. It also helps explain why nearly ten years of militancy and social disorder has left virtually no institutions controlled by radicals, no nationally prominent radical leaders, no functional mass-based radical party, and no established doctrines by which to measure and maintain one's own radicalism. Although Mills' *The Power Elite* was known to the New Left, its members' acquaintanceship with Veblen and Dewey was very slight. Consequently, their lack of familiarity with a substantial part of the American radical intellectual tradition has contributed to the movement's theoretical and programmatic deficiencies. But liberals who were older and had more time to absorb the radical legacy have also fared badly in recent years even though they have strong ties with a mass-based Democratic Party.

Mills and Veblen in particular never confused the liberal desire to ameliorate social relationships within a system of organized social inequality with the truly radical desire to abolish social inequality. Indeed, as Dewey finally recognized in his later years, liberalism all too often was satisfied to rationalize social relationships within a system of structured social inequality and consequently was incapable of dealing effectively with egalitarian concerns. In fact, much of what passed for liberalism was incapable of utopian criticism in that it could not envision a society appreciably different from what now exists. For that reason our three central figures all believed that American liberals had betrayed important parts of the liberal heritage. Today, when any attempt at all is made to distinguish varieties of liberalism, it is usually done on the basis of classical or laissez-faire versus modern or welfare liberalism.[4] While many contemporary liberals accept this distinction, Mills and Veblen, to their credit, rejected many of the basic premises of the liberal creed because they were not consistent with the findings of modern social science nor normatively adequate. Dewey's own belief in the inadequacies of liberalism in his time was well summarized in his claim that "the gulf between the future and the actual state itself is so great that it cannot be bridged by piecemeal policies undertaken ad hoc."[5]

According to C. B. Macpherson, perhaps the most eminent contemporary socialist theoretician in the English-speaking world, the concept of individualism is the basis of all liberal social theory. The appetitive, competitive, egoistic, self-seeking individual is assumed to be the human norm, as in the writings of Hobbes, Locke, and Bentham. In their attacks on classical liberalism Mills, Veblen, and Dewey argued that political order based upon self-interest could not sustain any relevant sense of community. Nor did they believe that utility maximization could ever be an adequate measure of community. They shared the belief that American intellectual life was largely privatized, competitive, and careerist and that alienation was widespread among academics, whose sophistry and opportunism were the order of the day. Our three central figures believed that the intellectual should be able to practice good craftsmanship, which meant that he should also be capable of discriminating between social values. Thus they attacked the moral agnosticism that is so characteristic of modern secular liberalism. In their view liberals too often assumed that people should remain indecisive about what sort of life was best so the liberals could be left alone to pursue their own life style. This also explained why liberals feared the consequences of an expanded connection between morality and politics. Like the contemporary political philosopher John Schaar and without being elitist, Mills, Dewey, and Veblen rejected the "squalid promiscuity that says anything goes and all desires are equal."[6] Appetitive individualism, avaricious transactionalism, and the social disorders associated with these pathologies could not be legitimized by uncritically sanctioning the expression of subjective preferences in the free market place of goods and ideas and thus equating price with value and value with subjective preference.

Our three central figures were aware that liberalism was a class ideology in that it once served as a legitimizing device for the interests of a particular class and still functioned in part to protect those interests. Veblen saw little of permanent value in liberalism; to him it was largely a transient phenomenon that was rapidly becoming obsolete. To Mills and Dewey, liberalism represented an historically transcendent set of values useful or even essential to the good life. They understood that while liberalism had a class bias its formulation had provided standards that could benefit all of society. Mills and Dewey, especially the former, could be savagely critical of contemporary liberalism, but, unlike Veblen, they never claimed that it was devoid of value for society.

PRAXIS

Mills, Dewey, and Veblen all believed that political intellectuals had their own distinctive place, which was an important one. In their judgment the intellectual's special job was to be the caretaker of ultimate values, so that he could represent the cultural and political conscience of the larger society. All three agreed that a man of thought could also be a man of action even if they disagreed as to how this action was to be accomplished. Taken together, their ideas suggest an important recognition of the necessity for transforming political and cultural criticism into an effective social theory.[7]

Although the differences between the three probably reflect personal temperament and historical circumstance as well as political divergence, they all searched for a group or class capable of leading a major social reconstruction. Although none of them ultimately found what he was looking for, it is instructive to observe the way their ideas evolved over time. Mills abandoned his early faith in the working class for a belief in the responsibility of political intellectuals to act as agents of social change. His later writings also give evidence of a growing faith in racial minorities, activist students, and foreign revolutionaries. Veblen, too, searched for a group capable of leading a radical reconstruction. At first, he entrusted the future to manual workers under the influence of the machine process. When revolution failed to materialize with the proletariat acting as catalyst, he began to focus on the change potential of the engineers and technicians, although his tongue-in-cheek endorsement of their radical potential belies the claim that Veblen was a technocratic elitist. Dewey, and probably Mead, preferred a multiclass coalition of men of good will supported by informed and coherent publics combined with technical experts to serve as the primary agents of social change. Since Dewey set his sights a bit lower than Mills and Veblen, his search for a leadership group, while ultimately not successful, was less futile.

Mills shared Dewey's belief that men must engage in those forms of social praxis that enable each individual to be an actor rather than a spectator, a willing participant rather than a creature of external control. It is thus easy to recognize pragmatic themes in Mills' own work. Consider, for example, his claim that it is the task of the sociological imagination to translate personal troubles into public issues. But Mills' often unwitting support for Dewey's attempt to unite theory and practice also illustrated his disagreement with instrumentalism. Mills complained that Dewey did not adequately comprehend how the particular structure of a society distributes power. Whenever opposing groups confront each other because of the structural antagonisms of society what "we get from Dewey is not a choice in support of one or the other."[8] Instead, Mills argues, we get "the plea that when social science develops like physical science, we can solve or obviate such problems."[9] It is also clear that Mills has Dewey in mind when he complains that "liberal practicality" tends either to be "apolitical" or to explain conflicts in terms of such pathological features as the "antisocial" or "corruption." In short, Dewey's political analysis is not radical enough because instrumentalist concepts of method, intelligence, and "problematization" prevent a more adequate realization of the political problem. Mills' attacks on pragmatic social thought both for its disregard of power and social class and its loss of critical perspective may seem perverse when directed at the later Dewey, yet these attacks remain a potent indictment of contemporary liberalism.

Mills' stance on the praxis issue was intermediate between the organizational hyperactivism of Dewey and the social detachment of Veblen. Although Mills did not eschew involvement in political movements to the degree Veblen did, he preferred to speak primarily through his written work. But speaking through his books always meant going to the root of the problem like Veblen rather than avoiding it as he alleged Dewey did. The amount of organizational activism in which the individual engaged was less important to Mills than that the political intellectual be consistently radical in his work. It is interesting to note that Mills was highly critical of Dewey for his inadequate understanding of praxis, but had little criticism of Veblen in this respect despite Veblen's aloofness from political organizations of any sort.

COMMUNITY

Neither Dewey nor Mills shared Veblen's enthusiasm for primitive communal orders, as in his admiring description of those peaceable "savage" communities characterized by "a certain amiable inefficiency when confronted with force or fraud."[10] Nevertheless, they prized human solidarity and believed it could not exist without a high degree of equality of condition. All three men, and especially Mills and Dewey, well recognized that the intellectual origins of the American radical tradition were rooted in efforts to make a way of life at once both free and communal. None of the three saw genuine community as a threat to freedom.

Mills' *The Power Elite* and Dewey's *The Public and Its Problems* both contain utopian arguments for a society committed to participation and to rejuvenated community. Both felt that the moral and political discipline of local publics was essential, but possible only if there were greater citizen participation. Otherwise, society could not avoid becoming a creature of the vested interests. Veblen was markedly more pessimistic on this score than either Mills or Dewey and he vacillated between abandoning society to "blind drift" (because human intelligence could not overcome structural rigidities) and advocating wholesale assault on absentee ownership (since only its destruction could restore communal solidarity).

Running throughout the work of all three is the vision of a utopian decentralized communal society not unlike that found in much contemporary New Left thought.[11] Veblen often articulated this vision in his praise of the old Scandinavian "small-scale, half-anarchistic, neighborhood plan of society," "a conventionally systematized anarchy regulated by common sense" in which justice meant a readiness "to live and let live" and "no public authority and no legally concerted action ordinarily is called in to redress grievances."[12] These little utopias had been destroyed by technological advance, but ever since men

> passed the technological limit of tolerance of that archaic scheme of use and wont they have been restlessly casting back for some workable compromise that would permit their ideal of "local self-government" by neighborly common sense to live somehow in the shadow of the large-scale coercive rule that killed it.[13]

The idea of community has exercised a considerable fascination for the radical mind, perhaps because genuine community is regarded by radicals as the ultimate repository of moral values. The development of a large number of common values requires free sharing and this the division into a privileged and a disadvantaged class makes impossible. Consequently, in order for it to be genuine, the community must be cleansed of class and racial distinctions, invidious status comparisons, and emulatory consumption patterns. Veblen's "vested interests" and "leisure class," Mills' "power elite," and Dewey's "privileged classes" all have a common significance; for in radical eyes it is only through the abolition of social inequalities that real community can develop.

Our three central figures also believed that community requires not only more numerous and varied points of shared common interest, but in addition a greater recognition of mutual interests in solving problems related to social control. This combination means open interaction between social groups and such interaction clearly requires a free interchange of opinion and information. The interchange in turn implies a medium of communication free from the taint and control of the vested interests, for community cannot be achieved without eradicating the blockages that prevent unhindered and undistorted exchanges of communication. This need for a free medium requires removal of the bias of commercial elites from the news media to permit a more disinterested exchange of information and to encourage an environment in which a genuinely critical exchange of ideas might occur.

The chronic political impotence of the American left has been attributed to the willingness of liberals to accommodate reform programs, government repression, and the alleged prevalence of occupational mobility. In addition, there can be no denying the relevance of ideological and cultural factors whether or not one is a devotee of Gramsci and his doctrine of ideological hegemony. Indeed, Mills, Veblen, and Dewey focused much of their analysis on the cultural, moral, and intellectual aspects of capitalist hegemony in the United States. They were not so naive as to think that basic changes in the system of power and property relations could be achieved without massive changes in the way that Americans perceived themselves and their social environment. Indeed, it is questionable that Veblen in his later years thought it possible to ever eradicate the vestiges of capitalist hegemony. Mills, too, believed that "lack of awareness of objective self-interest" or "false consciousness" was prevalent in the middle and lower classes. Neither Mills nor Dewey nor Veblen ever went so far as Lenin, in the direction of intellectual elitism, but they believed that the American public was susceptible to hoodwinking, brainwashing, and manipulation and thus was conditioned to systematically misperceive its own self-interest.

The problem of media control raises the question concerning which values are ultimately to be embedded in the moral repository of the community. All three men have a decided preference for community values that are secular, scientific, and altruistic. Such values make obligatory the diffusion of social intelligence and the dissemination of egalitarian values. To these must be added the values of competence and efficiency in the performance of one's work. However, these are not meant in the crude technocratic sense, which implies approval of efficiency for its own sake without regard for the social ends or purposes it serves. For all three men it is important that work be done well, but it is even more important that the work be socially beneficial. To illustrate further, Dewey maintained that no cooperative enterprise can be sustained without some basic understanding on the part of the individual of the meaning of the total activity in which he is engaged. Dewey pointed out that work would become a mere mechanical routine unless workers saw the technical, intellectual, and social relationships involved in what they did, and engaged in their work because of the motivations provided by such understanding.

It is important to recognize the intimate relationship that exists between their views of community and Veblen's instinct of workmanship, Dewey's notions of ethicized work, Mills' ideas regarding general craftsmanship, and Mead's philosophy of the act.[14] In earlier chapters the common emphasis in Veblen, Dewey, and Mills on the aesthetic qualities of work has been stressed. The values they share in this regard are evident although they have never been explored before in any detail. It is apparent, however, tht they share these similarities not only with each other but also with Mead. The connection is most obvious in his *The Philosophy of the Act*, where he explains the relationship between impulse, perception, manipulation, and consummation. To paraphrase Mead, the need to satisfy impulses leads to the stage of perception, where the individual calculates which objects are to be singled out as possible sources of satisfaction. The stage of manipulation follows, in which objects are identified as real, not imagined, and are shown to be manipulable. The final phase of the act in Mead's treatment is that of consummation. For example, the food that has been prepared is eaten or the courting partner coupled. In summation, the manipulatory stage of the act is the world of means while the consummatory stage is the world of ends. These ends or consummations, of course, have their value in their relation to the impulses that are the initial stage of the act. Consummations are satisfactions or dissatisfactions of the original impulses and have little value apart from those impulses.

Mills, following Mead's lead, believed that if the three parts of the act—perception, manipulation, and consummation—are too far separated from each other, the worker will suffer boredom and retreat into revery. Instead of finding work a source of gratification, the worker will seek escape. Thus Mills and Mead emphasize enriching the work environment through structural changes in the nature and organization of the work process, for one of the primary foundations of community must be a more satisfactory system of social relations in the workplace. In this sense Mills' "craftsmanship," Veblen's "workmanship," Dewey's "ethicized work," and Mead's philosophy of the act may be secular forms of redemption for mankind, but they can be experienced only in direct proportion to the actualization of community.

THE INDIVIDUAL AND SOCIETY

Veblen was a methodological collectivist who was far less interested in individual behavior than in understanding group processes, group problems, and group phenomena. Dewey and Mills, too, in functioning as social analysts, were methodological collectivists but differed from Veblen in that they emphasized the manner in which individualism was fostered by the social environment. Even though they begin their analysis from an institutional or group perspective, they do not submerge the individual into the social order to the degree Veblen does. For example, Dewey was not unaware of the emulatory, status-oriented nature of much consumption but, unlike Veblen, he thought that consumer behavior was in part an expression of genuinely different tastes and preferences that ought to be respected. Veblen was more concerned with the adoption of aims and purposes that were intially oriented toward community serviceability than Dewey and Mills, both of whom hoped that individual goals could be brought in line with socially desirable ends so as to achieve harmony without undue sacrifice on the part of the individual.

Individualism, too, may refer to the social and economic context of behavior, such as the ability of individuals to act alone in their own interests in free markets that permit and reward such activity. Again, while Dewey had serious doubts about the effectiveness of such behavior in raising the general standard of living, Veblen went further in his belief that economic individualism of this kind is usually predatory and exploitative.

Individualism can also refer to a social theory in which the members of society conceive the social pivot of change to be individual rather than group action and where the significant context of behavior is believed to be the individual acting alone, rather than in a group.[15] None of the three men were given to such individualism as a whole, but occasionally this idea creeps into Dewey's work, especially before 1900, whereas Veblen's work is devoid of such "Robinson Crusoe" notions.

In a closely related view, "individualism" is related to the qualities of an independent, self-reliant personality type. The ability of people to develop themselves as unique personalities is likewise called "individualism." Again, all three of the men we are contemplating valued such qualities in their fellow men as manifest in Veblen's praise of "masterless men," but they doubted the capacity of existing social structures to produce many such specimens. Veblen was particularly pessimistic in this regard, while Dewey hoped through reform to create a new social environment in which such personality traits would become more abundant. In this same vein Mills and Dewey shared a preference for political intellectuals who engaged in praxis because of individual commitment although they did not believe this required the individual's total submergence in the organization.

The question as to what extent the individual is a product of the social environment is one that divided Veblen from Mills and Dewey and from Mead, also. Veblen provides insight into man as a social phenomenon, but tells little about man as a unique personality. Veblen emphasized the social nature of man because he believed that most individuals cannot rise above their environment because individuality develops in a social context and remains subordinate to it. He gave significantly less emphasis than Mills and Dewey to the self-conscious, self-reflective, autonomous self although he neither believed in the total plasticity of behavior patterns nor completely obliterated the role of individual volition. As Charles Chandler put it:

> Dewey stresses the free, rational, autonomous individual in much of his work. If such a conception sometimes downplays the claims of the cultural environment, Veblen's philosophy goes to the opposite extreme for he makes society the primary datum. The individual as such has no substantial reality. The society is ultimately real, whereas the individual is an abstraction from this reality.[16]

Veblen's position rests upon the assumption that within biological limits, man's personality, individuality, and selfhood are social phenomena. Man has no being apart from his social interactions. In the early twentieth century this view was a necessary corrective against nineteenth-century atomistic conceptions of man which portrayed him as an isolated, self-sufficient individual upon whom the social environment had little impact.[17] However, Dewey and Mills argued that while selfhood does originate in a social context, this does not imply that selfhood cannot transcend its social origin. The community is a necessary condition for selfhood, but it does not completely mold and determine the character of selfhood. For Veblen, however, the self is derivative, mediated and reflected from within the society in which it is formed. The autonomous, differentiated, self-starting—in short the "unique"—individual—is conspicuous by his absence from the Veblenian social order.

Of course, Mills and Dewey neither advocated rugged individualism nor did they uncritically admire collectivism, for they were as much committed to fostering the virtues of individual autonomy as they were to analyzing the social determinants of human behavior. In the final analysis their ideal of community was significant, since it left individuals free to realize their inner desires and aspirations. For Dewey, in particular, collectivism was just a new label for the American dream, which for him was synonomous with individual fulfillment.[18] Dewey, Mills, and Veblen were all "collectivists" in the sense that they wished to transcend atomistic individualism. They recognized that society had become corporate and interdependent although its mind set remained individualistic. All shared a belief that men were inherently social beings, and insisted that the genuine needs of the community took priority over those of the individual. Where they differed was over the degree to which the individual was submerged in the community and was thus a by-product of the larger social order.

Mead's notions about individualism are more subtle, elaborate and convincing than those of the other three for social psychology was his forte. Essentially, he believed that individualism is socially induced so that any attempt to set the individual off from society is likely to result in a false dualism. In complex industrial settings like our own what we call "individualism" is the result of a person's developing an objectivity and detachment from observing the performance of many different social roles. This social process gradually conditions the individual to be able to "take" the roles of significant others but simultaneously enables them to remain aloof from them. Mead's characteristic "individual" is not submerged into the community to the vanishing point *à la* Veblen but their unique traits are nevertheless socially induced. To Mead "individualism" is not a figment of the imagination; it is a result of the broader social environment.[19]

Indeed, much of the interesting social thought in the decade between Dewey's passing in 1952 and Mills' death ten years later focused on the decay of individual autonomy and rationality. Mills often echoed Dewey's lament for the fate of individual moral values and rationality in a bureaucratized social structure, where the individual lacked any broad understanding of the social order in which he lived and where independence represented only a choice among already structured alternatives. Together, Mills and Dewey offered a critique of major institutions from the point of view of their consequences for individual lives, while suggesting that early nineteenth-century ideals of individualism were now irrelevant.

The American Radical Tradition

In the work of the three men there is a common moral tone, an important distinction between instrumental and noninstrumental knowledge,[20] and a broad ethical conception of the role of the political intellectual. It is in this sense that their doctrines bear unmistakable traces of an older American ideology. It is now evident that Mills was the most important single link between the radical tradition to which Veblen and Dewey belonged and the New Left when it emerged in the 1960s. The fact that the new generation of political activists which articulated his ideas did not understand the roots of Mills' thought is all the more reason for linking him to the past through a systematic delineation of the American radical tradition. The radicalism of the 1960s renewed concern for the American past by helping to produce a stream of studies analyzing and dissecting the roots of the American New Left. It is now evident that the cultural revolution of the 1960s sometimes served as an opiate that weakened the wills and softened the heads of its practitioners. Had Mills lived to observe it, it is doubtful if he would have mistaken its more bizarre traits and eccentric characters for a bona fide radicalism. Politics for him was too serious a matter to culminate in the idiosyncrasies of beats, hippies, and later yippies. And yet he could not have ignored its earnest moralism, its concern with inequalities of power and wealth, and its personal commitment to change. Nevertheless, had he lived, Mills likely would have been more impressed by the civil rights and peace movements than by the counterculture, for in the former he could find the fulfillment of cherished values with their roots far in the American past.

David De Leon has recently argued that the only genuine native radicalism has been "anarchism."[21] Certainly American radicalism has often taken the form of opposition to authority and to existing institutions, but De Leon exaggerated in confining radicalism to the anarchist camp. He was closer to the truth when he stated that American radicalism has been theoretically immature because it rested on unacknowledged premises that have never been articulated as a conscious social philosophy. As he puts it, "At times this allowed a powerful immediacy, but more often it prevents radicalism from perceiving its place within this culture, critically reappropriating from our heritage a clear and native identity."[22] De Leon's thesis is perhaps valid until the twentieth century when, with the instrumentalism of Dewey and the institutionalism of Veblen, one can witness theoretically self-conscious efforts to articulate a new position. Mills was thus able to develop a new radical theory of the American national power system by initially rooting his ideas in an indigenous critical tradition. He recognized that imported religious, political, economic, and social ideas had been successfully grafted onto our inherited radicalism, but he was also aware that the more exotic transplants like doctrinaire Marxism had withered or died in an alien environment. Indeed, the widespread impression of Mills as European in theoretical origin and focus

greatly overestimates the alien character of Mills' analysis. Despite his
fondness for certain non-American theorists, Mills often shows the pro-
vincial's home-grown distrust of European exotica. Time and again *The
Power Elite* reveals the author's aversion to European metaphysics.[23]

A common portrait of men like Mills and Dewey suggests that they
were overoptimistic concerning man and history because they were
wedded to the idea of progress. It also claims that they were ineffec-
tive in the analysis of politics. Naturally, these are typical criticisms of
leftist political intellectuals made by ideologues of the center, who
praise a politics of limited objectives and compromise. But the two
men knew that in the end a radical politics must respond to ethical
claims or else lose its sense of direction through obsession with narrow
strategies. Those who let strategic matters overwhelm ethical claims
and vision will lose sight of ultimate goals. On that score Mills and the
radical tradition to which he belonged stand up better than the interest-group pluralist tradition that has dominated the center of the
American political spectrum since 1933. To illustrate: Mills, like
Dewey before him, attacked the insufficiency of piecemeal ad hoc
policies that were devoid of systematic plan and direction. After all, it
was not Mills who acquiesced in mindless support of the Vietnamese
adventure or of the Cold War policies that led up to it. Nor was it he
who endorsed the growth of a military-industrial complex with its
exacerbation of international tensions and its enormous waste on military expenditures. It was not the author of *The Power Elite* who
ignored the waste caused by the emulatory consumption patterns so
effectively diagnosed by Veblen long ago. Nor can Mills be charged
with acquiescing in or sanctifying the existing distribution of income
and wealth, unlike the now emerging neoconservative movement that
includes so many of his former critics.[24]

Mills was certainly aware of the historical failure of an indigenous
radical movement to take permanent and substantial root in the
United States; yet this did not cause him to become estranged from the
core values of the radical tradition itself. Part of Mills' problem
stemmed from the fact that the American radical tradition he worked
within was not easy to identify. As David Marcell put it in a broader
context:

> there is considerable question as to the real influence early American
> thinkers had on late nineteenth and early twentieth-century thought;
> such implied continuity seems to meet organizational requirements of
> historians of thought more than it does to explain the development of
> philosophy.[25]

In view of the questionable degree of ideational continuity that exists between different periods of American intellectual history, perhaps the most that can be said about the radical tradition by way of generalization is that it has been (1) highly volitional in stressing the capacity of the individual will for promoting social reconstruction, (2) egalitarian in demanding the eradication of classes and of ethnic and racial barriers, (3) antiauthoritarian in attacking concentrations of private power, (4) antistatist in believing the existing government is under the control of the vested interests, (5) participationist in believing that individual involvement in the decision-making process is not just instrumental to other ends but a cherished value in and of itself, (6) communitarian in stressing the values of harmony and human solidarity without sacrificing the individual on the altar of false collectivism, (7) committed to the idea of progress in at least one of its forms,[26] (8) intellectually eclectic in seeking to absorb valuable insights from other perspectives and combine them into a new synthesis.

These characteristics of the American radical tradition distinguish it from both liberalism and Marxism and that give it a flavor of its own. That such values and doctrine were often present in the thought of American radicals is undeniable. But on account of the theoretical ambiguity and poorly congealed nature of this tradition a thinker such as Mills, despite his bravado, was sometimes uncertain of his bearing as well as his mooring. It was the difficulty of defining a legacy that incorporated Paine and Jefferson, Thoreau and Whitman, Lloyd and Bellamy, Dewey and Veblen, Haywood, Debs, and Thomas that is partly responsible for the unfinished ad hoc nature of much of Mills' work. Perhaps this is why characterizing the native radical heritage and showing how Mills fits into it is a tentative, improvisatory enterprise at best.

In Mills' view the American radical should not blithely ignore centuries of experience, for effective social criticism must be anchored in its own environment. Although there certainly were similar themes, traits, and values common to the American radical tradition, Mills' task was made more difficult by its vagueness. Indeed, the unfinished nature of his own work reflects the ambiguity and theoretical immaturity of the radical heritage bequeathed him. Mills was thoroughly self-conscious concerning the nature of his relationship with Veblen and Dewey, but he was far less so about the intellectual lineage of the rest of the American left. That it was no simple task to coagulate and use the divergent strands of the native radical tradition was evident in Mills' strenuously eclectic efforts to understand how its varied elements could be best reappropriated into a convincing new form. His task was made even more difficult because he also wished to draw upon the classical tradition in European social thought. It is evident, however, that Mills, Veblen and Dewey did not share Leslie Fiedler's belief that America's choice is always between living in a theoretical nontradition made for us by Europe, or in a synthetic European tradition of our fabrication. Rather, they looked for a doctrinal orientation that was specifically attuned to the American experience yet still linked with general European trends.

It may seem to the reader that this book unduly belabors the point that Mills was not a Marxist in any orthodox or traditional way. However, it is important to realize that the native American brand of radicalism to which we constantly refer is itself not basically Marxist. Since we are trying to place Mills within this tradition, we must recognize the limited role of Marxism both in it and in Mills' relationship to Marxism. Mills was aware that European-oriented radicals often were oblivious to the quality and diversity of American life in their dogmatic support for foreign doctrine at the expense of understanding their own history and culture. But, unlike many Marxists, Mills could never overcome his ambivalence toward the American liberal rejection of rigid social philosophies and fixed programs and liberal sympathy for the pluralistic and pragmatic. Yet, despite this ambivalence, Mills remained critical of liberalism because its criticism of American institutions lacked the kind of sustained economic analysis essential for understanding the system as a whole. As his more perceptive critics well understood, he was a radical liberal, not simply a radical *or* a liberal. Mills found the essence of American radicalism not in Stalin but in Norman Thomas and Thorstein Veblen, not in Russian or Chinese peasants but in the American farm laborers of the I.W.W., not in codified Marxism-Leninism but in eclectic radical thought. Yet Mills' intellectual outlook was complex, for he was clearly influenced by Marxism-Leninism and by foreign revolutionary movements. In fact, his later theoretical work represents a tentative groping toward a synthesis of both foreign and domestic radical traditions.

The Radical Attack on the Liberal Acquiescence

Partly because of Mills' influence on them in the 1960s and early 1970s, intellectuals displayed a growing sensitivity to inequalities of power and wealth, an easier acceptance of conflict as a positive force in politics, and a greater openness to radical doctrine. At the base of these changes was New Left disillusionment with the intellectual and cultural conformity so widespread among those who indulged in what

Mills called the "liberal acquiescence." Like Veblen earlier, Mills believed that liberal intellectuals were guilty of disseminating popular slogans and images that gave Americans a false sense of unity and common purpose. To Mills, this dependence on symbolic manipulation as a substitute for critical thought contributed to the ultimate failure of reform in the Cold War era. Mills' attack on the liberal acquiescence was thus based on his belief in the theoretical and programmatic poverty of liberalism. But it was difficult at times to tell whether, like Dewey, he simply wanted a more radical liberalism, or whether he wanted to abandon liberalism altogether on account of its irrelevance. His last pronouncements favor the latter interpretation but the rest of his life and work support the former. But Mills was angry because many former insurgents, finding change harder to achieve than they expected, had greatly lowered their expectations and were acquiescing in, if not positively accommodating themselves to the main drift. They had abandoned long-range, broad-scale programs of social reconstruction and often would not even exert themselves to influence immediate social priorities. Mills was appalled by the tendency of liberals to surrender their critical faculties and their imaginative zeal at precisely the moment when these were most urgently needed.

The past failure of the radical parties to develop realistic and concrete programs for the United States and the liberal's refusal even to think in ideological or broadly conceptual terms made structural change difficult to achieve. If Marxists sounded too exotic and doctrinaire to Mills, the liberals seemed too opportunistic and restrained in their analysis. Throughout his career Mills attacked liberals for their unwillingness to pursue a problem to its ultimate roots, for their fragmented view of society that focused on its discrete parts at the expense of the whole, and for a naive trust in education and social ameliorism. The radical Texan believed that liberals ignored the virtues of class struggle, were unable to see that the power elite was irresponsible and predatory, and failed to appreciate the extent to which capitalism had imprisoned the human intellect. Of course, a typical liberal response was to charge Mills with being attracted to either-or propositions and yes-or-no answers and with being unable to live with the ambiguity, paradox, and contradiction which is a normal part of the human condition. In buttressing these accusations Daniel Bell added his own list of Mills' sins, which included giving "equal weight to both sound and spurious evidence," "having a tone of 'resentment,'" and being "intellectually irresponsible."[27] But in recent years the gravitation of Bell and other centrist ideologues into the ranks of the "neoconservative" movement raises genuine doubt as to the degree to which they were ever really committed to the left values of equality and participation. In retrospect, it is apparent that the liberal antiradicalism of the 1950s had within itself the doctrinal seeds of the present neoconservative movement. It is to Mills' credit that he recognized early on that these seeds would sprout in favorable soil and climate and then blossom into the fruit of opposition to structural change.

MARXISM

It is also to Mills' credit that, like Dewey and Veblen, he refused to become a colonist of some other intellectual culture like Marxism. But his dislike of the obscurantism and sectarian conceit of Marxist splinter parties should not be taken as evidence of a doctrinal anti-Marxism, for his eclecticism made this impossible. He believed that Marxists did not understand that a major political movement capable of making a deep and lasting impression could not develop without building upon existing intellectual traditions and political culture. Thus, given the exclusivist cast of mind of many American Marxists the implicit groping toward an authentic American radicalism by Mills, Veblen, and Dewey is easily understood. The three could never overcome their common belief that Marxism was a mixture of fact and myth, sophisticated social theory and adolescent fantasy, inaccurate prophecies and messianic dreams. For these reasons, a monistic Marxism was not doctrinally adequate by itself to serve as the ideology of the American Left.

American radical scholarship has made inroads in the social sciences in the last decade, but because the newer radical journals often display a doctrinaire Marxism, they pay little attention to Mills.[28] Non-Marxian American radicalism is largely ignored and liberal aspects of the American intellectual tradition are treated negatively. The tendency to ignore or denigrate leading non-Marxist thinkers has grown as leftist political activism has declined and its base of social support has withered. As a consequence, much contemporary radical scholarship is largely devoid of any roots in American intellectual culture. This self-imposed ideological closure often stems from the belief that liberal intellectuals have irretrievably compromised themselves by support of incremental reformism. Through guilt by association, institutional economics and instrumentalism, two closely related schools of thought, are excluded from incorporation as part of a new radical paradigm. To a lesser degree the same holds true of a rich body of European social thought, part of the classical tradition of sociology, which Mills understood well. Although radicalism feeds on a more sophisticated and genuine Marxism than it did a generation ago, it cannot take full advantage of the doctrinal intersection at which it now rests. Diverse intellectual streams flow by, filled with insurgent potential, but many Marxist-inspired radicals will not imbibe. Six generations ago Emerson issued a declaration of cultural independence from European thought in his address on the American scholar. Still, what should be commonplace in radical circles, the ability of Americans to look on their unique experience with their own distinctive eyes and express it in their own ways, remains an unachieved ideal. An inclination exists in mainstream American culture, and in some academic circles, to regard radical ideas as foreign and therefore suspect. Part of the American Left has a similar bias based on an inferiority complex that exaggerates the sagacity of European intellectuals to the neglect of Americans of equal importance. Thus what is needed is an analysis which lays bare the radical roots of the American intellectual tradition by exposing its potential for promoting structural change. This is the largely unrecognized achievement of Mills, Veblen, and Dewey and it has received long overdue attention in these pages.

CONTEMPORARY CONCERNS AND THEORETICAL FUSION

It remains to situate the intellectual contribution of the three men in the context of relevant cultural, political, and economic concerns. If they are seen as shaped by historical forces now gone, why is this of more than historical interest? The answer lies in the fundamental continuities that exist between the capitalism they evaluated and the contemporary political economy. To illustrate the problem of inequality was of common concern to them. It is evident that the value conflicts inherent in the process of deciding how wealth and income are to be distributed are not resolved. Implicit in the thought of Mills, Veblen, and Dewey is the relationship between the problem of distribution and the larger issue of developing a more adequate social value theory.

The energy crisis and the arms race continue largely unabated. The economic waste that results is enormous. The work of the three men provides insight into the mechanisms that link these and related phenomena with broader structural aspects of capitalism in the United States. They may differ in their appraisal of the "wasteful" aspects of consumption, but all evince a keen interest in the pathological emulatory aspects of consumer behavior. Their arguments for a more deliberate and conscious social control of industry should be heeded by a society which is suffering from unemployment, inflation, and the other consequences of the inability to control business cycles adequately. Those social forces that have structural-change potential are still not adequately identified, and the decision as to which relationship, if any, political intellectuals and politicians might form with these forces is yet to be made. The withdrawn intellectual Veblen, who focused his efforts on promoting change primarily within the discipline of economics, can be contrasted with Mills' and especially Dewey's efforts to develop a more adequate praxis that would unite radical theory with social-change agents to transform the existing order. Ultimately, however, both the latter failed to achieve the unity of doctrine, program, class, and party they sought. Finally, both looked at social-science inquiry from the viewpoint of establishing more adequate methodological norms which, without sacrificing objectivity, would facilitate the study of pressing social problems. Thus Mills' encounter with Veblen and Dewey set the stage for many of the political and doctrinal issues that unite and divide what remains of the contemporary American Left.

Although the need for an indigenous critical theory is evident, what is to be its doctrinal core? American political realities and the intellectual environment dictate that this doctrine will develop from a culture different from that which fostered the Frankfurt School and other varieties of Marxism. Although a native critical theory could incorporate aspects of neo-Freudianism and Marxism, as did its European counterpart, it must also include important American elements. These might encompass Veblen's institutionalism, Dewey's instrumentalism, Mead's symbolic interactionism, and work subsequently done in these traditions, as well as other elements of European social thought.[29] To some this may smack of endorsing an eclecticism that will inevitably degenerate into reformist liberalism. However, the late C. Wright Mills accomplished part of this task, yet he avoided an ad hoc planless ameliorism. There are no adequate reasons why an indigenous critical theory cannot be properly attuned to the political and cultural realities of American life while maintaining a strong structural-change orientation. It is in the hopes of achieving such a theoretical synthesis that I recommend a careful scrutiny of Mills' encounter with the ideas of Thorstein Veblen, John Dewey, and George H. Mead.

10

Puritanism, Pragmatism and the American Radical Intellectual Tradition

Thus far Mills' background, his general intellectual position and his contribution to a theory of power and stratification in the United States have been described and analyzed. His relationship to European social thought has been delineated and it has been shown that he was influenced by various European thinkers although not to the extent claimed by many of his interpreters. His use and abuse of the ideas of Mead, Veblen, and Dewey have been evaluated and his position located in regard to the main body of their thought. Finally, Mills' own creative role in coagulating the various strands of radical thought has been explained. What remains to be done is to describe the institutional and intellectual linkage between Puritanism and Pragmatism on the one hand and our four central figures on the other.[1]

THE RADICAL TRADITIONS

In an age in search of "roots" it is gratifying to establish that Mills' work is part of an indigenous radical tradition with its origins deep in American political thought and practice. However, such a tradition is not easy to identify or describe. Indeed, Mills himself never fully succeeded in doing so, yet a native radical heritage in the United States does exist. However, the American radical tradition is complex and varied—its origins are populist and Marxist, Black and Hispanic, Christian Socialist, Jewish trade unionist and intellectual, labor radical, Catholic Worker, Transcendentalist, Anarchist and Anarcho-Syndicalist, Antinomian and Separatist, frontier prophetic, cultural bohemian, and, of course, Pragmatic and Puritan. Our radical tradition has still other attributes; but to neglect any of these named aspects of its heritage is to produce an unbalanced view of a rich legacy. However, our focus is on that part of the radical tradition with which Mills, Veblen, and Dewey had the strongest affinities.

PURITANISM TRANSMUTED INTO PRAGMATISM

Indeed, it is only when the residues of Puritanism were incorporated into Pragmatism that an important strand of indigenous intellectual radicalism reached fruition. Guy Stroh recognized the pervasive and enduring influence of the Puritans, including their impact on Pragmatism, when he wrote that:

> Though Puritanism has long since vanished from the American scene, its moral influence and significance persist. . . . Its importance derives in some measure simply because it came first. Its real significance, however, resides in the peculiar kind of tough-minded, practical idealism that it managed to transmit to later generations. Puritan ethics survived because it could be transformed and suited to the needs and aspirations of later times. In the process of this transformation and survival, its original meaning and theological structure were lost. But its moral purpose, seriousness, and tenacity remained remarkably intact.[2]

However, by the time the residues of Puritanism reached the cultural and intellectual milieu of Pragmatism it had been greatly modified, first by the Enlightenment, then by Transcendentalism, and finally, by Darwinism. That these intellectual movements had a secularizing impact on Puritan thought is undeniable, but important aspects of it were nevertheless incorporated into the Pragmatic tradition that Dewey and Mead helped to mold and that Mills and Veblen reacted to in their various ways.

The Puritan heritage is evident in the dualism that divides the world into the forces of good versus the forces of evil, the forces of light versus those of darkness, and the morality of Jesus versus that of Satan. Such dualism was assimilated by the American radical intellectual tradition and later embedded in Veblen's distinctions between the vested interests and the common man, between the predatory and the peaceful type, and between business and industrial pursuits. This dualism is also apparent in Mills' distinctions between the power elite and informed publics, intellectual entrepreneurs and social-science craftsmen, and Dewey's distinctions between science and supernaturalism and between the old and the new individualism. Thus what our central figures share is a belief that while dualisms have a hold on the popular mind, their impact on both intellect and society is pernicious. Their work points to the need for overcoming false dualisms, not sustaining them as urged by their conservative opponents. To Veblen this meant the triumph of industrial over business pursuits; for Dewey, it meant anticipating the victory of science over superstition; while for Mills it meant the resurgence of popular control over the power elite. In a characteristically Puritan way, although not in the literal doctrinal sense, Veblen, Mills, and Dewey viewed the world as a place for combat between the greedy and parasitical on the one hand and the men of genuine learning, industry, and morality on the other. For all three it was a question of whether the existing social structure would permit the emergence of the proper type or whether it would facilitate the production of predatory self-seekers. If the latter, social life in the future would be dominated by "imbecile institutions." Generations after Puritanism had transformed American intellectual life and been radically changed itself, its intellectual heirs such as Mills would view power as the most corrupting influence in modern societies. In a similar vein, Veblen's social criticism could be directed against unproductive idleness and waste in general, while Dewey and Mead, who shared Mills' and Veblen's dislike of waste and illicit power, focused on the philosophic dualisms that prevented systematic use of the method of intelligence.

THE PURITAN CONNECTION:
INTELLECTUAL AND INSTITUTIONAL

Veblen, Mead and Dewey were members of strong Protestant families, one Lutheran, the other two Congregationalist. It is interesting to note that while Veblen was iconoclastic and a womanizer, this lifestyle was tempered by much hard intellectual work on his part. Dewey and Mead were somewhat staid and straitlaced. Mills, whatever the nature of his personal life, had an intellectual style characterized by overtones of hellfire and damnation. The uncompromising Puritan bent on social perfectionism is abundantly evident in the Texan's intellectual work. Indeed, there is much less irony and humor in Mills' writings than in Veblen's although satirical qualities sometimes surface in them.[3]

Mills had studied the history of New England and also had considerable familiarity with its culture, religion, and early politics. In his three years at the University of Maryland he interacted on a regular basis with American historians like Frank Friedel, Kenneth Stampp, and Richard Hofstadter, all of whom later became eminent scholars. Although these men did not make their scholarly reputations as specialists in colonial American history they had far more than a passing interest in and familiarity with early New England. Perhaps they stimulated Mills to find in his own knowledge and admiration of Puritanism a catalyst for political action. He once indignantly asked in rhetorical fashion regarding Cold War policies that he loathed, "Do not these times demand a little Puritan defiance?"[4] His doctoral dissertation also had several complimentary references to the Puritans. Later, in *Character and Social Structure* Mills wrote approvingly of the Puritans that:

> The heroic Puritan of seventeenth-century England could methodically pursue his quest for salvation by disciplining himself for hard work and thriftiness, and thus by his success assure his religious worth and his salvation in the hereafter. He could, in short, relieve his anxieties by hard work, by work for work's sake, and under the appropriate premiums, take great pains to develop a new "contract morality" in business relationships. Thus perfectionism and moral rigor, punctiliousness, and pleasure-denying work, along with humility and the craving for neighbors' love all combine to shape the character structure of the classical Puritan who sought to master the world rather than adjust to it.[5]

But the most telling statement Mills' ever made about his feelings toward Protestantism and Puritans was this:

> In that which made them whatever they are, . . . and in that towards which [I am] trying to make myself, there are religious strains. Theirs may be a world without God, but it is not a world without religious influence. They recognize as their brothers the prophets of Judaism, all of them, from Amos, Sachariah—those first Men of Conscience who would obey their God rather than other men. . . . I know a little of what Luther was about, and . . . I am indeed full of the puritan ethos.[6]

Mills was thus influenced theoretically and experientially by the Puritan experience which sought for the achievement of a "city on a hill" that the rest of the world would admire and emulate.

Another link between Dewey, Mead, Veblen, and the Puritans is even more direct than that between the Puritans and Mills, for the link is institutional. Dewey, Mead, and Veblen studied in schools modeled after Harvard and Yale and many of the professors with whom they interacted were products of the New England Congregationalist tradition. Dewey did his undergraduate work at the University of Vermont where a large part of the faculty came from Congregationalist backgrounds. Burlington itself had originally been settled by Congregationalists, and most of its residents belonged to churches of British-Calvinist origin or influence. Veblen did his undergraduate work at Carleton College in Northfield, Minnesota. Carleton was affiliated with the Congregational Church and was founded by settlers of New England ancestry. Mead was a graduate of Oberlin and Harvard whose father was a Congregational minister. Both his parents taught in the Protestant seminary at Oberlin. Mills himself studied under several men who were products of this or closely related religious traditions. Perhaps the best example was that secularized Protestant moralist Clarence Ayres, who taught Mills at the University of Texas. Ayres was a graduate of Brown whose father was a New England Baptist minister.

PRAGMATISM AND PURITANISM: THE LINKAGE

Paul Conkin believes there are strong similarities between the Puritans and the Pragmatists, for in his view the Puritans of 1640 and the Pragmatists of 1930 were still much alike. He emphasizes their common moral tenor, instrumental conception of knowledge, and broad ethical conception of art.[7] The relationship between the two schools of thought may not be as close as Conkin thinks, but nevertheless there was a mind set of sorts common to both Puritans and Pragmatists. Mills himself recognized the values common to both the Puritan and Pragmatic traditions as underlying Veblen's own perspective when he admiringly wrote that:

> Veblen was a profoundly conservative critic of America: he wholeheartedly accepted one of the few unambiguous, all-American values: the value of efficiency, of utility, of pragmatic simplicity. His criticism of institutions and the personnel of American society was based without exception upon his belief that they did not adequately fulfill these American values. If he was, as I believe, a Socratic figure, he was in his own way as American as Socrates in his was Athenian.[8]

Mills' view of Veblen's work was shared by Dewey, who once commented that "I have always found Veblen's own articles very stimulating and some of his distinctions, like that between the technological side of industry and its 'business' aspects, have been quite fundamental in my thinking ever since I became acquainted with them."[9] This is an endorsement by Dewey of Veblen's dislike of waste, idleness, and exploitation which we can link with Mills' own sanctioning of Veblenian values. All three men shared the same values although they placed a somewhat different emphasis on them.

Puritans and Pragmatists alike believed every man should have a calling and work hard in it. Consequently, it is not surprising to find a dislike in Mills, Veblen, and Dewey of frivolous forms of recreation, entertainment, or art. Mills ridiculed the reading of comic books by adults as well as their lack of serious interest in good literature although he was well aware of the structural causes of such behavior. Veblen satirized games of chance and sports and the superstitions and brutalities that accompanied them. Dewey complained about the superficial quality of American movies and radio and their lack of any serious moral, cultural, or intellectual content. The conclusion is inescapable that the three men believed that socially useful work was a dignifying vocation requiring conscientious pursuit of a calling; for the doctrine of a calling was vital to Protestants and Pragmatists alike. Since they believed the real ends of work were aesthetic and moral, all three agreed that the separation of art and moral purpose from labor was alienating. In celebrating work, at least "socially useful work," they tried to give it a dignity they felt it had lost.

MORALITY AND SOCIAL ACTION

Although our four central figures were not moral absolutists, they clearly did not believe that the alternative to ethical absolutism was ethical anarchy, for the latter was to be avoided by infusing ethics with science. This attitude, with its emphasis on instrumental knowledge, led to a typical pragmatic stance toward problematic situations. Through use of proper methods society can reach correct moral choices to attain a degree of righteousness and progress. However, virtue is no moral attribute of an individual or a society unless there is a secular sphere for its enactment and this requires an environment in which the will is confronted with obstacles to be overcome. The literature of Puritanism has therefore stressed the importance of self-discipline and control: mastery of the environment by means of the will. This attitude can assume great political significance. For what Ralph Barton Perry once called a "moral athlete" becomes an intellectual combatant when the lines of political cleavage coincide with class and power struggles of the sort that Mills, Veblen, and Dewey analyzed in their work.

Moral individualism is the essence of Puritan ethical doctrine, for the Puritan respected private judgment and conscience above authority. It was characteristic of the Puritans to give their loyalties to ideas rather than to persons or institutions which made it a highly individual matter. While the Pragmatists all recognized the importance of the social and scientific aspects of ethics, they, too, emphasized the right of the individual to come to recognition of truth in his own way. Mills, Veblen, and Dewey did not deny that morality had been institutionalized but they refused to sanction moral codes that were authoritative only because they were conventional. This view was a source of their radicalism within the academic community and, indeed, within their own academic disciplines.

Mills, Veblen, and Dewey continued not simply the Puritan but in a broader sense the Protestant evangelical tradition albeit in secular form. Part of this tradition has been rooted in moral individualism, which provided the philosophic underpinnings of social protest. The attacks of Henry David Thoreau upon social conformism, the fiery abolitionist poems of John Greenleaf Whittier, Walt Whitman's endorsement of the individual, the advice of Ralph Waldo Emerson to be uncompromising, all form a backdrop to their work. Mills' sociology, in particular, was influenced by both the Pragmatic and Protestant models of the individual from whence he derived an individualistic normative theory. This theory is at the foundation of his criticism of power in hierarchically structured societies. The image of the morally and intellectually autonomous individual favored by pragmatism contrasted with the constraints imposed by a complex social order, and that order is found wanting by Mills. Thus, because of its fundamentally moral meaning, Mills' idea of alienation is Protestant-Pragmatic in orientation. It is the "morally free" in man that is obscured in American society, a society in which moral alienation is the condition of success.[10]

PROTESTANTISM AND PRAGMATISM: DECAY OR RESURRECTION?

During the greening of the New Left in the 1960s and early 1970s, the cultural alienation of the younger generation manifested itself in a negative view of such values as work, rationality, self-mastery, and control of the physical environment. In short, the core values of the Protestant Ethic came under increasing attack from disenchanted radical youth. Our three central figures might have agreed with the New Left in their mutual recognition of the impossibility of building community where the belief was prevalent that all social conflict can be harmonized through consumption. A perverse paradise whose goal was materialism, whose aesthetics were consumerized, and whose ethics consisted of Samuel Gompers' cry for "more, more, more" was unlikely to produce strong social bonds. However, had Mills, Veblen, and Dewey been alive, the wholesale onslaught of the New Left on the Protestant Ethic would have distressed them since a secularized version of it formed the core of their own moral values. They could agree with New Left indictment of Protestant moral rigidities and hypocrisy, but they would not acquiesce in dogmatic assaults on the virtues of hard work, self-discipline, and self-mastery. However, the social perfectionism of the New Left had certain elements in common with Puritanism even if its vision of a "city on the hill" differed in certain respects from the Calvinist. Nevertheless, it must be asked why so many American radicals looked to the more exotic metaphysics of the New Left and the counterculture for intellectual leadership and succor? Tom Hayden may well have been a legitimate heir to the radical tradition, but where are the yippies now that we need them? Or did we ever need them?[11] The remnants of the New Left now include Jesus freaks, converts to Mormonism, stockbrokers, devotees of oriental religion, and gays. They compete with social dropouts, dopers, hedonists, and other ideological enemies of the Protestant Ethic for our attention. But fortunately the American radical intellectual tradition and a newly resurgent radical politics, when and if it occurs, will have better sources of inspiration. Indeed, this book focuses on three of them.

However, it is evident that the baser aspects of American Protestantism have become sour, crabbed, apologetics for economic individualism in its most predatory forms. Its worst traits have resurfaced in the rhetoric and policies of Ronald Reagan although, since Jews and Catholics render him support, his is not merely a fundamentalist manifestation. What is most debased and squalid in the American Protestant traditions are the qualities once described by Sinclair Lewis in *Elmer Gantry*—of which there has been a resurgence. The anti-intellectualism, demagoguery, opportunism, and moral stultification Lewis analyzed now reach their apex not in Billy Graham's inanities but in the belligerent avoidance of social conscience by Jerry Falwell and the Moral Majority. How is it that the subverted residues of Protestantism now congeal in the moral Davy Jones's locker and intellectual squalor of the American Right? Related to this question is another one of equal importance. Given the principled commitment of Mills, Veblen, and the later Dewey to active theoretical and practical support of large-scale structural change, why has "pragmatism" come to denote little more than opportunism and expediency and to be associated with policies that are often alleged to be unprincipled? Lewis Feuer's "principle of wings" provides insight into the ideological evolution of a subverted pragmatism from a doctrinal change orientation of the political Liberal-Left to a moderate-conservative perspective of the Center and Right.

> The principle of wings . . . affirms that every philosophic unit-idea in the course of its career makes the passages through the whole spectrum of ideological affiliations. A philosophical doctrine which begins at the left will move rightward, and if at the right, it will diffuse toward the left. In the course of its life-history, every philosophic standpoint and unit-idea will therefore be associated with contrary political standpoints.[12]

In accord with Feuer's principle of wings, pragmatism—a perspective once noted for its moral commitment, opposition to intellectual dogmatism, and autonomy from the prevailing power system—may have assumed an apologetic intellectual and political role. The question is whether or not contemporary liberalism's ill-defined ethical standards, ideological closure, and affiliation with the powers-that-be owes these traits to the founders of pragmatism? Or are they derived from other intellectual sources and the result of complex institutional pressures?

One recent Left critic of American liberalism, Bruce Miroff, does not perceive any direct intellectual links between the "pragmatic liberals" and Dewey. Miroff does not attribute their policy errors directly to deficiencies in instrumentalism. Indeed, though his book *Pragmatic Illusions* is a critique of the "pragmatic liberal" political style and belief system, no mention is even made of Dewey.[13] What Miroff describes is little more than a limited conversion of the residues of the American pragmatic tradition into an ideological rationalization of the *modus operandi* of New Frontier and Great Society. However, it is evident that Protestantism and Pragmatism have aspects capable of being subverted or even converted into the ideological and doctrinal support of political conservatism. Precisely why they have would take a book-length study to explain. Yet it is evident that the radical legacy draws on doctrinal sources whose values are ambivalent and whose politics are mixed. But there is no denying the influence of these intellectual cultures on the environment that produced Veblen, Mills, and Dewey. They found what they were looking for in selected aspects of Protestantism and Pragmatism, but they put it to radical not conservative use. In this same vein of loyalty to an older America, Ralph Barton Perry once wrote tellingly that:

There is a tragic irony in the fact that American critics have helped to create the very impoverishment which they so bitterly lament. The political and religious traditions, even the economic tradition, of America are as rich as any human society has ever enjoyed. America does not lack tradition but fidelity.[14]

At the end of his famous essay "Ludwig Feuerbach and the End of Classical German Philosophy," Friedrich Engels wrote that "The German working class movement is the inheritor of German classical philosophy."[15] In a related sense those social classes that stand to benefit from a rejuvenation of radical politics are the inheritors of classical American social philosophy. Charles Wright Mills more than any other thinker in recent years synthesized these strands of thought and then wove them into a radical theory. The ultimate difference between Mills and many of his mainstream critics is that he chose to articulate ideals instead of hiding behind the subterfuge of methodological ritual or engaging in grantsmanship. He chose the path of social responsibility and moral freedom rather than the pursuit of power, economic self-interest, and professional respectability. In this sense his career and his ideas show what it means to be an authentic American radical. For this alone we are in his debt.

Citations

Complete publishing information appears in the Bibliography.

INTRODUCTION

1. William A. Williams, "Radicals and Regionalism," pp. 87–98.
2. When it was suggested that Mills be offered a professorship at Stanford University, the chairman of the sociology department said, "But Mills is not a sociologist, he is a Marxist." Paul Sweezy and Leo Huberman, eds., *Paul A. Baran: A Collective Portrait*, p. 53.

CHAPTER 1

1. For information on Mills' early life see Richard A. Gillam, "The Intellectual as Rebel: C. Wright Mills, 1916–1946." Gillam's other study of Mills, many years in progress, when and if it is published, will undoubtedly provide vastly more detail about his life. Gillam has conducted interviews with persons I do not know and has had access to unpublished manuscripts I have not seen, since not all Mills' writings are in the Mills Collection at Austin, Texas.
2. Clarence Ayres to Charner Perry, 2 March 1939, Ayres Collection.
3. Ibid.
4. Benjamin Smith, "The Political Theory of Institutional Economics," p. 230.
5. Mills to his parents, 18 March 1961, Mills Collection.
6. George Novack to Natalia Trotsky, 20 September 1961, Mills Collection.
7. See Edward Shils, "Imaginary Sociology," p. 78. Also, see Lipset and Smelser, "Change and Controversy in Recent American Sociology," pp. 41–51. The scurrilous review of *The Power Elite* by Daniel Bell, "The Big Bad Americans," is a good example of the depths to which leading sociologists sometimes descended in their efforts to discredit Mills. Although Mills did not publicly vent his personal animosity to the same extent as his conservative and centrist critics, he gave as good as he got in his personal correspondence. In a letter to his friend and co-author Hans Gerth, he commented as follows: "Dan Bell is here now with Fortune [Magazine]. I've seen him only once and don't look forward to meeting him again. He's full of gossip about how he met [Henry] Luce for lunch and what Luce said. [Bell is a] real little corkscrew drawn by power magnets; really pretty vulgar stuff." Undated letter, Mills to Gerth, Mills Collection.
8. Edward Shils, "The Great Obsession," pp. 20–21.
9. H. Malcolm MacDonald, review of *The Power Elite*, p. 1168.

CHAPTER 2

1. Mills, "The Value Situation and the Vocabulary of Morals," Mills Collection.
2. This important point is made by Irving Howe, "On the Career and Example of C. Wright Mills," in *Steady Work*, p. 250.

3. John Dewey, in *Contemporary American Philosophy* II, p. 22.

4. Mills, *Sociology and Pragmatism*, p. 314.

5. Mills, *Power, Politics and People*, p. 532.

6. Mills, review of Gordon W. Allport's *The Nature of Prejudice*.

7. See Joseph Scimecca's *The Sociology of C. Wright Mills* for a treatment of Mills as a "hard" systematic theorist who successfully fused pragmatic theories of personality formation with the Weberian theory of social structure.

8. Darla June Johnson, "The Place of Sociology of Knowledge in the Early Development of the Theoretical Viewpoint of C. Wright Mills," p. 10.

9. Richard Peterson, "The Intellectual Career of C. Wright Mills: A Case of the Sociological Imagination," pp. 21–22.

10. Mainline American sociologists ignore or dislike Veblen because he assumes that political power, class, and social status are closely linked in most societies. They often quote Weber against Marx (and Veblen) because Weber believes that analytically and conceptually power, class, and status can be separated. They usually fail to note that Weber's fragment "Class, Status and Party," although it does separate class, status, and power for analytic and conceptual purposes, in fact uses many historical examples of how the three overlap and are thus causally bonded. Mills, too, believed that analytically and conceptually class, status, and power are separate from each other; but Mills, like Veblen before him, recognized that as a matter of social reality they are usually linked together.

11. Mills, *Power, Politics and People*, p. 307.

12. Ibid., pp. 306–7.

13. Mills, *The Men of Power*, p. 252.

14. Mills, *White Collar*, p. 7. There are interesting similarities between Mills' treatment of rural America and Veblen's analysis of it in "The Independent Farmer" and "The Country Town" in *Absentee Ownership*.

15. Mills, *White Collar*, p. 35.

16. Ibid., p. 63.

17. Mills, *The Power Elite*, p. 18.

18. Ibid., p. 7.

CHAPTER 3

1. See Raymond S. Franklin and William K. Tabb, "The Challenge of Radical Political Economics," p. 128. Also, William T. Bluhm, *Theories of the Political System*, p. 435, T. B. Bottomore, *Critics of Society: Radical Thought in North America*, pp. 53–54, 63–64. John Plamenatz views Mills' analysis in *The Power Elite* as being influenced considerably by Marxist ideas although he believes correctly that Mills' "attack" on American democracy differs greatly from the Marxist attack on "bourgeois democracy." See his *Democracy and Illusion*, pp. 131–41. Talcott Parsons labels Mills "neo-Marxian" in his "Comment on Llewelyn Gross: Preface to A Metatheoretical Framework for Sociology," p. 138.

2. See Edwin Berry Burgum, "American Sociology in Transition," p. 319. Also see Paul Sweezy's critique of Mills in Ballard and Domhoff, eds., *C. Wright Mills and the Power Elite*, pp. 115–32. Mills' incomplete conversion to the ruling-class theory of orthodox Marxism-Leninism is stressed by Herbert Aptheker in his *The World of C. Wright Mills*.

3. Irving Zeitlin says, inaccurately, in reference to the influence of Marx and Weber on Mills, "those two giants contributed most to Mills' intellectual consciousness," (Zeitlin, "The Plain Marxism of C. Wright Mills," in George Fischer, ed., *The Revival of American Socialism*, p. 230). Mills did state on one occasion that Marx and Weber were the two outstanding figures in the history of sociology. It does not follow, however, that they had the greatest influence on his work. See Mills, *Images of Man*, pp. 12–13, and G. B. Sharp, "Mills and Weber: Formalism and the Analysis of Social Structure," p. 128.

J. A. Sigler calls Mills a "post-Marxian and post-Weberian." See his "The Political Philosophy of C. Wright Mills," pp. 32–33.

4. See Benjamin Smith, "The Political Theory of Institutional Economics," p. 263. Another writer who sees Mills as working in the institutionalist tradition is Wendell Gordon, in his *Economics from an Institutional Viewpoint*, p. 6. Also see J. R. Smith, "Politics from the Economic Point of View: An Analysis of the Political Theoretic Significance of the Writings of Thorstein Veblen," pp. 180–89.

5. William F. Warde emphasized Mills' commitment to pragmatism as a method in his "The Marxists," pp. 68, 95. Also see Henry Aiken, "C. Wright Mills and the Pragmatists," p. 10, and John Carbonara's "Critical Empiricism in C. Wright Mills," pp. 23, 32, 38, 68; Joseph Scimecca, in his "Paying Homage to the Father: C. Wright Mills and Radical Sociology," pp. 180–96, emphasized the synthesis of Weber and pragmatism in Mills' work.

6. Two studies which emphasize the impact of both Marx and the Franco-Italian elite theorists on Mills are Geraint Parry's *Political Elites*, p. 27, and Kenneth Prewitt and Alan Stone, *The Ruling Elites*, p. 175. For an interpretation of Mills' *The Power Elite* as a fusion of neomachiavellianism with the work of Weber see Charles G. Moskos, "The Concept of the Military-Industrial Complex: Radical Critique or Liberal Bogey?" pp. 498–512. Also, see David R. Segal, *Society and Politics*, p. 178. For a negative appraisal of the influence of Mosca on Mills see James Meisel, *The Myth of the Ruling Class: Gaetano Mosca and the Elite*, pp. 360–65.

7. See John Rex, *Sociology, Demystification and Common Sense*, pp. 13, 137. Rex also emphasizes the impact of Marx and the Frankfurt School on Mills.

8. See Randall Collins and Michael Makowsky, *The Discovery of Society*, p. 199.

9. The difficulty of "classifying" Mills' thought is pointed to by Ralph Miliband in his "C. Wright Mills," p. 20. Howard Sherman believes that Mills can be considered either a radical non-Marxist sociologist or a nondogmatic Marxist. See his *Radical Political Economy*, p. 5.

10. For examples of the view of Mills as an eclectic, see: Trent Schroyer, "The Critical Theory of Late Capitalism" in George Fischer, ed., *The Revival of American Socialism*, pp. 301–2; George Lichtheim, "Rethinking World Politics," pp. 255–57; Daniel Bell, "The Power Elite Reconsidered," in Hoyt Ballard and G. William Domhoff, *C. Wright Mills and the Power Elite*, p. 191; and Edward Shils, "Imaginary Sociology," pp. 20–21. Also, see Immanuel Wallerstein's "Mills, C. Wright," pp. 362–64.

11. See Mills, "Reflection, Behavior and Culture," pp. 57, 60, 66, 93, 105, 123.

12. See Pamela Mills, "The Dialectic of C. Wright Mills," p. 5.

13. Ibid., p. 12.

14. For a brief statement by Mills concerning the Frankfurt School, see *Power, Politics and People*, p. 572.

15. That Mills remained critical of Marx in fundamental ways at the time of his death is documented in Sal Landau's "C. Wright Mills: The Last Six Months," pp. 46–54.

16. Mills, review of Howard Selsam's *Socialism and Ethics*, p. 28.

17. Mills to Hallock Hoffman, 7 October 1959, Mills Collection.

18. Ibid.

19. George Novack to Natalia Trotsky, 20 September, 1961, Mills Collection.

20. Memorandum from Barrington Moore to the publisher of *The Sociological Imagination*, 6 May 1958, Mills Collection.

21. Mills, "Letters From Readers, Organization Men," p. 581.

22. Mills, *The Marxists*, p. 130. However, Mills also asked: "Has the value of Marx's method of work been destroyed? . . . No. His method is a signal and lasting contribution to the best sociological ways of reflection and inquiry available. . . . Marx himself never explained anything by the 'laws of dialectics,' although he did not avoid, on occasion, the dialectical vocabulary of obscurantism. Dialectics was, after all, the vocabulary of the Hegelian-trained man, and Marx did put this vocabulary to good substantive use: in terms of dialectics he rejected the absurdity of eighteenth-century views of 'natural

harmony,' achieved a sense of the fluidity and many-sided nature of history making; saw the 'universal interconnection' of all its forces; consistently maintained an awareness of perennial change, of genuine conflict, of the ambiguous potentialities of every historical situation." Mills, *The Marxists*, pp. 129–30.

23. Ibid., p. 129. Mills once wrote: "Marx wrong for advanced nations (1) Not the wage workers that increase but the white-collar. (2) Not increased misery but comforts. (3) Not class consciousness but political apathy. (4) Not slump but prosperity: the long boom. (5) Not *class* struggle in the open but *status* struggle. (6) Not only *class*, but *power* and *status*. (7) Not 'international' but nationalist closure." Unpublished manuscript, no title, Mills Collection.

24. Mills, *The Marxists*, p. 98.

25. Ibid., p. 99.

26. Irving L. Horowitz, "The Unfinished Writings of C. Wright Mills," p. 17.

27. Both works are cited on p. 26 of *The Marxists*. As early as 1940 he reviewed *The German Ideology* for a major journal. See his unsigned booknote in the *American Sociological Review*, 10 (June 1940), 466.

28. Mills, *The Marxists*, p. 102.

29. Robert Michels, *First Lectures in Political Sociology*, p. 106.

30. Mills explicitly recognized the pseudoscientific nature of much of the Machiavellian analysis when he wrote that: "Pareto's is one of the tougher, even cynical, styles of thought; he seems to relish this posture for its own sake, although he disguises it . . . by supposing it to be an essential part of science. Of course it is nothing of the sort. As a whole, I find his work pretentious, dull and disorderly." Mills, *Images of Man*, p. 14.

31. Mills, *The Marxists*, p. 10.

32. James Burnham, *The Machiavellians*, p. 234.

33. See Robert Putnam, *The Comparative Study of Political Elites*, p. 168.

34. Mills, *The Power Elite*, p. 20.

35. Ibid., p. 367.

36. Ibid., p. 20.

37. Ibid., pp. 14–15.

38. James Meisel, *The Myth of the Ruling Class*, p. 361.

39. Mills, *Images of Man*, pp. 14–15.

40. Mills, *The Power Elite*, p. 308.

41. Mills, "Comment on Criticism" in Hoyt Ballard and C. William Domhoff, eds., *C. Wright Mills and The Power Elite*, pp. 247–48.

42. Ibid.

43. See Mills' and Gerth's analysis of Burnham's *The Managerial Revolution* entitled "A Marx for the Managers," originally published in *Ethics* in 1942 and later reprinted in *Power, Politics and People*, pp. 53–71. Lasswell's influence on Mills and Mills' analysis of his work is also found in three unpublished manuscripts entitled "Types of Imperialism," "Contrasted Contributions" and "Lasswell's Theory of Symbols in Political Change," in the Mills Collection. See Mills, *The Power Elite*, pp. 375–77, for a statement about Lundberg's work.

44. Mills, *Images of Man*, pp. 12–13.

45. Ibid.

46. Mills, *Power, Politics and People*, p. 572.

47. Mills, *Images of Man*, p. 13.

48. Mills, *White Collar*, p. 357.

49. See Robert P. Jones, *The Fixing of Social Belief*, p. 139, for a discussion of this.

50. Gerth and Mills, *Character and Social Structure*, p. 307.

51. Ibid.

52. Ibid., p. 328.

53. Ibid., p. 324.

54. Ibid., p. 322.

55. On this point see Mills, *The Power Elite*, pp. 3–29.

56. Nelson Polsby, *Community Power and Political Theory*.

57. Gerth and Mills, *Character and Social Structure*, pp. 340–41.

58. Ibid., pp. 234–36, 360–63.

59. Ibid., pp. 408–9.

60. Ibid., p. 277.

61. Mills, *Power, Politics and People*, pp. 443, 448.

62. Gerth and Mills, *From Max Weber*, p. 25.

63. Ibid., pp. 77–128.

64. This is a central theme in Scimecca's *The Sociological Theory of C. Wright Mills*.

65. Gerth and Mills, *Character and Social Structure*, xvii. Also see Don Martindale, *The Nature and Types of Sociological Theory*, p. 370; Mills and Patricia Salter, "The Barricade and the Bedroom," pp. 313–15, and Robert P. Jones, *The Fixing of Social Belief*, pp. 48–49.

66. Gerth and Mills, *Character and Social Structure*, pp. 150–51. However, on this point see Dennis Wrong, "The Oversocialized Conception of Man in Modern Sociology," pp. 191–92.

67. Gerth and Mills, *Character and Social Structure*, p. 96.

68. This quotation is from an early draft of *Character and Social Structure*, Mills Collection.

69. Gerth and Mills, *Character and Social Structure, p. 96.*

70. I am indebted for this insight to Ernest Becker's "Mills, Social Psychology and the Problem of Alienation," in I. L. Horowitz, ed., *The New Sociology*, p. 110.

71. Mills, *Power, Politics and People*, p. 447.

72. See Darla Johnson, "The Place of Sociology of Knowledge in the Early Development of the Theoretical Viewpoint of C. Wright Mills," p. 49.

73. Mills, *Character and Social Structure*, p. 113. In Deweyan terms Mills is attacking a "false dualism" contained in both Freudian and neofreudian thought when he charged them with believing that: "Emotions, urges, or various physiological processes are 'the real' motivating factors of conduct; the rest is sham, or at any rate distorted and ungenuine expressions of the real motives of the real individual."

74. Ibid., xvii.

75. Ibid., iii.

76. Ibid., p. 85.

77. Ibid., p. 113. Mills also complains that: "It is true that Karen Horney sees inner conflicts as resulting from conflicts in human relations, but she does not lay bare the structure of these relations within the larger social framework of modern capitalism. As her books have come out . . . her original drive to disclose the larger social causes of neuroses has diminished." Mills, review of Karen Horney's *Our Inner Conflicts*, pp. 84–85. Mills wrote, "Sullivan's psychiatry makes him stress the human milieu. But it is not a psychiatry of the *individual* person (?) and, for all of its talk of 'culture,' it does not include an understanding of *social structure*." Mills, "Sullivan's Psychiatry of Milieu," Mills Collection.

78. Mills to Robert Merton, 13 February 1941, Mills Collection. Nevertheless, Mills wrote shortly after this that his article "The Methodological Consequences of the Sociology of Knowledge" "is the eventuation of looking at Dewey for about two years through the eyes of C. S. Peirce and Mannheim." Mills to Bill Kolb, 24 April 1941, Mills Collection.

79. Mills, *Images of Man*, p. 12. Mills also commented that "The theory that ideas evolve from one another in some kind of inherent continuity, is often called the 'immanent model of intellectual change.' Its refutation . . . as an adequate conception of intellectual history is perhaps the major burden of Karl Mannheim's work." Ibid., p. 10.

80. The broad variety of sources from which Mills drew in formulating his sociology of knowledge, including French social theory, is evident in his study of the "Language and Ideas of Ancient China," posthumously published in *Power, Politics and People*. His eclecticism is also apparent in his correspondence with other leading sociologists of the day about the problem of the sociology of knowledge, especially in letters to Florian Znaniecki, 25 March 1940, and to Robert Merton, 23 January 1940, Mills Collection.

81. Collins and Makowsky, *The Discovery of Society*, p. 199.

82. Mannheim, *Essays on the Sociology of Knowledge*, p. 289. However, there have

been few attempts to conduct empirical research utilizing methodologically adequate means on the subject of false consciousness. This problem deserves to have more attention paid to it in the future than it has in the past. Some progress has been made in recent years through development of cultural critique of capitalism which analyzed the systemic fostering of false consciousness through the cultural apparatus.

83. See the selection of Mannheim in Mills' *Images of Man*, pp. 508–28. Mannheim is so ambiguous in his use of "substantial rationality" that he has been interpreted to mean not only the ability to analyze larger and more complex sets of relationships, but also to be "a mode of thought that takes into account the morality of the goals and the human worth of the means used to achieve them." See, for example, Salvador Giner, *Mass Society*, p. 83.

84. Mills, *Power, Politics and People*, p. 608.

85. Mills, review of Mannheim's *Man and Society in an Age of Reconstruction*, p. 967.

86. Ibid., p. 968. Contrary to Mills, Mannheim places his faith in responsible elites as far as the planning process in concerned. They should plan for the whole society and then take the responsibility for what they have done. See Mannheim's *Man and Society in an Age of Reconstruction*, p. 75.

87. See Mills' "Language, Logic and Culture," "Situated Actions and Vocabularies of Motive," "Methodological Consequences of the Sociology of Knowledge," and "The Professional Ideology of Social Pathologists." All are reprinted in *Power, Politics, and People*, and are so cited throughout the text.

88. Mills to Robert Merton, 13 February 1941, Mills Collection.

89. Mannheim, *Ideology and Utopia*, pp. 84–85.

90. For a comparison of Mills' and Mannheim's work on the sociology of knowledge see Derek Phillips, "Epistemology and the Sociology of Knowledge: The Contributions of Mannheim, Mills and Merton," p. 82.

91. Mannheim, *Essays on the Sociology of Knowledge*, p. 61.

92. Mannheim, *Man and Society in an Age of Reconstruction*, p. 185.

93. Mills, review of Mannheim's *Man and Society in an Age of Reconstruction*, p. 966.

94. Ibid.

95. Mills, *The Marxists*, pp. 36–37.

CHAPTER 4

1. Dorfman, *Thorstein Veblen and His America*, p. 450.

2. Ibid.

3. Ibid., pp. 196–97.

4. Mills, introduction to Veblen's *The Theory of the Leisure Class*, pp. vi, xi.

5. Ibid., vi.

6. Mills, *Images of Man*, p. 13.

7. For an analysis of this tendency in New Left economists see Charles Leathers and Joseph Pluta, "Veblen and Modern Radical Economics," pp. 125–46.

8. For example, see the essay on Veblen and Mills by Douglas Dowd in Irving L. Horowitz, ed., *The New Sociology*, and Richard A. Gillam, "The Intellectual as Rebel: C. Wright Mills, 1916–1946," p. 41.

9. Leo Huberman to Mills, 4 April 1958, Mills Collection.

10. For an analysis of Ayres, see my "Value Theory, Planning and Reform: Ayres as Incrementalist and Utopian," pp. 689–706. Also see William Breit's "The Development of Clarence Ayres' Theoretical Institutionalism," pp. 244–57.

11. Mills, *Images of Man*, p. 336.

12. Gillam, "The Intellectual as Rebel," p. 40. William N. Leonard, who was a friend and fellow student with Mills, has offered these revealing comments about Ayres, the man and intellectual, and his environmental setting at Austin: "When I first encountered

Ayres in 1937, he was an unflagging liberal, zealous for civil liberties and completely fearless. Of course, the fact that he attacked Marxism, in which many students and faculty were interested in those days, feeling it was a kind of religion (he always referred critically to the long lines of worshippers at the grave of Lenin), helped him from becoming more of a target of criticism. I recall that the Texas Legislature conducted an investigation of 'atheism and communism' on the campus, coming up with a geologist who taught evolution and economist Robert Montgomery, a New Deal Democrat, who was accused of being "socialist" which the honorable legislators could not distinguish in those days from a 'communist.' Montgomery had to define socialism for them, discuss the various brands, and when asked if he believed in the "profit motive," answered that he believed passionately in profits—'profits for 130 million Americans.' That was our population at that time, I believe. His answer brought down the galleries, and we students were evacuated by the sergeant-at-arms. Later the investigation was dropped." William N. Leonard to Rick Tilman, 24 January 1975, p. 1.

13. Clarence Ayres to Charner Perry, 2 March, 1939, C. E. Ayres Collection.

14. Mills was aware at an early age of the influence of pragmatism, institutionalism, and symbolic interactionism on his thinking. He put it this way in the fall of 1938: ". . . most of my criticism has been laid from what I come to call a 'sociologistic' corner. This corner is constituted primarily by a social psychological orientation having at its center an ontological assumption: the 'social' is real. Given impetus by Mead, I was 'prepared' for him by a fairly adequate knowledge of American social psychology. The other major constituent of my sociologism is a standpoint I have derived from certain scattered passages of Thorstein Veblen, the pragmatists (especially Peirce) and from Karl Mannheim." Mills, "The Value Situation and the Vocabulary of Morals," Mills Collection.

15. See Allan Gruchy, *Contemporary Economic Thought: The Contribution of Neo-Institutional Economics*, pp. 1–87, 287 ff.

16. Mills' utilization of economic concepts and literature in his work are clearly indicative of the influence of institutionalism on him. This is apparent in his use of the "managerial revolution" thesis popularized by Berle and Means, but discovered in rudimentary form by Veblen a few years earlier. Mills was concerned as to how to interpret the effect of the separation of ownership from management on the exercise of corporate power. He finally concluded that it had made less difference than its proponents imagined, because formal changes in the corporate power system at the administrative level had little impact on corporate behavior. Relevant to the problem of corporate power was the literature written by institutionalists on the subjects of industrial concentration, oligopoly, and price administration. Mills shows familiarity with this literature in his writing on labor unions, the national power system, competition, and the middle class, not to mention his extensive work on corporate elites and the upper classes. The pervasive influence of institutionalism is also found in his criticism of classical and neoclassical economics. A good example of the influence of Ayres and Veblen in this regard is evident in Mills' negative attitude toward the hedonistic psychology of Economic Man. See Mills, "Psychology and Social Science," pp. 204–9.

17. Although Mills was not an economist, it is not uncommon for neoinstitutionalists to recognize parallels between his work and theirs. See Wendell Gordon's *Economics From an Institutional Point of View*, p. 6.

18. See especially Mills' introduction to Veblen's *The Theory of the Leisure Class.*

19. Immanuel Wallerstein, "Mills, C. Wright," p. 363.

20. Mills wrote that "The first thing that must be got clear about him is that he was generally a Marxist who adopted the elements of this general perspective for presentation to the academic publics of his generation." Unpublished manuscript, no title, Mills Collection.

21. Mills, "On Intellectual Craftsmanship" in *Symposium on Sociological Theory*, ed. Llewellyn Gross, p. 52.

22. See Veblen's two essays entitled "The Socialist Economics of Karl Marx and His Followers," I and II, reprinted in *The Place of Science in Modern Civilization and Other Essays.*

23. Mills, *Images of Man*, p. 12.

24. Ibid., p. 13.

25. Ibid. Another similarity in Veblen and Mills is that both distrusted Hegelian dialectics.

26. John Diggins has recently compared Veblen and Marx at great length in his *The Bard of Savagery: Thorstein Veblen and Modern Social Theory*.

27. Gerth and Mills, *Character and Social Structure*, p. 388. At times Ayres went even further than Mills and Veblen in his emphasis on the human skill aspect of technology. For example, he once wrote that "technology is organized skill." See *The Theory of Economic Progress*, p. 105. The moral and distributional significance of this conceptualization is evident when it is recognized that ownership patterns determine who is able to exchange the exercise of their skills for a living and on what terms. This is a point of common concern to institutionalists, political sociologists like Mills, and Marxists.

28. See Allan Gruchy, *Contemporary Economic Thought: The Contribution of Neo-Institutional Economics*, pp. 95–99.

29. Veblen, *Absentee Ownership and Business Enterprise in Recent Times*, pp. 205–6.

30. Mills, *Power, Politics and People*, p. 546.

31. Ibid.

32. Ibid., pp. 544–45.

33. Ibid., p. 454.

34. Ibid.

35. "[Veblen] had always seemed to me very loose, even vague about his 'business' and 'industrial' employments." Mills in "On Intellectual Craftsmanship" in Llewellyn Gross, ed., *Symposium on Sociological Theory*, p. 52. It is interesting to note Mills' recognition that Veblen had derived his two social types from Herbert Spencer and then employed them in anti-Spencerian manner: "Then, Veblen assimilated Spencer's two types into one society by making their coexistence horizontal. The militant type with its predatory traits became identified with the upper class, the 'captains' of industry; the industrial type with its amiable craftsmanship became the lower class. / This simple manipulation of Spencer's types and the view of life which resulted, therefore, is the nerve of Veblen's conception of modern American society. The element of protest in his style of vision and thought rests on his retention of the canons of 'efficiency' and its associations with industry conceived as technology, for his use of the two types in a consistent manner required that he make his prime distinction between business and industry, between money makers and industrial workers, between the pecuniary and the industrial—between the industrial society and the militant state." Mills, "Types of Imperialism," Mills Collection.

36. Mills, *Power, Politics and People*, p. 437.

37. Mills, *The Power Elite*, p. 168. The dichotomy is also found in a reference to the difference between physical and financial capital in *Power, Politics and People*, p. 437. This is a characteristic formulation of Ayres and Veblen that Mills adopted.

38. Mills, *The Causes of World War III*, p. 105.

39. Mills, "Science and Society." Mills Collection.

40. Ibid.

41. Mills, "The Contribution of Sociology to Studies of Industrial Relations," p. 19. This was one of Mills' few contributions to organization theory and was published posthumously.

42. Mills, draft of *Character and Social Structure*, Mills Collection. It is interesting to note that the published manuscript does not contain the reference to Ayres.

43. Gerth and Mills, *Character and Social Structure*, p. 397.

44. Ibid., p. 396.

45. Mills, draft of *Character and Social Structure*, Mills Collection.

46. Mills, *Sociology and Pragmatism*, p. 419.

47. Mills, unpublished Manuscript, no title, Mills Collection.

48. See Ayres, "Gospel of Technology" in *American Philosophy Today and Tomorrow*, ed. Horace Kallen and Sidney Hook.
49. See Benjamin Smith, "The Political Theory of Institutional Economics," p. 82.
50. Gerth and Mills, *Character and Social Structure*, p. 396.
51. Mills to Parents, 21 December 1939, Mills Collection. In this same letter Mills also commented that: "From my mother I have gotten a sense of color and air. She showed me the tang and feel of a room properly appointed, and the drama of flowers. She gave me feel. She also tried to teach me manners, but I fear I have forgotten many of them."
52. C. Wright Mills, "Work Milieu and Social Structure," Address to the Mental Health Society of Northern California, Asilomar, California, 13 March 1954.
53. Ibid.
54. Ibid.
55. See Mills' summary in *White Collar*, p. 220. This synthesis of Mills' analysis of craftsmanship is based on his essay "On Intellectual Craftsmanship" in *Symposium on Sociological Theory*, ed. Llewellyn Gross, and on the appendix in *The Sociological Imagination* entitled "On Intellectual Craftsmanship." Also see Chapter 10, entitled "Work," in *White Collar*. Also see "The Unity of Work and Leisure" and "Man in the Middle: The Designer," both reprinted in Mills, *Power, Politics and People*.
56. As quoted in Mills, "Work," Mills Collection. The quotation itself is from George H. Mead, *The Philosophy of the Act*, p. 457: "This is the root connection between work and art; as aesthetic experiences, both involve the power 'to catch' the enjoyment that belongs to the consummation, the outcome, of an undertaking and to give to the implements, the objects that are instrumental in the undertaking, and to the acts that compose it something of the joy and satisfaction that suffuses its successful accomplishment." Mead, *The Philosophy of the Act*, p. 454.
57. The claim that Veblen was a technocratic elitist who wanted to install a soviet of engineers and technicians in power in order to institutionalize craftsmanship is mistaken. See Tilman, "Veblen's Ideal Political Economy and Its Critics."
58. Mills, "Repossession of Cultural Apparatus," Mills Collection.
59. Mills, *Power, Politics and People*, p. 240.
60. Ibid., p. 150.
61. There is considerable evidence of the influence of Veblen's notion of "idle curiosity" on Mills, especially in his unpublished writings. See Mills, "Science and Society," Mills Collection. The relationship between Veblen's "instincts" (idle curiosity, workmanship and parenthood), Mills' "craftsmanship," and Marx's "unalienated labor" is a close one. The terms, although not equivalents, have a common significance. Nevertheless, the language Mills uses, his earlier and more sophisticated understanding of Veblen than Marx, and his unusual emphasis on the role of "idle curiosity" give "intellectual craftsmanship" a stronger Veblenian than Marxian flavor.
62. Veblen's choice of the word "instinct" is an unfortunate one, but he does distinguish behavior that is environmentally induced from physiological and neurological traits that he calls "tropisms." See his *The Instinct of Workmanship*, pp. 2, 3, 4, 25–27, 38.
63. Allan Gruchy, *Modern Economic Thought: The American Contribution*, p. 65.
64. At times in Mills' writings on craftsmanship there is a state of mind that borders on religious ecstasy.
65. Veblen, *Essays in Our Changing Order*, pp. 11–12.
66. Mills, *The Sociological Imagination*, pp. 72–73.
67. Mills, introduction to Veblen's *The Theory of the Leisure Class*, p. x. It is also evident that in the realm of methodology Mills and Veblen were alike in their use of evolutionary analysis and ideal types to determine the social main drift, the essentials of an historical epoch, and the characters of the typical persons within it. In these ways, there is, however, little to distinguish them from Marx and Weber.
68. Ibid., p. 70.
69. As quoted by Mills in *White Collar*, p. 256.

70. Mills, *The Power Elite*, p. 164.

71. Mills, *Power, Politics and People*, p. 288.

72. See Mills' critique of Veblen in this regard in *The Power Elite*, p. 88.

73. Ibid., p. 46.

74. Ibid., p. 85.

75. Ibid., p. 91.

76. Ibid., p. 74.

77. See Veblen's *Absentee Ownership and Business Enterprise in Recent Times*, p. 130, and Mills, *The Power Elite*, p. 262.

78. Mills, *White Collar*, pp. 256–57.

79. William T. Bluhm, *Theories of the Political System*, pp. 435–40. In any case, as Norberto Bobbio has recently shown, there is no such thing as a "Marxist" theory of the state. See his "Is There a Marxist Theory of the State?", pp. 5–16.

80. It is interesting to note that Clarence Ayres probably did not agree with Mills' thesis in *The Power Elite* as evidenced by a cryptic but critical review he wrote of it. See Ayres, "Two Approaches to Our Imperfections," pp. 23–24, 34.

81. See Mills, *The New Men of Power*, p. 247.

82. Mills, "The Power Elite: Military, Economic and Political" in *Problems of Power in American Democracy*, ed. Arthur Kornhauser, pp. 146–47.

83. Mills, *The Causes of World War III*, p. 21.

84. Veblen, *Absentee Ownership and Business Enterprise in Recent Times*, p. 374.

85. Ibid., pp. 374–75.

86. Ibid.

87. Ibid., p. 360.

88. Ibid., pp. 226–28.

89. Ibid.

90. See Robert P. Jones, "The Fixing of Social Belief," pp. 154–55.

91. Veblen, *Absentee Ownership and Business Enterprise in Recent Times*, p. 129.

92. Mills, *Power, Politics and People*, p. 265.

CHAPTER 5

1. Examples of this interpretation are found in Daniel Bell, "Veblen and the New Class," p. 638; David Riesman, "The Social and Psychological Setting of Veblen's Economic Theory," p. 459; and Lev Dobriansky, *Veblenism: A New Critique*, p. 389. This view has been challenged by Tilman in "Veblen's Ideal Political Economy and Its Critics," pp. 307–17.

2. See Clarence Ayres, *The Theory of Economic Progress*, p. 202; John Gambs, *Beyond Supply and Demand*, p. 273; and Douglas Dowd, *Thorstein Veblen: A Critical Reappraisal*, p. 11. This interpretation is critically evaluated by Tilman in "Thorstein Veblen: Incrementalist and Utopian," pp. 155–69.

3. This is a common theme in much of the literature on Veblen but, as will be shown, it rests on some fundamental misconceptions about the Veblenian system.

4. See Donald Walker, "Thorstein Veblen's Economic System," pp. 220–32.

5. See Karl Mannheim's *Man and Society in an Age of Reconstruction*, p. 58. Mannheim criticizes Veblen for his failure to distinguish between functional and substantial rationality, and for his belief that the machine process will produce both in industrial workers.

6. Veblen, *The Instinct of Workmanship*, p. 184.

7. Mills, *The Power Elite*, pp. 108–9.

8. Mills, introduction to Veblen's *The Theory of the Leisure Class*, p. xvi.

9. Ibid., xv.

10. Mills, *The Power Elite*, pp. 90–91.

11. Ibid.

12. Mills, introduction to Veblen's *The Theory of the Leisure Class*, pp. xvi, xvii.

13. Benjamin Smith, "The Political Theory of Institutional Economics," pp. 86–88.

14. Mills, *The Marxists*, pp. 34–35.

15. Mills, *Power, Politics and People*, pp. 56–67.

16. Ibid., p. 56. Veblen early in his career apparently believed that the engineers' training in scientific and technical knowledge would liberate them morally to perceive things as they really are, matter of factly, and hence achieve ascendancy because of their access to privileged epistemology. Later this was no longer an article of faith with him.

17. See Gerth and Mills, "A Marx for the Managers," in *Power, Politics and People*, pp. 53–71.

18. Mills, introduction to Veblen's *The Theory of the Leisure Class*, p. xvii.

19. Ibid., xiv.

20. For an analysis of this point see Benjamin Smith, "The Political Theory of Institutional Economics," pp. 69–71.

21. Henry Kariel, *Saving Appearances: The Re-establishment of Political Science*, p. 98.

22. Mills, introduction to Veblen's *The Theory of the Leisure Class*, viii.

23. Mills, *Power, Politics and People*, p. 54.

24. See Allan Gruchy, *Contemporary Economic Thought: The Contribution of Neo-Institutional Economics*, p. 101.

25. Mills, "Moral Intersections of Science and Society," Mills Collection.

26. See Mills' inclusion of a segment on rationality from Mannheim's *Man and Society in an Age of Reconstruction* in *Images of Man*, esp. p. 512.

27. Veblen, *The Theory of Business Enterprise*, p. 148. See Chapter 9 for a lengthy analysis of the effects of the machine process on human rationality and the inculcation of socialism in the work force.

28. Mills, introduction to Veblen's *The Theory of the Leisure Class*, xviii.

29. Mills, "Labor in the United States," May 1952, written for publication in the *Encyclopedia Americana*, but never published, Mills Collection. Also see Mills, *The New Men of Power*, p. 117.

30. Veblen's views are found in *Absentee Ownership in Recent Times*, pp. 292–95, 402. Mills' views are summarized in his "Unions and Politics," Mills Collection.

31. Ibid. Also see Mills, *The New Men of Power*, p. 237.

32. Mills, "Labor in the United States," Mills Collection.

33. Mills, *Power, Politics and People*, pp. 108–10.

34. Veblen, *The Engineers and the Price System*, introduction by Daniel Bell, p. 97.

35. See E. H. Downey, introduction to Robert F. Hoxie, *Trade Unionism in the United States*, p. xxxiii.

36. Mills, *Power, Politics and People*, p. 99.

37. Perlman's perspective at the time is summarized in A. L. Riesch Owen, *Selig Perlman's Lectures on Capitalism and Socialism*.

38. Mills, "A Note on Professor Perlman's Theory of Unionism," Mills Collection.

39. Ibid.

40. Ibid.

41. Ibid.

42. Mills, *Images of Man*, p. 15.

43. Mills, "A Note on Professor Perlman's Theory of Unionism," Mills Collection.

44. Ibid.

45. Ibid.

46. Ibid.

47. Ibid.

48. Ibid.

49. See A. L. Riesch Owen, *Selig Perlman's Lectures on Capitalism and Socialism*, p. 126. These lectures are based on notes taken in Perlman's class by a student in 1941–1942.

CHAPTER 6

1. Mills, "The Value Situation and the Vocabulary of Morals," Mills Collection.

2. The academic environment and the intellectual atmosphere of the University of Chicago during this period, as well as the pervasive influence of the pragmatic movement there, is dealt with by Darnell Rucker in his *The Chicago Pragmatists*. The influence of the pragmatists on Mills is evident in his M.A. thesis "Reflection, Behavior and Culture," which uses a sociology of knowledge perspective to analyze Dewey and Mead.

3. The links between the great American pragmatic philosophers, the Texas pragmatists under whom Mills worked, and Mills' own ideas are very significant. For example, under acknowledgments to a draft of *Character and Social Structure* Mills thanked George Gentry for introducing him to the ideas of Mead and Peirce. He also acknowledged Clarence Ayres and David Miller for contributing to his intellectual development. In a letter to W. H. Sanders written on 16 November 1940, Mills was effusive in his praise for Gentry. "Whatever else Texas can give a man or not give him it can give him George Gentry on C. S. Peirce. Get that. There is no better basis for any man in social science anywhere." Later, in a letter to Gentry, Mills explained to him why he was impressed by American pragmatism: "It has not been difficult for me to show that the central content of the pragmaticism of Peirce is a philosophical awareness of his occupational practices. Two things make for his pragmaticism: his occupation plus an interest in philosophy, but always an outsider from its dominant circles. The history of pragmatism after Peirce is the history of an enlarging public and the reflex that thinking with such publics produced in James, Dewey, and Mead. I become more and more convinced that the category of action in Dewey is intrinsically connected both to educational practices, and the kind of action involved in educating in an expanding educational system, and the ethical context in which the concept of action first arises for Dewey. I now know that the category of the social is in all the pragmatists, yes even in Mead, as fishy as the fish we didn't catch in the summer of '39." Mills to G. V. Gentry, 11 November 1941.

4. In this vein Herbert Blumer recently wrote that: "I am not able to recall any impression of the influence of Mead on C. Wright Mills; I would have to go back and review his writings to say anything with assurance. I had conversations with Mills off and on over the years, particularly during one summer when he attended a seminar that I was giving at the University of Chicago, which he was visiting. Yet, try as hard as I can, I am not able to recall any discussions with him about Mead. The meetings were many years ago and clear memories of them have vanished." Blumer to Rick Tilman, 2 March 1982.

5. Mead's only published writing that deals with Veblen is his lengthy review in 1918 of Veblen's *An Inquiry into The Nature of Peace and the Terms of Its Perpetuation* in the *Journal of Political Economy*, pp. 752–62. Veblen never mentions Mead in any of his published work. Dewey and Mead were close friends and intellectual compatriots and wrote a good deal about each other's work. How well they understood each other, and the relationship their ideas bear to one another, is a matter of dispute among social theorists and philosophers. For example, David Lewis and Richard Smith contend Mead was a sociological and philosophical realist rather than a nominalist. They claim that since the main thrust of his thinking is toward realism the tendency to associate him with the nominalist Dewey is a mistaken one. If their thesis is true, it probably places Mead closer to Veblen in this respect than to Dewey. Clearly, Veblen was not a nominalist insofar as his psychology, philosophy, and social theory are concerned. However, in the broader sense Herbert Blumer was probably correct when he wrote to the author that: "I cannot recall that Mead ever referred to Veblen, either in or out of the classroom. I seriously doubt that Mead was influenced in any significant way by Veblen or gave him any special consideration in his thinking." Herbert Blumer to Rick Tilman, 2 March 1982.

6. Mills, *Sociology and Pragmatism*, pp. 464–67.

7. Mills, of course, recognized the marked similarities in Dewey's and Mead's social

psychology when he wrote: "We are explaining behavior socially when we utilize social economic, political structures and processes in constructing the allegedly necessary conditions of that behavior. . . . In 1909 G. H. Mead gave substantive notice of the social as strict counterpart to the physiological, and his entire work is strongly conditioned by it. Dewey, in his 1917 paper, 'The Need for Social Psychology,' embraces the view . . . 'all psychology is either biological or social psychology.'" Mills, "A Note on the Classification of 'Social Psychological' Sciences," p. 10, Mills Collection. However, Mills preferred Mead's social psychology to Dewey's because: "Mead developed a social theory of reflection applicable to this type of gross situation. Or better . . . it seems that the empirical elements of Mead's theory are of such a conversational level. Moreover, the model of action underpinning Mead's theory of reflection (the action in terms of which he formulates it) is a social interactional schema, and not, as with Dewey, a biological adjustment model. His theory is developed as a strict counterpart to physiological science." Mills, "Reflection, Behavior and Culture," p. 90.

8. Gerth and Mills, *Character and Social Structure*, p. xv.
9. Gerth and Mills, *Character and Social Structure*, p. xvi.
10. Ibid., p. 409–10.
11. Ibid., p. 394.
12. Ibid., p. 124.
13. Ibid., p. 191.
14. Ibid., p. 102.
15. Ibid., p. 98.
16. Ibid., p. 448. Western European "critical theory" takes Marx to task for overlooking the symbolic interactionist dimension of how people relate to one another, not as workers and capitalists, but as agents who communicate via symbols and gestures. Many European intellectuals are stimulated by this discovery and look to Jürgen Habermas as a guru, but, of course, Mead and Peirce did pathbreaking work in this area long before critical theory as such even existed.
17. Ibid., p. 100.
18. Ibid., p. 96.
19. Ibid., p. 86.
20. Ibid., p. 96.
21. Ibid., p. 174.
22. Ibid., p. 181.
23. Ibid., pp. 81–82.
24. Ibid., p. 276.
25. Ibid., p. 101.
26. Ibid., pp. 416–17.
27. Ibid., p. 83. Mills summarizes and endorses what is essentially a Meadian perspective on roles and role-playing: "A person is composed of an internalization of organized social roles; language is the mechanism by which these internalizations occur. It is the medium in which these roles are organized. Now we have defined role as a conduct pattern of a person which is typically expected by other persons. It is an expected pattern of conduct. The roles a person plays thus integrate one segment of his total conduct with a segment of the conduct of others. And this integration of persons, and of the roles they expect of one another, occurs by means of language. For it is largely by a language of vocal gestures that we know what is expected of us. We meet the expectations of others by calling out in ourselves a response similar to the response which the other person has called out in himself . . . that is, both respond similarly to the same vocal gesture."
28. Ibid., p. 450.
29. Mills, *Power, Politics and People*, pp. 426–27. Interestingly, Mills also wrote: "It seems strange that no one has explicitly raised the questions of the data drawn upon by Mead in the construction and elaboration of his social theory of mind. Mead mentions dog fights in connection with the conversation of gestures and the rise of the self. And he did have a dog that followed him about and fought other dogs so that Mead would be

stimulated to thought. But after the days at Leipzig, Mead did not prosecute 'research' in the laboratory manner. He was trained, or rather, had trained himself, in the history of general ideas. He knew the history of Western philosophy and of physical science thoroughly, intimately. / I think his theory of mind is informatively oriented with reference to these histories; they were his subject matter and his data. His work on the histories of science and philosophy is less an 'application' of a developed theory of mind than they are bases for it. Recall his extended discussion of the romantics: Hegel, Fichte, Schelling, and the definitive essay of science. If you will read Mead from this angle he is more understandable, and certain of his obvious inadequacies are explainable: particularly the naive view of the reactions of the individual thinker to 'the community.' Only if 'community' is read to mean 'scientific or intellectual community' do certain portions of Mead's work appear adequate." Mills, *Power, Politics and People*, pp. 471–72.

30. Ibid., p. 429.

31. Ibid., p. 433.

32. See Tom Goff's *Marx and Mead*, and Richard Lichtman's "Symbolic Interactionism and Social Reality: Some Marxist Queries" for suggestive insights into the possibility of a theoretical fusion between Mead and structural sociology.

33. Jones, "The Fixing of Social Belief," pp. 54–55.

34. "I still think Mills did not fully understand Mead's generalized other. Actually Mills was not one who studied thoroughly many authors. He was most intelligent and made many marvellous suggestions, but I do not believe he was considered a thorough scholar. He did have respect for Mead, and learned about Mead—and other pragmatists—while here in Texas." David Miller to Rick Tilman, 19 February, 1982.

35. Mills, "Reflection, Behavior and Culture," pp. 106–7.

36. See Cronk, "Symbolic Interactionism," p. 315.

37. Mills, *Power, Politics and People*, p. 434.

CHAPTER 7

1. For a detailed study of the differences between Veblen and Dewey during and after the Progressive Era see my "Dewey's Liberalism versus Veblen's Radicalism: A Reappraisal of the Unity of Progressive Social Thought."

2. Mills was influenced more by the work of Dewey, Peirce, and Mead than by William James for James was not "a genuine pragmatist." The traditional interpretation of pragmatism which located James as the center of diffusion for pragmatic doctrine was "mistaken and intellectually unfortunate." Mills to Ernest Mannheim, 4 September, 1938, Mills Collection.

3. I. L. Horowitz, introduction to Mills' *Sociology and Pragmatism*, pp. 13–14.

4. Ibid., p. 23.

5. Horowitz perceptively commented that "throughout Mills' earlier efforts there is a dialogue with Dewey—sometimes direct and conscious, at other times elliptical and unconscious. Interestingly, getting beyond Dewey generally meant moving from an epistemological to a sociological perspective, and not, as might be imagined, moving away from pragmatism as such." Ibid., p. 17.

6. Henry Aiken, "C. Wright Mills and the Pragmatists," p. 10.

7. Mills, "Fragments," Mills Collection.

8. How else can the following statement be accounted for since it contradicts what he wrote elsewhere during the same period? ". . . we are beginning to believe that the kind of mediation, integration afforded by fact, is of entirely different nature than that afforded by moral or value factors." Mills, "The Value Situation and the Vocabulary of Morals," Mills Collection.

9. John Dewey, "Some Questions about Value," p. 414.

10. Mills, *The Sociological Imagination*, p. 77.

11. Ibid.

12. Mills, no title, 30 January 1939, Mills Collection.

13. Mills, "The Value Situation and the Vocabulary of Motives," Mills Collection.

14. John Carbonara, "Critical Empiricism in C. Wright Mills," p. 63. Also see pp. 64–66. Both Mills and Dewey had a dual value test built into their epistemology. A statement was true for them: (1) if it worked as a performative, that is, accomplished a task; and (2) more abstractly, if it added something valuable to mankind's store of knowledge about itself—to humanity's betterment in an evolutionary sense.

15. Darnell Rucker, *The Chicago Pragmatists*, pp. 161, 162.

16. I am indebted to Robert P. Jones for pointing this out. See his "The Fixing of Social Belief," p. 106. Also see Mills, *The Sociological Imagination*, appendix.

17. Mills, *Power, Politics and People*, p. 464.

18. Mills, "A Note on the Classification of 'Social Psychological Sciences,'" Mills Collection.

19. Ibid., p. 466.

20. Ibid.

21. Mills, "Sociological Methods and Philosophies of Science," Mills Collection.

22. Mills, "The Value Situation and the Vocabulary of Morals," Mills Collection.

23. Dewey, *Logic: The Theory of Inquiry*, pp. 492, 493.

24. Dewey, *Freedom and Culture*, p. 172.

25. Mihailo Marković, *From Affluence to Praxis*, pp. 53, 64.

26. See Mills' article on "The New Left" in *Power, Politics and People*, pp. 247–62.

27. Mills, *Power, Politics and People*, p. 606.

28. Mills, *Sociology and Pragmatism*, p. 405.

29. Mills, "For Ought," Mills Collection.

30. Ibid.

31. See Orion White, "The Concept of Administrative Praxis," in *The Dimensions of Public Administration*, ed. Joseph Uveges, pp. 96, 97.

32. Mills, *Sociology and Pragmatism*, pp. 368–69.

33. Dewey, *The Public and Its Problems*, pp. 202.

34. Mills, *Sociology and Pragmatism*, p. 405.

35. This is a summation of the prescriptions Mills makes in *The Power Elite*, pp. 293–304, and in *The Causes of World War III*, pp. 118–120.

36. However, as Richard Bernstein has pointed out, Dewey and Marx's conceptions of praxis have many similarities. Marxist "critics recognize how close in spirit the pragmatists are to Marx himself. Social praxis becomes the dominant category for Dewey as it does for Marx. Dewey also maintains that our practical activity shapes the entire range of our human activities, including our cognitive functions, and that this practical activity is itself shaped by social institutions in which we participate. Like Marx, Dewey believed that the only way to bring about a freer, more humane society in which creative individuality can flourish is by the transformation of objective social institutions. Like Marx, Dewey calls for a criticism of criticisms that is directed toward controlled change. And both agree that action which is not informed by correct understanding becomes futile and self-defeating. From a Marxist perspective these similarities between Marx and Dewey are not a basis for praising Dewey's philosophy, but for condemning it. Dewey's main failure is that failure to be genuinely radical, to get at the 'root.'" Bernstein, *Praxis and Action*, pp. 227–28. Mills' critical assessment of Deweyan social praxis can be found on pp. 394, 417 of *Sociology and Pragmatism*.

37. See Dewey's *Liberalism and Social Action*, pp. 54–55, 62, 70–73, 88–91 for a critique of the inadequacies of New Deal liberalism. For a critique of Marxism and Communist practice see his contribution to *The Meaning of Marx: A Symposium*, pp. 54–56. Mills' own conception of praxis is most clearly revealed in *The Power Elite*.

38. Mills, *Sociology and Pragmatism*, pp. 392–93.

39. The nature of Dewey's conception of individual moral autonomy is treated in more detail by Sara Garrigan-Burr in her "C. Wright Mills: His Political Perspective and Its Pragmatic Sources," p. 127. Also see John Carbonara, "Critical Empiricism in C. Wright Mills," pp. 84–87.

40. See Gerth and Mills, *Character and Social Structure*, pp. 112–129.

41. See Dewey's *Human Nature and Conduct*, p. 290.

42. Mills, *Sociology and Pragmatism*, p. 453.

43. Dewey, *The Public and Its Problems*, p. 12–13.

44. Mills, *The Power Elite*, pp. 302–3.

45. Dewey, *The Public and Its Problems*, p. 77.

46. Ibid., p. 131.

47. Ibid., p. 137. Both Dewey and Mills were critical at times of Walter Lippmann's thesis that publics do not exist.

48. Ibid., pp. 208–9. Dewey's concern is with the role of experts while Mills devoted more attention to political, corporate, and military elites.

49. Ibid., pp. 123–24.

50. Ibid., pp. 208–9.

50. See the excellent analysis of this and related problems by William J. Meyer, *Public Good and Political Authority*, pp. 37–38.

CHAPTER 8

1. Unfortunately, the Dewey-Mills correspondence sheds no light on their ideological differences. Instead, their letters deal primarily with the question of which philosophers were pragmatists. See Mills to Dewey, 29 October 1941, and Dewey to Mills, 3 November 1941, Mills Collection.

2. Marxist-Leninist interpretations to this effect are found in Howard Selsam, *Socialism and Ethics*, and Harry Wells, *Pragmatism: Philosophy of Imperialism*. Other radical interpretations include: George Novack, *Marxism and Pragmatism;* V. J. McGill, "Pragmatism Reconsidered: An Aspect of John Dewey's Philosophy," pp. 289–322; and Ernest Sutherland Bates, "John Dewey, America's Philosophic Engineer," pp. 387–96, 404.

3. Niebuhr argues that the development of scientific experimental procedures for the purposeful control of social changes is impossible in a community where there are "dominant social classes who are trying to maintain their special privileges in society." These pragmatic moralists fail to realize the "stubborn resistance of group egoism to all moral and inclusive social objectives." See *Moral Man and Immoral Society*, xi–xxxv. Also see Joan Huber Rytina and Charles P. Loomis, "Marxist Dialectic and Pragmatism: Power as Knowledge," p. 316.

4. See Randolph Bourne, *War and the Intellectuals*, edited with an introduction by Carl Resek, especially the essays entitled "A War Diary" and "Twilight of Idols." Of course, Bourne died before Dewey's growing radicalism became fully apparent. For a similar analysis see Lewis Mumford in *Pragmatism and American Culture*, ed. Gail Kennedy, pp. 36–49, 54–57.

5. Alfonso J. Damico, "Analysis and Advocacy: Pragmatism and the Study of Politics," p. 205.

6. Harold Stearns, *Liberalism in America*, pp. 180–84. Sterns also says (ibid.) that "The plain truth is that method and technique are subsidiary to ends and value in any rational philosophy either of politics or life, and that the pragmatists were so busy studying method that they had small time left for studying the purposes to which that method was to be applied." Also see A. E. Murphy, "John Dewey and American Liberalism," pp. 420–36. Unfortunately such analyses ignore the fact that the pragmatist's test for a good method is whether or not the method serves as a device for social betterment, progressive social evolution, or social reconstruction.

7. Morton White, *The Revolt against Formalism*, pp. 195, 200–202.

8. A. J. Somjee, *The Political Theory of John Dewey*, p. 174.

9. Howard B. White, "Political Faith of John Dewey," p. 361. There are other criticisms of Dewey by Arthur Lovejoy, George Santayana, Waldo Frank, Bertrand Russell, Lewis Mumford, and Joseph Wood Krutch. However, they are less relevant than those cited above.

10. Dewey, *Liberalism and Social Action*, p. 34.

11. Ibid, p. 32.

12. Ibid., pp. 47–48.

13. See especially "The Preconceptions of Economic Science," "Professor Clark's Economics" and "The Limitations of Marginal Utility" in Veblen's *The Place of Science in Modern Civilization and Other Essays*.

14. Mills, "Science and Society," Mills Collection.

15. Mills, *The Power Elite*, pp. 247–48.

16. Mills, *Sociology and Pragmatism*, p. 382.

17. Dewey, *Experience and Education*, p. 81.

18. See Mills' analysis in Chapter 11 of *The Power Elite*, entitled "The Theory of Balance."

19. Ibid., p. 246.

20. Dewey, *Liberalism and Social Action*, pp. 63–64. Also, see Lawrence L. Haworth's "Dewey's Philosophy of the Corporation," pp. 345–63.

21. Ibid., pp. 54–55. Also see p. 88.

22. See Frederick Swan's treatment of this in his "Toward a Relevant Social Science in the Work of C. Wright Mills," pp. 27–28.

23. Mills, *The Power Elite*, p. 299.

24. Ibid., p. 305.

25. In an early publication Mills characterized liberal ameliorism (incrementalism) in this manner: "The 'informational' character of social pathology is linked with a failure to consider total social structure. Collecting and dealing in a fragmentary way with scattered problems and facts, of milieux, these books (on social pathology) are not focused on larger stratifications or upon structured wholes." Mills, *Power, Politics and People*, pp. 526–27.

26. Mills, *Sociology and Pragmatism*, p. 382.

27. This is the interpretation of Mills' conception of incrementalism put forth by John Carbonara in his "Critical Empiricism in C. Wright Mills," pp. 23, 90–91.

28. Jim Cork quotes from a letter he received from Dewey in which Dewey said "I can be classed as a democratic socialist. If I were permitted to define 'socialism' and 'socialist,' I would so classify myself today." As quoted in Cork's "John Dewey, Karl Marx, and Democratic Socialism," p. 450. Consult the following Dewey sources: "America's Public Ownership Program," p. 1; "Taxation as a Step to Socialization," pp. 1–2; "The Imperative Need for a New Radical Party," in *Challenge to the New Deal*, ed. Alfred M. Bingham and Selden Rodman, 269–73; "No Half Way House for America," p. 1; "You Must Act to Get Congress to Act," p. 1; "Voters Must Demand Congress Tax Wealth Instead of Want," p. 1; "President's Policies Help Property Owners Chiefly," pp. 1–2; "The Drive against Hunger," p. 190.

29. Dewey, *Liberalism and Social Action*, p. 62.

30. Dewey, *Individualism Old and New*, pp. 119–20. Again, note the ambiguity and vagueness of the first sentence in the quotation.

31. Edward J. Bordeau, "John Dewey's Ideas about the Great Depression," pp. 78–79, 83–84.

32. Perhaps the strongest statement he made during this period is to be found in his "My Pedagogic Creed," p. 80.

33. George Dykhuizen, *The Life and Mind of John Dewey*, p. 221.

34. Dewey, "Why I Am for Smith," p. 320.

35. Ibid., p. 321.

36. See Charles F. Howlett, *Troubled Philosopher: John Dewey and the Struggle for World Peace*, pp. 124–25.

37. Dewey, "You Must Act to Get Congress to Act," pp. i, 1, 11. For a more detailed analysis of Dewey's political views during the 1930s see Edward Bordeau, "John Dewey's Ideas about the Great Depression," pp. 67–84.

38. *New York Times*, October 20, 1944, p. 32.

39. Mills wrote to his parents that "I am this November voting for Norman Thomas. I know he will not win but that does not mean the vote is lost. You both vote for him too.

His is the only anti-war party in the running." Undated letter, Mills to parents, Mills Collection.

40. Charles F. Howlett, *Troubled Philosopher*, p. x.

41. Ibid., pp. 28–29, 147–48.

42. Mills, *Sociology and Pragmatism*, p. 393. Also see pp. 343, 351–53, and Joseph Scimecca, *The Sociological Theory of C. Wright Mills*, p. 61. But also see Gary Bullert, "John Dewey in Politics," p. 300.

43. Mills, "Sum Up of J. D.," Mills Collection.

44. Mills, *Sociology and Pragmatism*, pp. 434–38.

45. See *The Power Elite*, pp. 259–74. Also see *White Collar*, p. 1.

46. Mills, "Reflection, Behavior and Culture," p. 45.

47. Mills, *Sociology and Pragmatism*, p. 380.

48. Mills, "The Conceptions and the Outcomes of Reflection," Mills Collection.

49. I am indebted to Sara Garrigan-Burr's study of Mills for this suggestion. See her "C. Wright Mills: His Political Perspective and Its Pragmatic Sources," p. 127.

50. See Lewis E. Hahn's "Dewey's Philosophy and Philosophic Method" in *Guide to the Works of John Dewey*, ed. Jo Ann Boydston, p. 34.

51. Dewey, *Reconstruction in Philosophy*, p. 1.

52. Dewey, *Logic: The Theory of Inquiry*, pp. 42–43.

53. Ibid., pp. 43–44. Also see p. 45.

54. Mills to Florian Zaniecki, 25 March 1940, Mills Collection.

55. Dewey, *The Quest for Certainty*, pp. 199–200.

56. Dewey, *The Public and Its Problems*, p. 36.

57. Ibid., p. 7.

58. Dewey, *The Quest for Certainty*, p. 213.

59. This is a paraphrase of Dewey's language in his *Logic: The Theory of Inquiry*, p. 499.

60. Ibid., pp. 104–5.

61. For a more elaborate treatment of this point see A. J. Somjee, *The Political Theory of John Dewey*, pp. 2, 3, 7.

62. Ibid., p. 61.

63. Dewey, *A Common Faith*, pp. 77–78.

64. "Outlines of a Critical Theory of Ethics," in *The Early Works of John Dewey, 1882–1898*, Vol. III, p. 320.

65. Mills, *Sociology and Pragmatism*, p. 441.

66. Dewey, A Common Faith, p. 81.

67. Dewey, *The Public and Its Problems*, p. 174.

68. Dewey, *Liberalism and Social Action*, pp. 80–81.

69. See Dewey, *Experience and Education*, p. 5.

70. See, for example, H. S. Thayer, *Meaning and Action: A Critical History of Pragmatism*, p. 182.

71. Mills, *Sociology and Pragmatism*, pp. 418–19. But for a rebuttal of such claims see Dewey's *A Common Faith*, pp. 77–78, and his "Authority and Social Change" in *Authority and the Individual*, p. 187.

72. Mills, *Sociology and Pragmatism*, p. 410.

73. Dewey, *The Quest for Certainty*, p. 265. In this respect another Dewey comment is illuminating: "The thesis that the operation of cooperative intelligence as displayed in science is a working model of the union of freedom and authority does not slight the fact that the method has operated up to the present in a limited and relatively technical area. On the contrary, it emphasized that fact. If the method of intelligence had been employed in any large field in the comprehensive and basic area of the relations of human beings to one another in social life and institutions, there would be no present need for our argument. The contrast between the restricted scope of its use and the possible range of its application of human relations—political, economic, and moral—is outstanding and depressing. It is this very contrast that defines the great problem that still has to

be solved." Dewey, "Authority and Social Change," in *Authority and the Individual,* p. 187.

74. Mills, *Sociology and Pragmatism,* p. 434.

75. Ibid., p. 394.

76. Ibid.

77. Ibid., p. 400.

78. Ibid., p. 410. "But when in ethics itself he comes to examine the normative we get a method. It is a formal method without specific content; ethics becomes engineering. All these *normative* concerns of Dewey tend strongly to be without specific content . . . this 'method' shies away from all value hierarchies, that is, specific commitments to specific contents. It legitimized this hesitancy in terms of the processual character of the world; the implication of 'evolution' for pragmatism, as this implication lies in the political sphere, is hesitancy and a type of tentativeness which can be and has correctly been called expediency . . . that leads into one, perhaps the most central feature of the Deweyan rational style of thought and strategy: he *methodized* everything." Mills, "Sum Up of J. D.," Mills Collection.

79. Dewey, *Reconstruction in Philosophy,* p. 175.

80. Ibid., p. 176.

81. Dewey, *Human Nature and Conduct,* p. 282.

82. Dewey, *Democracy and Education,* pp. 89–90.

83. Ibid., 118–29.

84. Dewey, *Human Nature and Conduct,* p. 282.

85. On this last point see Dewey's "Philosophies of Freedom" in *Freedom in the Modern World,* ed. Horace Meyer Kallen, p. 261.

86. See George E. Axtelle and Joe R. Barnett, "Dewey on Education and Schooling" in Boydston, 1970.

87. Dewey, *Democracy and Education,* pp. 59–60.

88. Mills, *Sociology and Pragmatism,* p. 456–57.

89. Ibid., p. 458.

90. Dewey, *Experience and Education,* p. 36.

91. Ibid., p. 84.

92. Dewey, *Democracy and Education,* pp. 114–15.

93. Ibid., p. 90.

94. Ibid., pp. 60, 62.

95. For a more elaborate treatment of this aspect of Dewey's thought see George E. Axtelle and Joe R. Burnett, "Dewey on Education and Schooling," p. 288–89.

96. See Sidney Hook's summation in "John Dewey—Philosopher of Growth," pp. 1017–18.

97. Dewey, *The Public and Its Problems,* pp. 107–8.

98. Dewey, *Human Nature and Conduct,* p. 276.

99. Ibid., pp. 76–77.

100. Dewey, *Liberalism and Social Action,* pp. 74–75.

101. Ibid., pp. 75–76.

102. Ibid., pp. 64–65.

103. Mills, *Sociology and Pragmatism,* p. 333.

104. Mills, "Reflection, Behavior and Culture," p. 54.

105. Mills, *Sociology and Pragmatism,* p. 382.

106. Dewey, *Freedom and Culture,* p. 143.

107. Ibid., p. 165.

108. Dewey, *Liberalism and Social Action,* p. 74.

109. Mills, *Sociology and Pragmatism,* pp. 416–17.

110. See Paul Sweezy and Herbert Aptheker in G. William Domhoff and Hoyt Ballard eds., *C. Wright Mills and the Power Elite,* pp. 115–64. Also see Aptheker's *The World of C. Wright Mills.* Mills elaborates on this theme: "The character which Dewey gives action may be, in part explained by tacit awareness, or a desire to avoid the conse-

quences foretold in the truism that when thought gets hitched to political action, it tends strongly to become rigid, to ignore factual matters which would embarrass it by changes. Such a situation also goes into the explanation of why Dewey has been rather liberally mugwumpish in politics and why 'action' is not linked with a sizable organization, a movement, a party with a chance at power. The concept of action in Dewey obviously does not cover the kinds of action occuring within and between struggling, organized political parties. . . . Politically, pragmatism is less expediency than it is a kind of perennial mugwump confronted with rationalized social structures." Mills, *Sociology and Pragmatism*, p. 394.

111. Ibid., p. 324.

112. James H. Tufts to Mills, 6 December 1941, Mills Collection.

113. Dewey was instrumental in organizing and/or leading numerous organizations. Since Mills was aware of this he was probably criticizing Dewey for vacillating in his support between liberal and radical organizations instead of consistently adhering to a "radical" line.

CHAPTER 9

1. See Joseph Dorfman's *Thorstein Veblen and His America* and George Dykhuizen's *The Life and Mind of John Dewey.*

2. Mills, Veblen, and Dewey were aware of the claim that history, in being a process of change, generates change not only in details but also in the method of directing social change. See Dewey, *Liberalism and Social Action*, p. 83. For Dewey, this meant the gradual realization on the part of the public that the method of social intelligence was the only effective way of permanently altering and directing the present as history. For Veblen it meant a wholesale, but probably futile, onslaught on the vested interests at both the ideological and institutional levels; for Mills it implied both, but it also required that the political intellectual, as recommended by Dewey, locate the sources of evil, propagandize their nature and existence, and mobilize a political coalition to defeat them.

3. John Walton makes several of these same points in "The Sociological Imagination of Thorstein Veblen," pp. 418–64.

4. For an important exception to this generalization, see Phillip Abbott's *Furious Fancies: American Political Thought in the Post-Liberal Era.* Abbott distinguishes in Chapter 1 between four forms of liberalism in addition to classical laissez-faire. They are welfare liberalism, utopian liberalism, pluralist liberalism, and scientific liberalism.

5. Dewey, *Liberalism and Social Action*, p. 62.

6. John H. Schaar, "The Case for Patriotism," pp. 97, 98.

7. Richard Pells makes this point repeatedly in his excellent study of left intellectuals in the 1930s. See his *Radical Visions and American Dreams.*

8. C. Wright Mills, *Sociology and Pragmatism*, p. 405.

9. Ibid.

10. Veblen, *The Theory of the Leisure Class*, p. 24.

11. For a treatment of this theme in Dewey see Arthur Lothstein, "Salving from the Dross: John Dewey's Anarchocommunalism" pp. 55–111.

12. Veblen, *Imperial Germany and the Industrial Revolution*, pp. 291–325.

13. Ibid., 326–327. Although Mills and Dewey shared Veblen's admiration for a decentralized communal social order, they were more optimistic than he about utilizing centralized governmental power to implement programs to aid the common man. This difference reflects the belief of Dewey and Mills that government is potentially capable of acting on behalf of groups that presently lack status and power. This was a view Veblen did not share since he held that government, as the instrument of the ruling class, was not likely to aid the powerless.

14. Compare these central themes in Mills, *Power, Politics and People*, p. 347–53,

and *The Sociological Imagination*, pp. 195–226, with Veblen, *The Instinct of Workmanship;* Dewey, *Art as Experience;* and Mead, *The Philosophy of the Act.*

15. This discussion of the forms "individualism" can take owes much to Frederick L. Pryor's review, p. 133.

16. Chandler, "Institutionalism and Education: An Inquiry into the Implications of the Philosophy of Thorstein Veblen," p. 252. Although Veblen's primary orientation lay in the community, he was not oblivious to the individual, for his entire social philosophy is directed toward the fuller realization of man's potential. However, since the Veblenian individual is completely socialized, he has no independent being. He is an abstraction from the reality of society. Thus, when Veblen on rare occasion writes of the individual, he is in fact writing of the community, since in his view the community and the individual are almost identical ways of looking at society. Because Veblen submerges the individual so deeply in the community, the individuals he writes about lack unique traits. The only exceptions to this are the uncommon instances of the "Marginal Man," usually an intellectual in pursuit of idle curiosity, who calls into question the mores and beliefs of the community.

17. This is also an important theme in Dewey's *Individualism Old and New.*

18. Ibid.

19. See Mead's *Mind, Self and Society.*

20. Paul Conkin believes these two traits are characteristic of the thought of other leading figures in American intellectual history. See his *Puritans and Pragmatists*, p. v.

21. This is the central thesis in his *The American as Anarchist: Reflections on Indigenous Radicalism.*

22. Ibid., 154.

23. Richard Gillam, "C. Wright Mills and the Politics of Truth: The Power Elite Revisited," p. 471.

24. See Peter Steinfels, *The Neoconservatives* for an excellent analysis of the origins and characteristics of the present neoconservative movement.

25. David Marcell, *Progressives and Reform*, pp. x–xi.

26. Veblen's attitudes toward progress were ambivalent, because while he viewed scientific and technological innovation as progressive, he was skeptical that moral and institutional progress were also occurring. His view can be contrasted with the intermittent claim of Dewey and Mills that social growth is occurring and that it provides the moral criterion whereby both social evolution and individual action can be called progressive. Veblen came at last to the conclusion that the atavistic continuities that he satirized might indeed overwhelm mankind, whereas Mills believed the radical intellec-tual and his allies were at least potentially capable of bringing the high and the mighty to their knees. Dewey, of course, usually saw a glimmer of light even in the most tragic and desperate situation—although, contrary to popular opinion, he did not believe the golden era was about to be ushered in.

27. See Daniel Bell, "The Big, Bad Americans," p. 116.

28. There are Marxist journals published in the United States, such as *Telos* and the now defunct *Marxist Perspectives*, which are less afflicted by ideological closure and intellectual sectarianism. Nevertheless, *Telos* is a good example of a journal that is open to such European intellectual currents as critical theory, existentialism, phenomenology, and structuralism, yet largely ignores the American doctrines such as instrumentalism and institutionalism, which influenced Mills.

29. See J. L. Simich and Rick Tilman, "Critical Theory and Institutional Economics: Frankfurt's Encounter with Veblen," pp. 631–45.

CHAPTER 10

1. I am indebted to Mary Kraetzer, *The Sociology of Knowledge of Thorstein Veblen and C. Wright Mills*, and to Paul Conkin, *Puritans and Pragmatists*, for their earlier exploration of several of the themes on which this chapter focuses.

2. Guy Stroh, *American Ethical Thought*, p. 21.

3. Mary Kraetzer, "The Sociology of Knowledge of Thorstein Veblen and C. Wright Mills," p. 7.

4. Mills, *The Causes of World War III*, p. 171.

5. Mills, *Character and Social Structure*, p. 188.

6. Unpublished manuscript, no title, Mills Collection. The pamphleteering of the Puritans against social and political evils led to the emergence of written criticism as an important form of protest against oppression and provides still another link with our central figures. The Puritans used the critical essay in its pamphlet form as a device to attack religious and political exploitation and it became part of the American radical intellectual heritage. Mills specifically referred to his *The Causes of World War III* and *Listen Yankee* as "pamphlets." Veblen's *The Vested Interests and the Common Man*, *The Engineers and the Price System*, and *The Higher Learning in America*, and Dewey's polemical writing in *Individualism Old and New*, and *The People's Lobby Bulletin* may also be viewed in this light.

7. See Conkin's *Puritans and Pragmatists*. An important bond between all four of our central figures is that they had a considerable knowledge of early Protestant thought and practice. It is also worth noting that they were not satisfied with interpreting it through secondary sources or through the lens of earlier intellectual movements. Instead, they went to the original source material.

8. Mills, introduction to *The Theory of the Leisure Class*, p. xi.

9. As quoted in Joseph Dorfman, *Thorstein Veblen and His America*, p. 450.

10. On this point see Garrigan-Burr "C. Wright Mills: His Political Perspective and Its Pragmatic Sources," pp. 23–24. In pragmatic thought, the general conception of personhood rejected determinism. Mills with the relativism characteristic of a pragmatist resisted any claims that history, like a law of science, operates inevitably. He denied there were any historical "laws" when he wrote that: "Just as there is a variety of social structures, there is a variety of principles of historical change . . . for we don't know any universal principles of historical change." Mills, *The Sociological Imagination*, p. 150.

11. In recent years, by his own account, ex-Yippie Jerry Rubin has tried (in alphabetical order) acupuncture, bioenergetics, EST, Fischer-Hoffman therapy, Gestalt therapy, health foods, hypnotism, jogging, Reichian therapy, rolfing and yoga. Rubin, born in 1938 and an ex-stockbroker in 1983, operates a singles club in New York. He recently stated approvingly that "People now want connections, contacts, money. They want to translate their dreams into money . . . money is power." As quoted in the *Los Angeles Times*, 27 November 1982, Part I, p. 6.

12. Lewis Feuer, *Ideology and the Ideologists*, pp. 56–57. I endorse only the part cited. The rest of Feuer's book is an intellectually and politically irresponsible tirade against the left.

13. Bruce Miroff, *Pragmatic Illusions: The Presidential Politics of John F. Kennedy*.

14. Ralph Barton Perry, *Puritanism and Democracy*, p. 60.

15. Friedrich Engels, "Ludwig Feuerbach and the End of Classical German Philosophy," p. 242.

Bibliography

Most of the best writing on Mills' background has been done by graduate students. Indeed, with few exceptions, more mature scholars have shown little knowledge of Mills' intellectual antecedents. As a result this book owes far more to authors of dissertations and theses than it does to the luminaries of the sociology profession. I have found five doctoral dissertations on Mills to be of particular value. They are Robert P. Jones, "The Fixing of Social Belief: The Sociology of C. Wright Mills"; Sara Garrigan-Burr, "C. Wright Mills: His Political Perspective and Its Pragmatic Sources"; John Carbonara, "Critical Empiricism in C. Wright Mills"; Benjamin Smith, "The Political Theory of Institutional Economics"; and Mary C. Kraetzer, "The Sociology of Knowledge of Thorstein Veblen and C. Wright Mills." These dissertations are considerably better than the average level of work done by American doctoral candidates. I have used them extensively and often cited them.

As of July 1977, only a handful of other scholars had used the C. Wright Mills Collection, which is housed at the Barker Texas History Archive at the University of Texas at Austin. It was organized as Mills left it at his death, and although important for understanding how he worked, it was awkward to use—letters, notes, manuscripts, books and articles were often dumped indiscriminately into the same box with little semblance of order.

I have also used the Clarence Edwin Ayres Collection, which also is housed at the Barker Texas History Archive. It is an invaluable aid in understanding the intellectual milieu that existed at Austin when Mills was a student there in the late 1930s.

The bibliography does not contain a complete list of writings by and about Mills. The best sources of this information are Mills' *Power, Politics and People,* and John Anson Warner's "The Critics of C. Wright Mills: Ideology and the Study of Political Power in America." Nor does it list the unpublished manuscripts that are in the Mills Collection. The best source of information regarding these is

Robert Paul Jones' dissertation "The Fixing of Social Belief: The Sociology of C. Wright Mills," which lists the manuscripts by title and gives a brief summary of the contents of each.

No effort is made to list all of the voluminous published material on or by Dewey and Veblen. Only the Dewey-Veblen scholarship that played a direct role in the organization and research of this book is mentioned. A bibliography of Dewey's writings has been compiled by Milton Halsey Thomas: *John Dewey, A Centennial Bibliography* (Chicago: University of Chicago Press, 1962). This volume also contains extensive listing of works about Dewey, reviews of his books, and pertinent unpublished theses and dissertations. Another excellent source of information on Dewey scholarship is Jo Ann Boydston and Kathleen Poulos: *Checklist of Writings about John Dewey 1887–1973* (Carbondale: Southern Illinois Press, 1974). A comprehensive listing of Veblen's published work is found in Joseph Dorfman: *Thorstein Veblen and His America* (New York: Viking Press, 1947). An annotated bibliography of writings about Veblen is contained in Rick Tilman and J. L. Simich: *Thorstein Veblen: A Critical Guide* (Boston: G. K. Hall and Company, forthcoming).

ARTICLES

Adorno, T. W. "Veblen's Attack on Culture." *Journal of Philosophy and Social Sciences* 9, April 1941.

Aiken, Henry. "C. Wright Mills and the Pragmatists." *New York Review of Books* 3, March 11, 1965.

Ayres, Clarence. "Economic Essentials of a Lasting Peace." Southwestern Social Science Quarterly 24, June 1943.

———. Gospel of Technology," in Kallen and Hook, 1968

———. "Two Approaches to Our Imperfections." *New Leader* 34, June 18, 1956

———. "What Should Teachers Swear?" *Southwestern Review* 35, Autumn 1950.

Axtelle, George, and Joe R. Burnett. "Dewey on Education and Schooling," in Boydston, 1970.

Baran, Paul. "The Theory of the Leisure Class." *Monthly Review* 3 and 4, July–August 1957.

Bates, Ernest Sutherland. "John Dewey, America's Philosophic Engineer." *Modern Monthly* 7, August 1933.

Batiuk, Mary E., and Howard L. Sacks. "George Herbert Mead and Karl Marx: Explaining Consciousness and Community." *Symbolic Interaction* 4, Fall 1981.

Becker, Ernest. "Mills' Social Psychology and the Problem of Alienation," in Horowitz, ed., 1964.

Bell, Daniel. "The Power Elite Reconsidered," in Ballard and Domhoff, eds., 1968.

———. "Veblen and the New Class." *American Scholar* 32, Autumn 1963.

Bobbio, Norberto. "Is There a Marxist Theory of the State?" *Telos* No. 35, Spring 1978.

Bordeau, Edward J. "John Dewey's Ideas about the Great Depression." *Journal of the History of Ideas* 32, January–March 1971.

Breit, William. "The Development of Clarence Ayres' Theoretical Institutionalism." *Social Science Quarterly* 54, September 1973.

Burgum, Edwin Berry. "American Sociology in Transition." *Science and Society* 24, Fall 1959.

Corey, Lewis. "Veblen and Marx." *Marxist Quarterly* 2, Spring 1937.

Cork, Jim. "John Dewey, Karl Marx, and Democratic Socialism." *Antioch Review* 9, December 1949.

Cronk, George F. "Symbolic Interactionism: A "Left-Median" Interpretation." *Symbolic Interaction*, Fall 1981.

Damico, Alfonso J. "Analysis and Advocacy: Pragmatism and the Study of Politics." *Polity* 7, Winter 1974.

Davis, Arthur K. "Veblen, Thorstein." *International Encyclopedia of the Social Sciences*, vol. 16.

Dewey, John. "America's Public Ownership Program." *People's Lobby Bulletin*, May 1932.

———. "The Drive against Hunger." *New Republic* 74, March 1933.

———. "The Imperative Need for a New Radical Party." *Common Sense* 2, 1933. Reprinted in Bingham and Rodman, pp. 269–73.

———. "My Pedagogic Creed." *School Journal* 54, 1897.

———. "No Half Way House for America." *People's Lobby Bulletin*, June 1934.

———. "Outlines of a Critical Theory of Ethics," in *The Early Works of John Dewey, 1882–1898*, 1969, vol. 3.

———. "Philosophies of Freedom," in Kallen, 1928.

———. "President's Policies Help Property Owners Chiefly." *People's Lobby Bulletin*, November 1934.

———. "Some Questions about Value." *Journal of Philosophy* 41, August 17, 1944.

———. "Taxation as a Step to Socialization." *People's Lobby Bulletin* 4, March 1935.

———. "Voters Must Demand Congress Tax Wealth Instead of Want." *People's Lobby Bulletin*, June 1932.

———. "Why I Am for Smith." *New Republic* 56, November 7, 1928.

———. "You Must Act to Get Congress to Act." *People's Lobby Bulletin*, May 1932.

Diggins, John P. "The Socialization of Authority and the Dilemmas of American Liberalism." *Social Research* 46, Autumn 1976.

Elliott, John. "An Approach to Political Economy." *Journal of Economic Issues* 12, March 1978.

Franklin, Raymond S., and William K. Tabb. "The Challenge of Radical Political Economics." *Journal of Economic Issues* 8, March 1974.

Giddens, Anthony. "Classical Social Theory and the Origins of Modern Sociology." *American Journal of Sociology* 81, January 1976.

Gillam, Richard. "C. Wright Mills and the Politics of Truth: The Power Elite Revisited." *American Quarterly* 27, 1975.

———. "Intellectuals and Power." *Center Magazine* 10, May–June 1977.

———. "White Collar from Start to Finish: C. Wright Mills in Transition." *Theory and Society* 10, January 1981.

Hahn, Lewis E. "Dewey's Philosophy and Philosophic Method," in Boydston, ed., 1970.

Haworth, Lawrence L. "Dewey's Philosophy of the Corporation." *Educational Theory* 20, 1970.

Hodder, H. J. "Political Ideas of Thorstein Veblen." *Canadian Journal of Economics and Political Science* 22, August 1956.

Hodges, Donald Clark. "The Fourth Epoch: Epilogue to the Unfinished Social Philosophy of C. Wright Mills." *Philosophy and Phenomenological Research* 29, March 1969.

Hook, Sidney. "John Dewey—Philosopher of Growth." *Journal of Philosophy* 56, December 1959.

Horowitz, Irving L. "The Protestant Weber and the Spirit of American Sociology." *History of European Ideas* 3, No. 4, 1982.

———. "The Unfinished Writings of C. Wright Mills," *Studies on the Left* 3, Fall 1963.

Howe, Irving. "An American Tragedy." *Dissent* 10, Spring 1963.

Kallen, Horace. "Individuality, Individualism and John Dewey." *Antioch Review* 19, Fall 1959.

Kassoff, Allen. "American Sociology through Soviet Eyes." *American Sociological Review* 30, February 1965.

Kennedy, Gail. "The Process of Evaluation in a Democratic Community." *Journal of Philosophy* 56, March 1959.

Kerbo, Harold R., and L. Richard Della Fave. "The Empirical Side of the Power Elite Debate: An Assessment and Critique of Recent Research." *Sociological Quarterly* 20, Winter 1979.

Klein, Philip A. "American Institutionalism: Premature Death, Permanent Resurrection." *Journal of Economic Issues* 12, June 1978.

Landau, Sal. "C. Wright Mills: The Last Six Months." *Ramparts* 4, August 1965.

Leathers, Charles and Joseph Pluta. "Veblen and Modern Radical Economics." *Journal of Economic Issues* 12, March 1978.

Lichtheim, George. "Rethinking World Politics." *Commentary* 28, September 1959.

Lichtman, Richard. "Symbolic Interactionism and Social Reality: Some Marxist Queries." *Berkeley Journal of Sociology* 15, 1970.

Lipset, S. M., and Neil Smelser. "Change and Controversy in Recent American Sociology." *British Journal of Sociology* 12, March 1961.

Lothstein, Arthur. "Salving from the Dross: John Dewey's Anarchocommunalism." *Philosophic Forum* 10, Fall 1978.

MacDonald, H. Malcolm. "The Revival of Conservative Thought." *Journal of Politics* 19, February 1957.

McGill, V. J. "Pragmatism Reconsidered: An Aspect of John Dewey's Philosophy." *Science and Society* 3, Summer 1939.

Metz, Joseph. "Democracy and the Scientific Method in the Philosophy of John Dewey." *Review of Politics* 31, April 1969.

Miliband, Ralph. "C. Wright Mills." *New Left Review*, No. 15, May–June 1962.

Mills, C. Wright. "Comment on Criticism," in Ballard and Domhoff, eds., 1968.

———. "The Contribution of Sociology to Studies of Industrial Relations." *Berkeley Journal of Sociology* 15, 1970.

———. "On Intellectual Craftsmanship," in Gross, 1959.

———. "The Power Elite: Military, Economic and Political," in Kornhauser, ed., 1957.

———. "Psychology and Social Science." *Monthly Review* 10, October 1958.

Mills, C. Wright, and Patricia Salter. "The Barricade and the Bedroom." *Politics* 4, October 1945.

Moskos, Charles G. "The Concept of the Military-Industrial Complex: Radical Critique or Liberal Bogey?" *Social Problems* 21, April 1974.

Murphy, A. E. "John Dewey and American Liberalism" *Journal of Philosophy* 57, June 1960.

Parsons, Talcott. "Comment on Llewelyn Gross: Preface to a Metatheoretical Framework for Sociology." *American Journal of Sociology* 67, September 1961.

Pells, Richard. "From Community to Conformity: Social Criticism in the Postwar Years." *Philosophic Forum* 10, Fall 1978.

Peterson, Richard A. "The Intellectual Career of C. Wright Mills: A Case of the Sociological Imagination." *Wisconsin Sociologist* 1, Fall 1962.

Petryszak, Nicholas. "The Biosociology of the Social Self." *Sociological Quarterly* 20, Spring 1979.

Phillips, Derek. "Epistemology and the Sociology of Knowledge: The Contributions of Mannheim, Mills and Merton." *Theory and Society* 1, 1974.

Portis, Edward. "Political Action and Social Science: Max Weber's Two Arguments for Objectivity." *Polity* 12, Spring 1980.

Riesman, David. "The Social and Psychological Setting of Veblen's Economic Theory." *Journal of Economic History* 23, Fall 1953.

Rytina, Joan Huber, and Charles P. Loomis. "Marxist Dialectic and Pragmatism: Power as Knowledge." *American Sociological Review* 35, April 1970.

Schaar, John. "The Case for Patriotism." *New American Review* 17, May 1973.

Schroyer, Trent. "The Critical Theory of Late Capitalism" in Fischer, 1971.

Scimeca, Joseph. "Paying Homage to the Father: C. Wright Mills and Radical Sociology." *Sociological Quarterly* 17, Spring 1976.

Sharp, G. B. "Mills and Weber: Formalism and the Analysis of Social Structure." *Science and Society* 24, Spring 1960.

Shils, Edward. "Imaginary Sociology." *Encounter* 16, June 1960.

———. "The Great Obsession." *Spectator*, 5 July 1963.

Sigler, J. A. "The Political Philosophy of C. Wright Mills." *Science and Society* 30, Winter 1966.

Simich, J. L., and Rick Tilman. "Critical Theory and Institutional Economics: Frankfurt's Encounter with Veblen." *Journal of Economic Issues* 14, September 1980.

———. "On the Use and Abuse of Thorstein Veblen in Modern American Sociology," II, *American Journal of Economics and Sociology*, forthcoming.

Smith, John. "The Value of Community: Dewey and Royce." *Southern Journal of Philosophy* 12, Winter 1974.

Tilman, Rick. "Dewey's Liberalism versus Veblen's Radicalism: A Reappraisal of the Unity of Progressive Social Thought." *Journal of Economic Issues*, forthcoming (1984).

———. "The Intellectual Pedigree of C. Wright Mills: A Reappraisal." *Western Political Quarterly* 31, December 1979.

———. "Thorstein Veblen: Incrementalist and Utopian." *American Journal of Economics and Sociology* 32, April 1973.

———. "Value Theory, Planning and Reform: Ayres as Incrementalist and Utopian." *Journal of Economic Issues* 8, December 1974.

———. "Veblen's Ideal Political Economy and Its Critics." *American Journal of Economics and Sociology* 31, July 1972.

Tilman, Rick, and J. L. Simich. "C. Wright Mills' Critique of John Dewey's Political Ideas." *American Journal of Economics and Sociology* 37, October 1978.

Walker, Donald. "Some Reflection on Veblenian Economics." *Economic Inquiry*, Fall 1977.

———. "Thorstein Veblen's Economic System." *Economic Inquiry* 15, April 1977.

Wallace, David. "Reflections on the Education of George H. Mead." *American Journal of Sociology* 72, January 1967.

Wallerstein, Immanuel. "Mills, C. Wright." *International Encyclopedia of the Social Sciences*, vol. 10. New York: Macmillan and Free Press, 1968.

Walton, John. "The Sociological Imagination of Thorstein Veblen." *Social Science Quarterly* 60, December 1979.

Warde, William F. "The Marxists." *International Socialist Review* 23, Summer 1962.

Weinstein, Michael, and Deena Weinstein. "Sartre and the Humanist Tradition in Sociology," in Warnock, 1971.

Werlin, Robert. "Marxist Political Analysis." *Sociological Inquiry* 42, Numbers 3 and 4 (Special Issue), 1972.

White, Howard B. "Political Faith of John Dewey." *Journal of Politics* 20, May 1958.

White, Orion. "The Concept of Administrative Praxis." In *The Dimensions of Public Administration*. Joseph Uveges, ed. Boston: Holbrook Press, Inc., 2nd ed., 1975.

Wolfinger, Raymond. "Rejoinder to Frey's 'Comment'." *American Political Science Review* 65, December 1971.

Wrong, Dennis. "The Oversocialized Conception of Man in Modern Sociology." *American Sociological Review* 26, April 1961.

Zeitlin, Irving M. "The Plain Marxism of C. Wright Mills," in Fischer, ed., 1971.

BOOKS

Aaron, Daniel. *Writers on the Left*. New York: Harcourt, Brace and World, 1961.

Abbott, Phillip. *Furious Fancies: American Political Thought in the Post-Liberal Era*. Westport, CT: Greenwood Press, 1980.

Anderson, Charles H. *The Political Economy of Social Class*. Englewood Cliffs, NJ: Prentice-Hall, 1974.

Aptheker, Herbert. *The World of C. Wright Mills*. New York: Marsani and Munsell, 1960.

Ayres, Clarence. *The Divine Right of Capital*. New York: Houghton Mifflin Co., 1946.

———. *Holier than Thou: The Way of the Righteous*. Indianapolis: Bobbs-Merrill Co., 1929.

———. *Huxley*. New York: W. W. Norton & Co., 1932.

———. *The Industrial Economy: Its Technological Basis and Institutional Destiny*. New York: Houghton Mifflin Co., 1952.

———. *The Nature of the Relationship between Ethics and Economics*. Chicago: University of Chicago Press, Philosophic Study No. 8, 1918.

———. *The Problem of Economic Order*. New York: Farrar and Rinehart, 1938.

———. *Science—The False Messiah*. Indianapolis: Bobbs-Merrill Co., 1927.

———. *The Theory of Economic Progress*. Chapel Hill: University of North Carolina Press, 1944.

———. *Toward a Reasonable Society: The Values of Industrial Civilization*. Austin: University of Texas Press, 1961.

Ballard, Hoyt, and G. William Domhoff, eds., *C. Wright Mills and the Power Elite*. Boston, Beacon Press, 1968.

Bernstein, Richard. *The Restructuring of Social and Political Theory*. Philadelphia: University of Pennsylvania Press, 1976.

———. *Praxis and Action*. Philadelphia: University of Pennsylvania Press, 1974.

Bingham, Alfred M., and Selden Rodman, eds. *Challenge to the New Deal*. New York: Falcon Press, 1934.

Bluhm, William T. *Theories of the Political System*. Englewood Cliffs, NJ: Prentice-Hall, 1965.

Bohlke, Robert H., and Kenneth Winetrout. *Bureaucrats and Intellectuals: A Critique of C. Wright Mills*. Springfield, MA: American International College, 1963.

Bottomore, T. B. *Critics of Society: Radical Thought in North America*. New York: Random House, 1968.

Bourne, Randolph. *War and the Intellectuals*, ed. Carl Resek. New York: Harper and Row, 1964.

Boydston, Jo Ann, ed. *Guide to Works of John Dewey*. Carbondale and Edwardsville: Southern Illinois Press, 1970.

Boydston, Jo Ann, and Kathleen Poulos. *Checklist of Writings about John Dewey 1887–1973*. Carbondale: Southern Illinois University Press, 1974.

Burnham, James. *The Machiavellians*. New York: Regnery, 1963.

Calhoun, Daniel H., *The Intelligence of a People*. Princeton: Princeton University Press, 1973.

Collins, Randall, and Michael Makowsky. *The Discovery of Society*. New York: Random House, 1972.

Commons, John R., et al. *History of Labor in the United States*. 4 vols. New York: Macmillan Co., 1935.

Conkin, Paul. *Puritans and Pragmatists*. Bloomington: Indiana University Press, 1976.

Corti, Walter R., ed. *The Philosophy of George Herbert Mead*. Winterthur, Switzerland: Amriswiler Bucherei, 1973.

Damico, Alfonso. *Individuality and Community: The Social and Political Thought of John Dewey*. Gainesville: University of Florida Press, 1978.

DeLeon, David. *The American as Anarchist: Reflections on Indigenous Radicalism*. Baltimore: Johns Hopkins University Press, 1978.

Dewey, John. *A Common Faith*. New Haven: Yale University Press, 1960.

———. *Art as Experience*. New York: G. P. Putnam's Sons, 1958.

———. *Authority and the Individual*. Harvard Tercentenary Publications, ed. Cambridge, MA: Harvard University Press, 1937.

———. *Contemporary American Philosophy*, II, ed. George Plimpton Adams and William P. Montague. New York: Macmillan Co., 1930.

———, et al. *Creative Intelligence: Essays in the Pragmatic Spirit*. New York: Henry Holt and Co., 1917.

———. *Democracy and Education*. New York: Macmillan Co., 1916.

———. *The Early Works of John Dewey, 1882–1898*, vol. 3. Carbondale: Southern Illinois University Press, 1969.

———. *Essays in Experimental Logic*. New York: Dover Publications, n.d. (first published in 1916).

———. *Experience and Education*. New York: Collier Books, 1963.

———. *Experience and Nature*. Chicago: Open Court Publishing Co., 1925.

———. *Experience and Nature*, second edition, revised. New York: Dover Publications, 1958.

———. *Freedom and Culture*. New York: G. P. Putnam's Sons, 1963.

———. *Human Nature and Conduct*. New York: Modern Library, 1930.

————. *Individualism Old and New.* New York: G. P. Putnam's Sons, 1962.

————. *Liberalism and Social Action.* New York: G. P. Putnam's Sons, 1963.

————. *Logic: The Theory of Inquiry.* New York: Holt, Rinehart and Winston, 1938.

————, et al. *The Meaning of Marx: A Symposium.* New York: Farrar and Rinehart, 1934.

————. *Philosophy and Civilization.* New York: G. P. Putnam's Sons, 1963.

————. *Problems of Men.* New York: Philosophical Library, 1946.

————. *The Public and Its Problems.* Denver: Alan Swallow, 1954.

————. *The Quest for Certainty.* New York: G. P. Putnam's Sons, 1960.

————. *Reconstruction in Philosophy,* enlarged edition. Boston: Beacon Press, 1959.

Dewey, John, and Arthur F. Bentley. *Knowing and the Known.* Boston: Beacon Press, 1949

Dewey, John, and James H. Tufts. *Ethics.* Revised edition. New York: Henry Holt and Co., 1932.

Diggins, John P. *The Bard of Savagery: Thorstein Veblen and Modern Social Theory.* New York: Seabury Press, 1978.

Dobriansky, Lev. *Veblenism: A New Critique.* Washington, DC: Public Affairs Press, 1957.

Dorfman, Joseph. *Thorstein Veblen and His America.* New York: Viking Press, 1934.

Dowd, Douglas. *Thorstein Veblen: A Critical Reappraisal.* Ithaca: Cornell University Press, 1967.

Drukman, Mason. *Community and Purpose in America: An Analysis of American Political Theory.* New York: McGraw-Hill, 1971.

Dykhuizen, George. *The Life and Mind of John Dewey.* Carbondale: Southern Illinois University Press, 1973.

Elliott, William Y. *The Pragmatic Revolt in Politics: Syndicalism, Fascism and the Constitutional State.* New York: Howard Fertig, 1968.

Feuer, Lewis. *Ideology and the Ideologists.* New York: Harper, 1974.

————, ed. *Marx and Engels: Basic Writings on Politics and Philosophy.* Garden City, NY: Doubleday, 1959.

Fischer, George, ed. *The Revival of American Capitalism.* New York: Oxford University Press, 1971.

Galbraith, John K. *American Capitalism.* Boston: Houghton Mifflin, 1952.

Gambs, John. *Beyond Supply and Demand.* New York: Columbia University Press, 1947.

Gans, Herbert, et al. *On the Making of Americans: Essays in Honor of David Riesman.* Philadelphia: University of Pennsylvania Press, 1979.

Gerth, H. H., and C. Wright Mills, eds. *Character and Social Structure: The Psychology of Social Institutions.* New York: Harcourt Brace Jovanovich, 1953.

————. *From Max Weber.* New York: Oxford University Press, 1946.

Giner, Salvador. *Mass Society.* New York: Academic Press, 1976.

Goff, Tom W. *Marx and Mead: Contribution to a Sociology of Knowledge.* London: Routledge and Kegan Paul, 1980.

Gordon, Wendell. *Economics from an Institutional Viewpoint.* Austin: University of Texas Press, 1973.

Gross, Llewellyn, ed. *Symposium on Sociological Theory.* New York: Harper and Row, 1959.

Gruchy, Allan. *Contemporary Economic Thought: The Contribution of Neo-Institutional Economics.* Clifton, NJ: Augustus M. Kelley, 1972.

———. *Modern Economic Thought: The American Contribution.* New York: Prentice-Hall, 1947.

Guarasci, Richard. *The Theory and Practice of American Marxism.* Washington: University Press of America, 1980.

Hobhouse, L. T. *Liberalism.* London: Oxford University Press, 1971.

Horowitz, Irving L. *C. Wright Mills: An American Utopian.* New York: Macmillan-Free Press, 1983.

———, ed. *The New Sociology.* New York: Oxford University Press, 1964.

———. Introduction to Mills' *Sociology and Pragmatism.* New York: Oxford University Press, 1966.

Howe, Irving. *Steady Work: Essays in the Politics of Democratic Radicalism, 1953–1966.* New York: Harcourt Brace Jovanovich, 1966.

Howlett, Charles F. *Troubled Philosopher: John Dewey and the Struggle for World Peace.* Port Washington, NY: Kennikat Press, 1977.

Hoxie, Robert F. *Trade Unionism in the United States.* Introduction by E. H. Downey. New York: Russell and Russell, 1966.

Johnpoll, Bernard. *The Impossible Dream: The Rise and Demise of the American Left.* Westport, CT: Greenwood Press, 1981.

Kallen, Horace M., ed. *Freedom in the Modern World.* New York: Coward-McCann, 1928.

Kallen, Horace M., and Sidney Hook, eds. *American Philosophy Today and Tomorrow.* Freeport, NY: Books for Libraries Press, 1968.

Kariel, Henry. *Saving Appearances: The Re-establishment of Political Science.* Belmont, CA: Duxbury Press, 1972.

Keller, Suzanne. *Beyond the Ruling Class.* New York: Random House, 1963.

Kolakowski, Leszek, and Stuart Hampshire, eds. *The Socialist Idea: A Reappraisal.* Introduction by Leszek Kolakowski. New York: Basic Books, 1974.

Kornhauser, Arthur, ed. *Problems of Power in American Democracy.* Detroit: Wayne State University Press, 1957.

Kraditor, Aileen. *The Radical Persuasion, 1890–1917.* Baton Rouge: Louisiana State University Press, 1981.

Lader, Lawrence. *Power on the Left: American Radical Movements since 1946.* New York: W. W. Norton & Co., 1979.

Laslett, John, and Seymour Martin Lipset, eds. *The Failure of a Dream?* Garden City, NY: Doubleday, 1974.

Lewis, J. David, and Richard L. Smith. *American Sociology and Pragma-tism*. Chicago: University of Chicago Press, 1980.

McWilliams, Wilson Carey. *The Idea of Fraternity in America*. Berkeley: University of California Press, 1974.

Mannheim, Karl. *Essays on the Sociology of Knowledge*. London: Routledge and Kegan Paul, 1952.

———. *Ideology and Utopia*. New York: Harcourt Brace Jovanovich, 1936.

———. *Man and Society in an Age of Reconstruction*. New York: Harcourt, Brace Jovanovich, 1940.

Marcell, David. *Progress and Pragmatism*. Westport, CT: Greenwood Press, 1974.

Marković, Mihailo. *From Affluence to Praxis*. Ann Arbor: University of Michi-gan Press, 1974.

Martindale, Don. *The Nature and Types of Sociological Theory*. Boston: Houghton Mifflin Company, 1960.

Mead, George H. *Mind, Self and Society*. Chicago: University of Chicago Press, 1967.

———. *Movements of Thought in the Nineteenth Century*. Chicago: Univer-sity of Chicago Press, 1936.

———. *The Philosophy of the Act*. Chicago: University of Chicago Press, 1972.

———. *Philosophy of the Present*. La Salle, IL: Open Court Publishing Com-pany, 1959.

———. *Selected Writings*. Edited, with an introduction by Andrew J. Reck. Indianapolis: Bobbs-Merrill, 1964.

———. *The Social Psychology of George H. Mead*. Edited with an introduc-tion by Anselm Strauss. Chicago: University of Chicago Press, 1956.

Meisel, James. *The Myth of the Ruling Class: Gaetano Mosca and the Elite*. Ann Arbor: University of Michigan Press, 1962.

Meyer, William J. *Public Good and Political Authority*. Port Washington, NY: Kennikat Press, 1975.

Michels, Robert. *First Lectures in Political Sociology*. New York: Harper and Row, 1964.

Miller, David L. *George H. Mead: Self, Language and the World*. Austin: University of Texas Press, 1973.

Miller, Donald L. *The New American Radicalism: Alfred M. Bingham and Non-Marxian Insurgency in the New Deal Era*. Port Washington, NY: Kennikat Press, 1979.

Mills, C. Wright. *The Causes of World War III*. New York: Simon and Schus-ter, 1958.

———. *Images of Man*. New York: George Braziller, 1960.

———. *Listen Yankee: The Revolution in Cuba*. New York: McGraw-Hill Book Company, 1960.

———. *The Marxists*. New York: Dell Publishing Co., 1972.

————. *The New Men of Power: America's Labor Leaders* (with the assistance of Helen Schneider). New York: Harcourt Brace Jovanovich, 1948.

————. *The Power Elite.* New York: Oxford University Press, 1959.

————. *Power, Politics and People,* ed. and with an introduction by Irving L. Horowitz. New York: Oxford University Press, 1967.

————. *The Puerto Rican Journey: New York's Newest Migrants* (with Clarence Senior and Rose K. Goldsen). New York: Oxford University Press, 1951.

————. *The Sociological Imagination.* New York: Oxford University Press, 1968.

————. *Sociology and Pragmatism.* New York: Oxford University Press, 1966.

————. Introduction to the Mentor edition of Thorstein Veblen, *The Theory of the Leisure Class.* New York: New American Library, 1953.

————. *White Collar.* New York: Oxford University Press, 1956.

Miroff, Bruce. *Pragmatic Illusions: The Presidential Politics of John F. Kennedy.* New York: David McKay Company, 1976.

Moore, Edward C. *American Pragmatism: Peirce, James and Dewey.* New York: Columbia University Press, 1961.

Moore, R. Laurence. *European Socialists and the American Promised Land.* New York: Oxford University Press, 1970.

Mumford, Lewis. In *Pragmatism and American Culture,* ed. Gail Kennedy. Boston: D. C. Heath & Co., 1950.

Niebuhr, Reinhold. *Moral Man and Immoral Society.* New York: Charles Scribner's Sons, 1960.

Novack, George. *Marxism and Pragmatism.* New York: Pathfinder Press, 1975.

Owen, A. L. Riesch. *Selig Perlman's Lectures on Capitalism and Socialism.* Madison: University of Wisconsin Press, 1976.

Parry, Geraint. *Political Elites.* New York: Praeger Publishers, 1969.

Pells, Richard H. *Radical Visions and American Dreams.* New York: Harper and Row, 1973.

Perlman, Fredy. *The Incoherence of the Intellectual.* Detroit: Black and Red Press, 1970.

Perlman, Selig. *A Theory of the Labor Movement.* New York: Augustus M. Kelley, 1949.

Perry, Ralph B. *Puritanism and Democracy.* New York: Harper and Row, 1964.

Plamenatz, John. *Democracy and Illusion.* London: Longman Group, 1973.

Pole, Jack R. *The Pursuit of Equality in American History.* Berkeley: University of California Press, 1978.

Polsby, Nelson. *Community Power and Political Theory.* New Haven, CT: Yale University Press, 1965.

Press, Howard. *C. Wright Mills.* Boston: Twayne Publishers, 1978.

Prewitt, Kenneth, and Alan Stone. *The Ruling Elites.* New York: Harper and Row, 1973.

Putnam, Robert. *The Comparative Study of Political Elites*. Englewood Cliffs, NJ: Prentice-Hall, 1976.

Quint, Howard. *The Forging of American Socialism*. Indianapolis: Bobbs-Merrill Co., 1964.

Raskin, Marcus. *Being and Doing*. New York: Random House, 1971.

Rex, John. *Sociology, Demystification and Common Sense*. Boston: Routledge & Kegan Paul, 1974.

Riesman, David. *The Lonely Crowd*. New Haven, CT: Yale University Press, 1961.

Rucker, Darnell. *The Chicago Pragmatists*. Minneapolis: University of Minnesota Press, 1969.

Scheffler, Israel. *Four Pragmatists*. New York: Humanities Press, 1974.

Schroyer, Trent. *The Critique of Domination*. New York: George Braziller, 1973.

Scimecca, Joseph A. *The Sociological Theory of C. Wright Mills*. Port Washington, NY: Kennikat Press, 1977.

Segal, David R. *Society and Politics*. Glenview, IL: Scott, Foresman & Co., 1974.

Selsam, Howard. *Socialism and Ethics*. New York: International Publishers, 1943.

Sherman, Howard. *Radical Political Economy*. New York: Basic Books, 1972.

Somjee, A. J. *The Political Theory of John Dewey*. New York: Columbia University Press, 1968.

Stearns, Harold. *Liberalism in America*. New York: Boni and Liveright, 1919.

Steinfels, Peter. *The Neoconservatives*. New York: Simon and Schuster, 1979.

Stroh, Guy W. *American Ethical Thought*. Chicago: Nelson-Hall Co., 1979.

Sweezy, Paul, and Leo Huberman, eds. *Paul A. Baran: A Collective Portrait*. New York: Monthly Review Press, 1965.

Thayer, H. S., *Meaning and Action: A Critical History of Pragmatism*. Indianapolis: Bobbs-Merrill Co., 1968.

Thomas, Milton Halsey, *John Dewey, A Centennial Bibliography*. Chicago: University of Chicago Press, 1962.

Tinder, Glenn. *Community: Reflections on a Tragic Ideal*. Baton Rouge: Louisiana State University Press, 1980.

Truman, David. *The Governmental Process*. New York: Alfred A. Knopf, 1964.

Veblen, Thorstein. *Absentee Ownership and Business Enterprise in Recent Times*. Boston: Beacon Press, 1967.

———. *The Engineers and the Price System*. New York: Viking Press, 1921.

———. *Essays in Our Changing Order*. New York: Viking Press, 1934.

———. *The Higher Learning in America*. New York: Augustus M. Kelley, 1965.

———. *Imperial Germany and the Industrial Revolution*. New York: Viking Press, 1939.

———. *An Inquiry into the Nature of Peace and the Terms of Its Perpetuation.* New York: Macmillan, 1917.

———. *The Instinct of Workmanship and the State of the Industrial Arts.* New York: B. W. Huebsch, 1914.

———. *The Place of Science in Modern Civilization and Other Essays.* New York: Russell and Russell, 1961.

———. *The Portable Veblen.* Edited and with an introduction by Max Lerner. New York: Viking Press, 1950.

———. *The Theory of Business Enterprise.* New York: Charles Scribner's Sons, 1904.

———. *The Theory of the Leisure Class: An Economic Study of Institutions.* New York: Modern Library, 1934.

———. *The Vested Interests and the Common Man.* New York: Viking Press, 1919.

———. *What Veblen Taught.* Edited and with an Introduction by Wesley Mitchell. New York: Viking Press, 1936.

Warnock, Mary, ed. *Sartre: A Collection of Critical Essays.* Garden City, NY: Doubleday Anchor, 1971.

Warren, Frank. *An Alternative Vision: The Socialist Party in the 1930s.* Bloomington: Indiana University Press, 1971.

Warshay, Leon. *The Current State of Sociological Theory.* New York: David McKay, 1975.

Wells, Harry. *Pragmatism: Philosophy of Imperialism.* Freeport: Books for Libraries Press, 1941.

White, Morton. *The Revolt against Formalism.* Boston: Beacon Press, 1957.

Zeitlin, Irving M. *Rethinking Sociology.* New York: Appleton-Century-Croft, 1973.

REVIEWS

Allport, Gordon W., *The Nature of Prejudice.* Review by C. Wright Mills. *New York Times,* 1 March 1954.

Dahl, Robert, and Charles Lindblom, *Politics, Economics and Welfare.* Review by C. Wright Mills. American Sociological Review 19, August 1954.

Horney, Karen, *Our Inner Conflicts.* Review by C. Wright Mills. *Briarcliffe Quarterly* 3, No. 9, April 1936.

MacFarlane, Alan, *The Origins of English Individualism: The Family, Property and Social Transition.* Review by Frederick L. Pryor. Journal of Economic Literature 18, March–June 1980.

Mannheim, Karl, *Man and Society in an Age of Reconstruction.* Review by C. Wright Mills. *American Sociological Review* 5, June 1940.

Mills, C. Wright, *The Power Elite.* Review ("The Big, Bad Americans") by Daniel Bell. *Time* 67, December 7, 1956, p. 116.

The Power Elite. Review by H. Malcolm MacDonald. *American Political Science Review* 50, December 1956.

Selsam, Howard, *Socialism and Ethics.* Review by C. Wright Mills. *Politics* 1, February 1944.

Veblen, Thorstein. *[An Inquiry into] The Nature of Peace and the Terms of Its Perpetuation.* Review by George H. Mead. *Journal of Political Economy* 26, June 1918.

ADDRESS

Mills, C. Wright. "Work Milieu and Social Structure." Address to the Mental Health Society of Northern California, Asilomar, California, March 13, 1954.

PUBLISHED LETTERS

Miliband, Ralph. "Letter to Editors." *Dissent* 10, Summer 1963.

Mills, C. Wright. "Letters from Readers, Organization Men." *Commentary* 23, June 1957.

Wakefield, Dan. "Letter to Editors." *Dissent* 10, Summer 1963.

DISSERTATIONS, THESES, AND PAPERS

Bray, Bernard L. "C. Wright Mills, Political Sociology and Substantive Politics." Diss., University of Kansas, 1973.

Bullert, Gary. "John Dewey in Politics." Diss., Claremont Graduate School, 1974.

Carbonara, John Charles. "Critical Empiricism in C. Wright Mills." Diss., State University of New York at Buffalo, 1967.

Chang, George W. "The Individual and Society in the Philosophy of John Dewey." M.A. thesis, University of Hawaii, 1966.

Chandler, Charles C. "Institutionalism and Education: An Inquiry into the Implications of the Philosophy of Thorstein Veblen." Diss., Michigan State University, 1959.

Cleere, Ford Wallace. "The Intellectual as Change Agent in the Writings of C. Wright Mills." Diss., University of Colorado, 1971.

Decker, David L. "C. Wright Mills and Social Definition of Reality." Unpublished manuscript, California State College, San Bernardino, Department of Sociology, 1976.

Garrigan-Burr, Sara. "C. Wright Mills: His Political Perspective and Its Pragmatic Sources." Diss., University of California Riverside, 1977.

Gillam, Richard. "The Intellectual as Rebel: C. Wright Mills, 1916–1946." Thesis, Columbia University, 1966.

Johnson, Darla. "The Place of Sociology of Knowledge in the Early Development of the Theoretical Viewpoint of C. Wright Mills." Thesis, University of Maryland, 1970.

Jones, Robert Paul. "The Fixing of Social Belief: The Sociology of C. Wright Mills." Diss., University of Missouri, 1977.

Kraetzer, Mary C. "The Sociology of Knowledge of Thorstein Veblen and C. Wright Mills: A Study of the 'Radical' Tradition in American Sociology." Diss., Fordham University, 1975.

Leary, Paul M. "The Romantic Reaction: Politics and Utopia in Contemporary Social Criticism." Diss., Rutgers University, 1966.

Mayer, Henry Charles. "The Theory of a State in the Philosophy of John Dewey." M.A. Thesis, University of Notre Dame, 1957.

Mills, C. Wright. "Reflection, Behavior and Culture." M.A. Thesis, University of Texas, 1939.

Mills, Pamela. "The Dialectic of C. Wright Mills." Unpublished manuscript, Barnard College, 1965.

Moore, Harold Francis. "Instrumentalism and the Assessment of Social Importance." Diss., Fordham University, 1971.

Nutch, Frank. "Pragmatism and the Professions: An Approach to a Sociological Imagination." Diss., York University, 1979.

Scimecca, Joseph. "The Sociological Theory of C. Wright Mills." Diss., New York University, 1972.

Smith, Benjamin W. "The Political Theory of Institutional Economics." Diss., University of Texas at Austin, 1969.

Smith, J. R. "Politics from the Economic Point of View: An Analysis of the Political Theoretic Significance of the Writings of Thorstein Veblen." Diss., University of California, Berkeley, 1977.

Swan, Frederick R. "Toward a Relevant Social Science in the Work of C. Wright Mills." Diss., University of Tennessee, 1977.

Warner, John Anson. "The Critics of C. Wright Mills: Ideology and the Study of Political Power in America." Diss., Princeton University, 1972.

Weinroth, George J. "The Political Philosophy of C. Wright Mills." M.A. thesis, Michigan State University, 1960.

Index

Adams, John, 92
Addams, Jane, 122
Aiken, Henry, 124
Allport, Gordon W., 15
American Federation of Labor, 21, 100, 101
Ayer, Alfred J., 125, 127
Ayres, Clarence, 6, 31, 63, 64, 67, 70, 71, 72, 73, 96, 107, 108, 146, 170, 197

Bell, Daniel, 8, 11, 189, 203
Bernstein, Richard, 217 n36
Biologism, 156, 157, 158
Bluhm, William T., 83
Blumer, Herbert, 217 n4
Bordeau, Edward, 151
Burnham, James, 38, 42, 94
Business unionism, 98

Calvinism, 46–47
Carbonara, John, 127, 225
Carleton College, 61, 197
Ceremonial-technological dichotomy, 67, 68, 70, 71, 92
Chandler, Charles, 183
Classical elitism, 38–39
Columbia University, 8, 122
Commons, John R., 31, 64, 100–6
Congregationalism, 108, 121, 197
Congress of Industrial Organizations, 21
Conkins, Paul, 197
Craftsmanship, 74–75, 76–77, 128, 176
Critical theory, 192, 215 n16
Cultural lag, 67–70, 167

De Leon, David, 185
Dewey, John, 12, 17, 31, 36, 49, 74, 89; and American radical traditions, 184–88, 193–94; background, 121–22; on community, 178–81; on the individual and society, 182–84; against Formalism, 174; on growth as a social end, 162–66; influence on Mills, 2–3, 14–15, 123–42, 218; and Mannheim, 57, 59; and Marxism, 10, 123, 190–91; and Mead, 109, 113, 118–20, 121–22; Mills' criticism of, 143–72; and praxis, 177–78; and Protestantism, 197–200; and Veblen, 61–65
Dial, The, 62, 122
Democratic Party, 22
Downey, E. H., 100

Eclecticism, 15–19, 29, 59, 142, 192
Engels, Friedrich, 34, 202
"Exploitative state," 83–84

"False consciousness," 38, 54, 95–96, 104
Feuer, Lewis, 201
Fiedler, Leslie, 188
Frankfurt School, 192
Freud, Sigmund, 31, 50–53
Fromm, Erich, 53
"Functional rationality," 55, 56, 74, 90, 96, 97

"Generalized other," 110–12, 113–20 passim
Gentry, George, 107–8, 214 n3
Gerth, Hans, 7, 43, 49, 50, 52, 54
Gillam, Richard, 5, 64, 203
Growth, as social end, 162–66
Gruchy, Allan, 64
Guild socialism, 21, 56, 172

Habermas, Jurgen, 215
Hale, Edward E., 31, 101

Hamilton, Walton, 64
Hardman, J. B. S., 21, 105–6
"Hemingway Man," 132–33
Hofstadter, Richard, 7, 28, 196
Horney, Karen, 53
Horowitz, I. L., 12, 123–24
Hoxie, Robert, 100–2
Huberman, Leo, 32, 63
Hull House, 122, 151

Individualism, 182–84
Industrial Workers of the World, 188
Instincts, 77–78
Institutionalism, 2, 9, 14, 59, 60, 63, 64–65, 107, 185, 190, 192, 223
Instrumentalism, 14, 49, 60, 63, 65, 128, 146, 157, 163, 172, 178, 185, 190, 192, 223
"Iron law of oligarchy," 41

James, William, 15, 31, 62, 108, 109, 123–124
Job consciousness vs. class consciousness, 100–6
Johnson, Darla, 17
Jones, Robert Paul, 118, 225

Kariel, Henry, 95–96

"Labor metaphysic," 21, 99, 100, 106, 136, 155
Labor theory of value, 33, 92
League for Independent Political Action, 122, 152
Lekachman, Robert, 34
Lenin, V. I., 32, 102–3, 180
Leonard, William N., 208–9 n 12
Liberalism, 30, 84, 89, 139, 144–49, 154, 171–78, 187–89, 192, 201
Liberty League, 152
Lippman, Walter, 218
Logical positivism, 125–29
Lundberg, George, 129, 131

MacDonald, H. Malcolm, 12
Machiavellians, 36–42
MacPherson, C. B., 176
Mannheim, Karl, 31, 46, 48, 53–59, 92, 96, 127
Marcell, David, 186
Markovic, Mihailo, 132

Marx, Karl, 2, 10, 17, 42, 45, 48, 53, 54, 58, 60, 63, 66, 68, 78
Marxism, 1, 2, 16, 19, 20–21, 29, 30–36, 42, 44–45, 56, 63, 92, 99, 118, 124, 170, 185, 187–93
Mass society, 56, 142
Mead, George H., 7, 31, 36, 49, 64, 75, 78, 139, 193; background, 108–9; compared with Freud and Neofreudians, 50–53; and Dewey and Veblen, 109, 121–22; on "generalized other," 110, 113–14; "I," "me" distinction of, 110, 115–16; individual and society, 182–84; influence on Mills, 2–3, 109–20; and method of intelligence, 195; Mills' criticism of, 119–20; and "particular other," 111; *Philosophy of the Act*, 181; in Pragmatic tradition, 194; and praxis, 177–78; and Protestantism, 195–97; and "significant other," 110, 113–14; sociology of knowledge, 116–17
Meisel, James, 40
Merton, Robert, 8, 54
Methodological inhibition, 130
"Method of intelligence," 124, 153, 158–62, 167–68, 195
Michels, Roberto, 17, 31, 37, 40, 41
"Military metaphysic," 27–29, 37
Miller, David, 107–8, 118, 216 n 34
Mills, C. Wright: and American radical traditions, 184–88, 193–94; Ayres' influence on, 62–74; background, 5–9; on biologization, 155–58; *The Causes of World War III*, 37, 138; *Character and Social Structure*, 44, 46, 50–53, 110, 139, 196; and classical elitists (Machiavellians), 36–42; and the Commons-Perlman thesis, 101–6; on idea of community, 178–81; critics of, 3–4, 9–13; on Dewey and American Liberalism, 143–72; on Dewey's audience, 154–55; on Dewey's incrementalism, 149–51; on Dewey's political sociology, 166–70; and Dewey's "publics," 140–42; eclecticism of, 15–19; on Freud and Freudians, 50–53; on growth as social end, 162–66; Hoxie's influence on, 100–1; *Images of Man*, 36–37, 42, 54, 59, 103; on the individual and society, 182–84; institutional economics of, 209 n 16; and intellectual craftsmanship, 78–

80; and Mannheim, 53–59; on Marx and Marxists, 31–36; *The Marxists*, 32, 34–36; and Mead, 107–20; on the method of intelligence, 158–62; *The New Men of Power*, 8, 20, 21–23, 29, 102, 106; periodization of influences on, 17–19; power and stratification theory of, 14–29; *The Power Elite*, 8, 12, 20, 26–29, 31, 39–40, 56, 59, 83, 84–85, 137, 155, 179, 186; Pragmatic influences on, 123–42; on praxis, 131–37, 177–78; and Protestantism, 5–6, 199–202; *The Sociological Imagination*, 33, 37, 79; *Sociology and Pragmatism*, 154; and Weber, 42–50; *White Collar*, 8, 20, 23–26, 29, 42–43, 81; critique of Veblen, 90–98; Veblen's influence on, 61–106; and Veblen's view of labor, 98–100

Mills, Pamela (daughter), 31
Mills, Yaroslava (wife), 9
Miroff, Bruce, 201
Moore, Barrington, 32, 33
Mosca, Gaetano, 17, 37, 39, 40–42, 48

Neoinstitutionalism, 64, 65
Neofreudians, 31, 50, 53, 192
New Deal, 14, 20–21, 23, 26–28, 98–99, 105, 134, 149–52
New England, 108, 121, 195–97
"New entrepreneur," 48
New Left, 99, 175, 185, 188, 199–200
Novack, George, 10, 33

Oberlin College, 108, 197
"One Big Union of Financial Interests," 86–87
"Overdeveloped society," 43, 76–77

Pareto, Vilfredo, 17, 31, 37, 38–42
Peirce, Charles S., 7, 31, 49, 59, 64, 109, 121
"Plain Marxist," 10, 33, 35, 36
Pluralism, 22, 37, 79, 147
Perlman, Selig, 7, 100–6
Perry, Ralph Barton, 198, 201–2
Peterson, Richard, 17
Phenomenology, 223
Polsby, Nelson, 45
Populism, 193
Pragmatism, 2, 10–11, 14, 29, 49, 57, 59,

107, 118, 123–24, 127–28, 132–34, 137, 142, 144, 153–54, 193–94, 200–1, 214 n3
Praxis, 131–37, 178, 192
Port Huron statement, 21
Protestantism, 5–6, 75, 193–202
"Publics," 140–42
Puritanism, 47, 91, 193–194

Radicalism, 1, 3, 18, 19, 30, 36, 140, 150, 151, 163, 175, 185, 190
Role theory, 115, 215 n27
Rubin, Jerry, 224 n11
Rucker, Darnell, 128

Scimecca, Joseph, 17, 50
Selsam, Howard, 32
Shils, Edward, 11
Smith, Al, 152
Socialist Party, 152, 153
Somjee, A. J., 144
Soviet Union, 8, 123
Stalin, Joseph, 116, 123
Status emulation, 80–83; in emulatory consumption, 22–23
Stroh, Guy, 194
Students for a Democratic Society, 21
Substantial (substantive) rationality, 55, 74, 76, 90, 92, 96–98
Symbolic interactionism, 10, 50, 52, 59, 108, 215

Technocratic elitism, 90, 94–95
Telos, 223 n28
Temporary National Economic Committee, 88–89
Texas A. & M., 6
Thomas, Norman, 152–53, 187–88, 219
Tool combination-tool accumulation principle, 68, 72
Trotsky, Leon, 8, 32–33, 123, 155
Tufts, James H., 170

University of Chicago, 63, 107, 109, 121–22
University of Maryland, 7, 8, 196
University of Michigan, 108, 122
University of Wisconsin, 7, 105
University of Texas, 6, 31, 63, 107

Veblen, Thorstein, 12, 14, 17, 19, 31, 36, 43, 59, 113; aristocratic and bourgeois

traits fused by, 90–92; background, 61–62; ceremonial-technological dichotomy, 70–71; and conservative institutionalism, 101–6; on cultural lag, 67–69; and Dewey, 109, 121; and Hoxie, 100–1; on industrial arts, 67; institutional and neoinstitutional economics influenced by, 64–65; and Marx(ism), 66–67, 190–91; Mills influenced by, 2–3, 14, 62–63; and Mills critique of Liberalism, 89, 146, 148–49; on nature of the state, 83–89; on organized labor, 98–106; parallels with Dewey and Mills, 173–92; on peaceful and predatory types, 77–78; and power-status relationship, 92–94; and Protestantism, 193–95; on technology and rationality, 95–98
Versailles Peace Conference, 153

Waco, Texas, 5, 6
Wallerstein, Immanuel, 65
Weber, Max, 17, 19, 31, 42–50, 53, 60, 66, 78, 204 nn3, 10
Williams, William Appleman, 1
White, Morton, 144
"Wobbley," the, 132–33
World War I, 144, 153
World War II, 20–21, 153–54